☆ THE BIRTH OF THE UNITED STATES ☆

The
BIRTH
of the
UNITED STATES

WITHDRAWN

BY JIM BISHOP

William Morrow and Company, Inc.
New York
1976

Printed in the United States of America.

1 2 3 4 5   80 79 78 77 76

Library of Congress Cataloging in Publication Data

Bishop, James Alonzo (date)
        The birth of the United States.

        Bibliography: p.
        Includes index.
        1. United States. Declaration of independence. 2. United
States. Continental Congress, 1776. I. Title.
E221.B63   973.3'13   75-38593
ISBN 0-688-03006-8

BOOK DESIGN: H. ROBERTS

Dedicated to
Adele Parmelee Steencken,
a loving, forgiving sister

☆ **Contents** ☆

FOR THE RECORD

It is my lifelong impression that history is poorly taught in the United States of America. In the primary and secondary schools, where the likes and dislikes are molded, the subject is a matter of dates, cardboard caricatures, and events. In my school studies I found that if I could remember a name, an event, and a proper date, I was given a passing grade.

I feel rewarded that my interest in history survived the dull, pontifical approach of the teachers. My gratitude is directed toward the free public library system, where I found the authors, the great fascinators who brought a flame of illumination to the dark caves of the past, men and women who researched a subject for years for little reward except the silent applause of young know-nothings like me.

The story which you are about to read is the culmination of years of reading and thinking about the Second Continental Congress and its adversaries in Great Britain. Most of all I have endeavored to present a close-up look at the first four days of July, 1776.

Hallandale, Florida JIM BISHOP

☆ July 1, 1776 ☆

THE TALL REDHEAD EMERGED FROM HIS PAR-
lor and bedroom with a big brass key and a large squarish
object which looked like an easel. He locked the door and
slipped the key into his waistcoat pocket. Thomas Jefferson,
an intellectual at age thirty-three, was disappointed with these
rooms. He had selected the new, three-story brick house at
Market and Seventh streets in Philadelphia because there
were no other homes or businesses near it and he had counted
on "a freely circulating air," which had not asserted itself in
the deathly stillness of hot June nights and the swarms of
mosquitoes which seemed addicted to human ears.

He stepped out into the brassy morning sun which
stood above the trees on the Delaware River. He walked down
Seventh Street toward the State House. Jefferson did not com-
plain to bricklayer Jacob Graff, the young man who had built
the house. Graff too was suffering with sultry nights, mosquitoes, and the thin wail of an infant whose fretful cry Jefferson
heard after midnight. He was not a complainer, even when he
had a legitimate complaint. His peers among the statesmen
of the Colonies saw Thomas Jefferson as a shy man, an intro-
vert who could write with a degree of majestic philosophy,
but who would not defend what he had written.

There was a chance, he knew, that if the Colonies voted independence of the British Crown, this city of Philadelphia might be the capital of a new nation, or of a conglomerate of states. The city, stretching a mile and a half in one direction and a mile in the other, was as busy as a hive. That small space, smaller than the 7,500 acres his father had left him at Monticello, Virginia, had a population of 38,000 —second only to the great metropolis of London. As he walked, his blue eyes captured the drays bringing produce to the city on Monday morning, the heavy wagons hauled by plodding oxen yanking hogsheads of beer and spirits; black slaves with hands on hips carrying baskets of laundry on their heads; the businessmen with broad-brimmed beaver hats hurrying to and from their offices; bearded sailors in rough homespun, gawking at the heat-shimmering skyline of Philadelphia.

Stout housewives in long swirling skirts, lace handkerchiefs pinned to their hair, curled by Jefferson on the pedestrian path, some turning to look at the "easel." They could believe that the freckled redhead was an artist; certainly he looked like any other stranger in the city except that his gray breeches and gray waistcoat with the robin's-egg blue facing were too proper a uniform for an artist. It was not given to any of them to know that the "easel" was an invention of Jefferson's. It was a portable desk with ratchets. When it was set upon the knees, the upper leaf could be raised to 35 degrees of upright.

Nor would any but Jefferson know that, this morning, the "easel" contained an instrument which he had devised entitled "THE UNANIMOUS DECLARATION of the thirteen united STATES OF AMERICA." It would be read today by the clerk of the Second Continental Congress. Afterward, few of the delegates would resist the temptation to shred, to alter, to obliterate the high-blown philosophical phrases. Every word would be at the mercy of fifty-four other delegates, assuming that all of them might be present in State House for the first time.

Jefferson would not ask recognition from the chair to defend it. Whatever he had to say was in the document. To the contrary, Thomas Jefferson would tell his friends that the Declaration was not the best of *his* thinking; "it is an expression of the American mind."

In a manner of speaking, Jefferson was lucky to have three noted sponsors among the delegates. Richard Henry Lee, of the Virginia Lees, was an elegant orator who suggested in open forum that the Colonies should give up trying to reach an "accommodation" with King George III of Great Britain. Rather, he said, the Colonies should unite and tell the King and his Parliament that the Americans proclaimed themselves free and independent states.

Lee, standing to speak, was almost as eloquent as Jefferson was, sitting with a quill. He was not popular with the members of Congress because he was aloof, an aristocrat among sullen revolutionaries. The prominence of his nose, which ran straight out of his forehead, was held too high for some of the delegates. Certainly the gentlemen of Pennsylvania, New York, and South Carolina were opposed to independence. New Jersey, which was soon to feel the wrath of the King's red-coated regiments, felt that the Lee resolution smacked of a traitorous heart and the possibility of a traitor's death. The delegation sent a courier home to ask explicit instructions on how to vote.

Meanwhile, Benjamin Franklin, who, at age seventy, studied Jefferson's portable desk through an invention of his own—bifocal spectacles—had sat with balding John Adams of the Massachusetts Bay Colony to urge the young man from Monticello to write the Declaration of Independence. Jefferson had declined. Adams, so stout that when he walked he looked like a pealing bell, insisted that Jefferson and only Jefferson had the gleaming phrases, the philosophy, to undertake the lonely writing of a correct document of independence.

13

Adams couldn't do it because he was known to all as a red-faced firebrand whose scornful words sometimes rattled the leaded windows in the big room at State House. He was disliked—yea, feared—by some delegates because of outbursts, the face reddening and swelling as Adams shouted his disenchantment with King and Mother Country. He was one of the reasons why the presiding officer, John Hancock of Massachusetts Bay, kept the windows closed.

The business of the Second Continental Congress was pledged by the delegates to remain secret. It wasn't. The gentlemen wrote long letters home to spouses, to friends pledged to keep the letters secret. John Adams used breakfast time (6 A.M.) to write detailed letters to his wife, Abigail, who in turn wrote long letters to her husband about the withdrawal of British forces from Massachusetts. The captains of the swift-running Yankee privateers assured her that the English had withdrawn to Halifax, there to regroup in greater strength for the next attack on the Colonies.

Adams had become a delegate certain that the spirit of revolution was in full flame only in Massachusetts Bay. Then he heard the aristocrats from Virginia and he realized that, though the men from the large plantations appeared to be slower to anger and were more discreet in their oratory, the spirit of revolution was so deeply ingrained that Virginia was already drawing up its own constitution. It was at this point that Adams, appointed to the committee with Franklin and Jefferson to draw up a declaration of independence, decided that the fateful words should be composed by a Virginian —Thomas Jefferson.

He could not persuade the redhead. Benjamin Franklin did. The old man pleaded that he was thinking of moving out of Philadelphia because it was "too noisy, too busy. I find myself repeating thoughts and utterances twice over." Jefferson was faltering. "You write so well," the old Pennsylvanian said. He would attempt to write it himself, but, in his advanced age, he found himself given to writing sallies and fripperies which might induce laughter. There would be no room for the light and careless phrase in the Declaration. At this point, June 11, 1776, Jefferson surrendered to the will of his seniors and began to write and rewrite, thinking, phrasing, revising, despairing; until, on June 28, he asked Adams and Franklin to come to his rooms to study "a draft."

They made few changes. Others were mechanical, corrections of Jefferson's poor spelling and execrable punctuation. Parts of it they read aloud, inducing rhapsodic comment from each other. Thomas Jefferson repeated that it was not to be regarded as his personal thought; he may have known that some of his critics would accuse him of having first read George Mason's recent "Declaration of Rights for Virginia." He could expect "Loyalists" to call upon Jehovah to witness the perfidy of His Majesty's blessed subjects.

John Dickinson and his Pennsylvania delegation were, while not precisely Tories, at least loyal to the King and desirous of blaming Parliament for past injustices rather than George III. John Adams referred to the host colony—and the Pennsylvania delegation—as "puling, pusillanimous cowards," which was akin to tossing a bucket of whale oil into a winter fireplace. Such appellations drove most delegates to a frenzy of standing, stomping, waving their arms for recognition from the chair, shouting at each other, interrupting the speaker with sarcasm, arguing, pleading—a babble of frothy tongues. Adams, beet red, seemed at times to be reduced to a resonant chant: "A union and a confederation of thirteen states, independent of parliament, of minister and of king!"

In spite of the disagreements, which were sometimes carried out of the room and up Walnut Street, the wealthy Quakers of Pennsylvania endorsed two petitions for redress to the King, the first of which he had refused to read. It is an earthy irony that the only point on which all delegates seemed to agree was a unanimous vote. No matter what the

15

measure before the delegations, each voted as a unit of one, and those who saw a vote going against them insisted that the clerk regard it as "unanimous." Dickinson's second plea to the King was mauled by the Congress, weakened, watered; until, when it was passed "unanimously," he got to his feet wearily and said, "Mr. Chairman, there is only one word in this paper of which I disapprove, and that is the word 'Congress.' " He sat. Benjamin Harrison of Virginia, the fifth in direct line to bear that name, stood. Under the rules he could not speak, because when the Congress sat as the Committee of the Whole, John Hancock stepped down as president so that he could participate in the debates, sending Benjamin Harrison up as president pro tem. Within or without the rules, Harrison glared at Dickinson and trumpeted, "There is only one word in this paper of which I approve and that is the word 'Congress.' "

Jefferson was aware of the furious independence of the protagonists. Grudgingly, he would admit that it was this quality which made the Second Continental Congress a great deliberative body. A year before this hot day, when George Washington of Virginia had accepted command of the Continental Army and had hurried off with his aides to Boston, Congressmen recalled a time when Washington was opposed to complete independence of the Crown, although he was ready to fight for complete liberty if that was the sense of the Congress. General Washington was certain that the Colonies, as constituted, were too weak to sustain a long war of attrition; too young to have nations as friends when the British imposed an embargo on American goods and services; too poor to build and man a navy to battle the might of Britain; too quarrelsome to forge the thirteen Colonies into a single unified state, or even to agree on common laws and trade.

Jefferson approached State House. Had he been blindfolded he would have known where he was by the odor of manure from the stable. For the first time in his memory, the big windows of the congressional room were open to small stirrings of air and the assault of buzzing horseflies. Had he been asked what he would like to do after delivering the Declaration of Independence to the clerk, it seems no risk at all to say that he would have liked to be in the cool hills of his home at Monticello, practicing his violin three hours a day. This was his habit, and there is no reason to believe that he would not have preferred the breeze-bent hummocks of pine and music to the assaults he was bound to sustain in Philadelphia.

His father had died, leaving 7,500 acres of wooded and farm land to be divided between Thomas and his younger brother, Randolph (with cash dowries for six daughters), and sixty slaves to work the plantation. The Jeffersons were not numbered among the wealthy plantation owners of the Colonies, but they too had much to lose in the gamble for freedom. For relaxation Thomas Jefferson perfected his ability to think and write in Latin, Greek, French, and Italian. Often, when he extended his thinking to its utmost, the young man was afflicted with headaches. Physicians were unable to give him a specific for this, although he believed one who said that if Jefferson bathed his feet in cold water every morning, he would be free of colds and rheumatic pain.

He turned into the building, bowing and bidding good morning to the delegates who were present. He sat on a chair in the back row and opened his portable desk on his legs. The clerk unlocked his desk, picked up the sheets of his copy of the Declaration, and took them inside the area where the presiding officer would sit this day.

It was 9 A.M. on the tall outdoor clock at the rear of the building, time to call the Congress to order. However, John Hancock knew that some members were chronically tardy, and he continued to chat with agreeable members. The room had originally been built for the deliberations of the

Pennsylvania Assembly, but the militia had picketed the gentlemen, protesting that they had not been paid and would not accept the printing-press script which the Continental Congress was using to replace good solid British pounds, shillings, and pence.

Cheerfully, the Pennsylvanians surrendered the ground-floor room to the Congress and moved to the second floor, where, much of the time, they did not meet to deliberate anything, worried about the muskets carried by the militia. The top floor was given to peaceable Indians for powwows, but their careless use of fire in the center of the floor worried the Congress on the ground floor.

And yet there was something in common between the Pennsylvania Assembly and the Continental Congress: procrastination and irresolution. Weary of it, Richard Henry Lee of Virginia took the final thunderous step by offering a resolution to appoint a committee to draft a declaration of independence. His marshaling of argument, his plea for complete severance from the Crown, was so brilliantly conceived that the Congress voted five men to the committee, and denied Lee membership. As gracefully as possible, he waited a week and then returned to Virginia, stating that he must take part in the drawing up of Virginia's constitution.

Thomas Jefferson received the highest number of votes, although he was young and a new member. He was followed by Benjamin Franklin of Pennsylvania, who favored the Declaration; Robert Livingston of New York, who had been ordered by the officials of the colony not to vote for independence; John Adams of Massachusetts, who hungered for a free nation; and the severely plain Puritan of Connecticut, Roger Sherman, who said he favored a revolution and freedom, but wanted to see some expression of the common will of the Colonies before voting for it.

Between June 11 and June 28, 1776, there is nothing

in history or historical notes to show that Livingston or Sherman visited Jefferson at his work, or that they assisted him when he was present at State House. Livingston, born of landed gentry in New York, was only twenty-nine years old. When he assumed the floor, he said that complete independence from Great Britain was inevitable and necessary, "but at this time inexpedient." Sherman was fifty-five, a cobbler of New Milford, who had moved to New Haven, studied law, and become rich. He dressed in homespun black and was pledged so deeply to the Puritan ethic that he refused to vote for violence, whether it be war or retribution. He was shrewd, not scholarly; if he planned to leave any mark on the Declaration, it would be his signature and nothing more.

The completed document was ready on June 28, but the committee of the whole had voted to postpone consideration of it until July 1. It is probable that Jefferson would have preferred to be in Virginia, where the largest of the colonies was drawing up a constitution which would be a model for others. The young philosopher-scientist sent a rough draft of a constitution to his native soil. It was not accepted by his peers, but Jefferson's combination of eloquent forbearance and bold confrontation ran like a thread of gold through the Virginia constitution. He wasn't able to be present at Williamsburg when Patrick Henry was elected first governor, and this too depressed his mood.

The fifty-five quarrelsome, and sometimes picayune, men endured dilatory tactics within their own body, but would not permit it in others. Maryland, which had been opposed to independence, asked for time to change its mind. The Continental Congress declined, sending word to Annapolis that it would take up the matter of a declaration of independence at the end of June. Samuel Chase, a Maryland delegate who was loud and rude and known as "Bacon Face" because of his complexion, rode back to Annapolis to tell the governing body

19

that unless it decided to instruct its delegates to vote for independence, the world-shaking event would escape Maryland. The governing body acted favorably at once.

The host colony, Pennsylvania, released its seven delegates so that they could vote for freedom—six were still opposed; only Benjamin Franklin would vote in favor. Under the unit vote, his vote was worthless.

Delaware sent three delegates. Two, McKean and Rodney, favored "Liberty instanter," and one, Read, was opposed. Caesar Rodney, a brigadier general in the Delaware militia, had to leave to serve with his unit. This left one favoring the Declaration, one opposed. Word was sent to Rodney, who was plowing a field on the morning of July 1, that he had better get to Philadelphia quickly or Delaware's vote would be canceled. He departed in a day-and-night downpour, a side of his face covered by a kerchief to hide the huge cancer which would take his life.

South Carolina sent four young sons of plantation owners. The colony was busy drawing up a constitution, and could not spare its mature minds to make the trip to Philadelphia. The average age of its delegates was under thirty. The gentlemen arrived with no admonition to vote for or against liberty and union, but they were as certain as their fathers in Charleston that independence was not an issue. When they were asked how they would vote, they said they didn't know. They were gentlemen of impeccable manners and generous speech. They said that "provincial and local independence" was the issue, as they saw it; a union with other colonies was something they had not foreseen.

The Virginians felt sorry that their leader, Richard Henry Lee, was in Williamsburg on this hot morning. His three succinct resolutions were on the desk of Clerk Charles Thomson, who ignored them as he had since they were read and tabled in committee June 7. Although few thought of

20

them as a historic document, they spelled out, in seventy-nine words, the strangulation of Great Britain as the motherland of the thirteen Colonies:

> That these United Colonies are, and of right ought to be, free and independent States, that they are absolved of all allegiance to the British Crown, and that all political connection between them and the State of Great Britain is, and ought to be, totally dissolved.
> That it is expedient forthwith to take the most effectual measures for forming foreign Alliances.
> That a plan of confederation be prepared and transmitted to the respective Colonies for their consideration and approbation.

Between June 7 and July 1, the Second Congress sat on the proposal, keeping it secret from the thirteen Colonies and their local governments. It was as though the delegates were determined to *sneak* the news to the Colonies after the event. It did occur to them that summaries of their meetings, their accomplishments, often required six weeks to reach Savannah, Georgia, by fast packet. It was with respect for this loss of time that North Carolina released its delegation to vote for independence if it came up on the floor, but not to introduce it if it didn't.

As John Hancock rapped the palm of his hand on his desk for order, vote counters such as Franklin and John Adams saw the result as seven in favor—New Hampshire, Massachusetts, Rhode Island, Connecticut, Virginia, North Carolina, and Georgia—and six against—Pennsylvania, New York, New Jersey, Delaware, Maryland, and South Carolina. Seven to six would hardly be a victory for freedom. Certainly not a mandate. If Hancock removed himself from his chair, and called a "meeting of the whole," the lusty, blustery joke teller who roared with laughter at his own amusement, Benjamin Harrison, would be chairing the weakest victory of his career. Benjamin Franklin stood, shoved his bifocals on his forehead, and sat in an empty chair beside Thomas Jefferson. He patted the young man's knee to reassure him.

The custodian closed and locked the door. A bowling-ball peal of thunder was heard, and another. The roomful of men remained quiet. Hancock announced that the Congress would first conduct its regular daily business, largely listening to a reading of letters and petitions. Delegates stared silently at the white walls, the two brassy fireplaces, or at Clerk Thomson. Rain hissed in the stable yard and splashed on the stone windowsills. A member rose quietly and tiptoed to close the windows. The custodian, as always, was outside the locked door, standing guard.

Before President Hancock, lightning flashed upon a wall decoration of British swords, a drum, and regimental banners captured last year at Fort Ticonderoga. As the storm darkened the city, the room lost some of its light and members were idly fascinated by the sporadic and swift pale-blue light on captured trophies. An omen? For or against? Others slapped at their silk stockings as the horseflies became enraged at being imprisoned. Ethan Allen and Benedict Arnold had captured those battle pennants. Everyone knew that was last year. This year Arnold had invaded Canada but failed to persuade the French and British trappers, tradesmen, and divines to join the Colonies in a fight for freedom. The British and French had resisted in battle; Arnold had been driven back into New York State with God knew how many losses.

The reading of missives droned on. A wind came up. The windows rattled, the dust on the fireplace floors emerged into the room like specters. The delegates listened, in varying degrees of lassitude, to confidential reports from General George Washington in New York; Generals Gates and Schuyler, Arnold and Sullivan, and from a few colonels and civilians of substance too. Clerk Thomson's voice had the sound of a file on a protruding horseshoe nail.

There was no good news in the mail. The Congress seldom received advice of a military triumph. The Colonies had not declared war on Great Britain; and the King had not declared war on the Colonies. British Parliament and George III saw the invasion as a police duty, an expedition to put down an unruly and ungrateful child. The brothers Howe—a general and an admiral—were entrusted to make peace with the Colonies, or such of them as repented their evil ways. The Howes and their spies found little to console them. The flames of freedom engulfed the land from the northern area of the Massachusetts Bay Colony to Savannah, Georgia. Most of the Colonies consisted of coastal lands, seldom extending far into timberland, although Pennsylvania had a remote western outpost called Fort Pitt. The British counted on assistance from Tories who begged to be listed in dispatches to London as loyal to Parliament and King. The numbers of Tories had dropped sharply; less than one-third of the 2,500,000 colonists had a kind word to say for George Rex. The waverers were overcome by the enthusiasm of militia, Minute Men, and tradesmen who insisted that there was but one choice: complete freedom or slavery to taxes.

General Washington stated that, beginning six days ago, lookouts at Gravesend had spotted a few British masts anchored inside Sandy Hook. A day later, more arrived. The third day lookouts were stunned to see what they called "a forest of masts" riding at anchor between Staten Island and the coast of New Jersey. Washington was not willing to entrust his plan of action or the disposition of his small army to a courier. The tactics of the Howes and the countertactics of the Continental Army appeared to be obvious. The Continental general staff guessed that the best stroke of the British would be to try to split the Colonies into halves, devouring one half at a time. The easiest landing to effect this would be at New York, where the harbor was great in size and there was sufficient landmass to establish a secure place on Staten Island.

When the English had replenished stores and water, they had two options. The first was to land at Long Island, across the Narrows from Staten Island, at night, and to fight their way across Brooklyn to the East River, risk a night crossing, and fight General Washington's main force at Manhattan. The second was to brave the batteries of cannon at Bowling Green and Paulus Hook, run the men-of-war under sail up to Washington Heights, and cut off Washington's retreat route up the Hudson and through White Plains. The cannon at the disposal of the Colonies could fire a ball little more than two hundred yards. Admiral Howe could sail his fleet up between those at Bowling Green and those on the Jersey shore at Paulus Hook with sufficient room to avoid being hit.

General Howe decided it would be better to invade across the Narrows, hoping to force Washington into battle. As long as his ragged army was intact, it would be a living threat to the British Crown. Neither of the Howes realized that George Washington had split his army—a dangerous practice —putting one force at Gravesend Bay to forestall a landing there, keeping the remainder based at Manhattan.

The Congress did not relish the news from Washington, or his pessimistic attitude about short-term enlistments. He would have preferred to draft every able-bodied man to serve for the duration of the conflict. Under the separate rules of the Colonies, militiamen were disbanding, going home to plow, plant, or reap. The Congress could not conscript men, and didn't have the power to pay them in hard currency. The Congress had no official standing except whatever ephemeral power was given to it by the colonies acting in concert. They sat in Philadelphia, which was not a capital of a nation because there was no nation. The Congress had the power to print money, which on the open market was worth less than a third of its face value in British pounds sterling. Even the delegates, in the main, were not considered to be the best mentalities of each colony; the most important men were kept at home to help organize the more important work of devising a state constitution.

It was almost noon when John Hancock set his mace on his desk and resolved the Congress into a Committee of the Whole. A spokesman for Maryland stood and asked the indulgence of the Congress to read a resolution passed by the governing body at Annapolis, to wit:

> That the instructions given to our deputies in December last be recalled, and the restriction contained therein, removed; and that the deputies to be authorized and empowered to concur with the other United Colonies, or a majority of them, in declaring the United Colonies free and independent States; in forming a compact between them and in making foreign alliances. . . .

A shout went up from Massachusetts and Virginia. The resolution was noted and accepted, and was placed on Clerk Thomson's desk as Hancock surrendered his power to Benjamin Harrison. The first of the Lee resolutions—calling for freedom of the united Colonies, and cutting all ties to Great Britain—was read and debated. Those who would favor Jefferson's Declaration of Independence would vote for the Lee resolution. It served as a sample of the formal document to come. The room had darkened so much that a member asked that candles be brought in. The windows were again secured as a high wind tore at Philadelphia under low slate-gray and black clouds. Heavy slanting drops of rain dimpled and blackened the outer walls. The candle flames swung to one side, then the other, precisely as some members found themselves fearing that the Colonies were moving too fast too soon, a consciousness that each was but a thin reed which could be blown away.

Until today, all that they had asked of the King was a restoration of the *status quo ante,* back to a time before 1773 and its outrageous taxes, back to a time when the Colonies were reasonably happy children of the British kingdom. King and Parliament and Prime Minister had ignored their pleas and had sent soldiers and ships against them. The delegates had a burning desire to think of themselves as being forced into forming a separate nation—backed into it by a callous monarch.

A few, like Franklin and John Adams, could remember earlier oppressive laws; they remembered the strict measures against smuggling; an order demanding that the Colonies pay the salaries and expenses of the British governors who ruled them; taxes on East India tea, paint, documents, playing cards, indigo dye. If that was not sufficient to light the fire of discontent, Britain did not want the Colonies to trade with other nations; the homespun Puritans could buy all their manufactured goods from England. In time, Adams and Franklin noted that almost all the taxes had been rescinded, all except tea. The tax would have sent eighty thousand dollars each year from the thirteen Colonies to England at threepence per pound. News of the tax caused Bostonians to demand that a ship full of tea be returned to England. The plea was refused. Men of Massachusetts disguised themselves as Indians and dumped ninety thousand dollars' worth of tea into Boston harbor. Ironically, the threepence tax was lower than the amount Americans had been paying. The colonists preferred to smuggle cheaper tea from Holland. It was this which had finally alienated the Colonies from the Crown, and it was this which united the thirteen Colonies behind Massachusetts when the British closed the Port of Boston.

The delegates hoped that debate on the Lee measure

would be limited to John Adams (for) and John Dickinson (against). There were murmurings that the Congress had listened to all the arguments a hundred times over and no one would be persuaded to change his vote today. New Jersey destroyed this aspiration by declaring that it was a new and radical group sitting for the first time. The five members would appreciate a capsule of the arguments for and against the Lee resolution, realizing, of course, that acceptance or rejection would determine the fate of the Declaration of Independence.

John Dickinson was recognized. He was tall, patrician, a wealthy Pennsylvania farmer as sincere and honorable in his opposition to liberty as John Adams was for it. There was no official stenographer, but few forgot how Dickinson, head bowed as though in sorrow, stuck his fingers in his waistcoat pocket and said, "My conduct this day I expect will give the finishing blow to my popularity, Yet, I would rather forfeit popularity forever than vote away the blood and happiness of my countrymen."

He remarshaled the old arguments that the Colonies, as presently constituted, were too weak to fight the Crown and all its minions. At this moment, George Washington was in New York in command of twenty-five regiments totaling nine thousand men. This was the Continental Army. It was hardly treasonable to question whether these untrained men could stand and fight the tremendous fleet that Admiral Howe had standing off New York. Or whether they could win a victory over General Howe's army, the highly skilled and trained British soldiers and the mercenary Hessians whom King George had hired from Europe.

Dickinson hit with the hardest blows of logic. He shook the most radical members of the Congress. Independence? It could mean nothing less than an all-out war for which the Colonies were unprepared—militarily, politically, economically. England had pledged the whole of its resources to put independence down. Where would the American settlers get the money to keep an army in the field? Who indeed would have the will to fight the gargantuan machine pitted against them year after interminable year?

"Independence!" he shouted, looking up, beseeching the members with his eyes. "It is like destroying our house in winter, before we build another shelter." Independence! America might well expect the destruction of her growing cities. The British would urge the Indian tribes to turn against the colonists. The frontiers would shrink, draw closer to the sea; "scalping parties will whoop along New York's Wall Street and Philadelphia's Market Street."

And suppose, he said softly, just suppose that England found the task of subduing the states a long and difficult one. The cost to the King in lives and treasure might well smash the British Empire. Then France and Spain would become emboldened to sweep back into the Colonies, asserting old claims to lands now used by Americans. Who could stem a second sweep of mighty arms? Who, indeed?

Trade had been cut off with England. Where did the Colonies have a foreign friend? Nowhere. France and Spain might be willing to trade with Boston, New York, Philadelphia, Baltimore, Norfolk, Charleston, and Savannah, but by God, gentlemen, how could they break the British blockade? Who would brave it? No one. If there was a time for independence, no man of sense would dare say it was now. There wasn't even a central government to husband the efforts of the Colonies. The Second Continental Congress was in being only at the sufferance of each colony. If the Congress took a firm stand, it could be disbanded to become a useless instrument at any time—at the whim of a group of colonies.

John Dickinson sat. His forehead was beaded with perspiration. Surely, he must have dwelled a moment on the one thing he did not say. He had told his family that if the delegates voted for independence, he would swallow his pride and enlist in the Continental Army as a private soldier.

John Adams stood. The bald and short lawyer from Braintree pointed his arguments with the plodding, tireless blows of a laborer hammering a spike into a rock. He had such poor regard for what he said that for the rest of his life he would state that his speech had been an "idle mispence of time." Outside, the lightning flashed again and the rain was noisy against the windows. Thomas Jefferson thought that Adams "came out with a power and thought and expression that moved us from our seats."

The New Jersey delegation, newly elected, sat entranced. Adams argued that the fight for freedom was already in being. The King was already at war with the Colonies. Must he be permitted to gobble them one by one? There was only one road to survival—fight and win, even if the effort required every able-bodied man, every growing boy. The enemy was already in our cities. America must seek help from France; France, in her own interest, had a score to settle with the British for the loss of big tracts of land on the new continent.

The Americans already had an agent, Silas Deane, at Versailles, waiting for a favorable word from Louis XVI and his malodorous ministers. Would it not be better to seek a friend now, rather than wait for victory, when foreign alliances would be cordially thrust upon a new and exhausted nation? It was no longer a question of whether the Colonies wanted to fight. Ask the people of Charleston, who had just rebuffed Cornwallis and his expeditionary force. Ask the Minute Men of Lexington and Concord whether they had asked for a resort to arms, or whether it was thrust upon them. Ask the Delaware militia, with their splendid uniforms, digging redoubts in New York City.

If war was a fact, and the subjugation of the Colonies

was the goal of George III, then why cower before him? Why not, this day and for all the days ahead, renounce the shelter of his scepter and utter a final cry for independence? Why count all that each of us, and all those we hold dear, might lose in this conflict? If the Colonies did not fight, they would lose all anyway at the hands of merciless Redcoats. Did anyone doubt that the British command already had a list of all leaders, in Congress and back home? The losses in home, property, business had long been itemized by the British.

It was the King who had set the date for independence. As long as the confederated states could field an army, even a small one, the King must send more soldiers, more ships, spend millions more in pounds sterling to keep the Americans subdued. If war was a fact, and indeed it was, then independence was the proper punctuation for the word.

The New Jersey delegation burst into huzzahs. They were silenced by the stares of men who had become accustomed to being statesmen for a whole year. Harrison pounded his desk with the palm of his hand. New Jersey was warmly appreciative of the sense of John Adams because the colony had made a political turn of 180 degrees in the past month. The earlier delegation to the Congress had been told not to vote for independence. A few weeks ago the political climate altered abruptly toward the radical. The royal governor had been placed under arrest. The three members sent to the Congress had been replaced by five—Richard Stockton, Chief Justice; Dr. John Witherspoon, president of the College of New Jersey at Prince Town; Francis Hopkinson, poet, painter, attorney; John Hart, a sixty-five-year-old farmer; and Abraham Clark, a short acidulous lawyer from Elizabeth Towne.

Except for the solitary outburst, the New Jersey group was inordinately shy. They had been present for two days, but they felt they were outside the ebb and flow of the tides of liberty. Within a day they had a champion. Edward Rutledge of South Carolina was the youngest man of all—twenty-six.

He had been in the shadow of his older brother John most of his life. Edward spoke nasally and shrilly; he needed friends as a desert traveler requires water. When John went back to South Carolina to expedite a new state constitution, Edward was sent as South Carolina's chief delegate to the Congress.

He spoke often and positively. Much of what he had to say was pedantic. He was fond of reminding the older delegates that he had studied law at Middle School in England. He failed to mention that this was true of the other three delegates from his state. John Adams did not appreciate Rutledge. In his diary Adams wrote: "Rutledge is a perfect bob-o-lincoln, a sparrow, a peacock, excessively vain, excessively weak . . . inane, puerile." And yet, on this day, it was Edward Rutledge who had entreated Adams to speak up for the cause of liberty once more—if not for the sake of South Carolina, then for the edification of New Jersey. After vain flutterings, Adams agreed to do it.

The clock was approaching 4 P.M. This was dinnertime at the local taverns for visiting delegates. Sitting as a Committee of the Whole, the Congress reported to itself as a deliberative body. John Hancock hurried back to his mace and clothed desk. He was a wigged popinjay, one of such property as to be building a man-of-war for the American Navy, one who aspired to be Commander in Chief of the American Army, a man always powdered, perfumed, and ruffed, who often walked the streets of Philadelphia with servants ahead and behind.

He was about to call a roll of the colonies when it was suggested that the hour was late, that Congress should acknowledge that it had received a report from the Committee of the Whole and would act on that report on the morrow. John Hancock did not wait for a second to the motion. He asked the delegates to confer quietly and to vote at once on the Lee resolution. As Thomas Jefferson recorded the tally on his portable desk, he wrote: "it was carried in the affirmative by the votes of N. Hampshire, Connecticut, Massachusetts, Rhode Island, N. Jersey, Maryland, Virginia, N. Carolina & Georgia. S. Carolina and Pennsylvania voted against it." Delaware, with two votes divided, had no vote; New York had to await further instructions. The tally was 9 to 2. Rutledge asked an adjournment until morning. It was seconded and granted. South Carolina required time to think.

It was the custom for radical members to coax, to cajole members such as George Read of Delaware, Lewis Morris of New York, Charles Carroll of Maryland, and such others as the radicals thought of as fence-sitters. The time, the arguments were mostly wasted. The delegates often wandered out into the streets of Philadelphia, shouting at each other as they approached a favorite tavern, and resorting to roars of displeasure when they got inside and sipped from copper flagons of still ale.

Livingston of New York said that, in a cautious way, he was for a declaration of independence, in spite of the fact that—or perhaps because of it—the Van Cortlandt family, the DePeysters, the DeLanceys were loyalists to King and Crown. He enjoyed "tweaking" the wealthy families. A courier had been sent to New York posthaste to state that if New York persisted in opposing a declaration of independence, it might find itself alone as the brothers Howe attacked. It must either join the majority of colonies now, or risk a hands-off attitude from the Congress when the battle for survival began. Livingston and others had demanded that the ruling clique transmit new instructions at once.

It was a blustery wind-swept afternoon. Thomas Jefferson, probably alone, walked back with his portable desk to his brick quarters. His flared jacket was wet; he held a large kerchief over the flame-red hair. Inside the desk his copy of the Declaration reposed, as it had in the morning of his hopes. It would be brought back again, matching word for word the one on the clerk's desk. If the Congress voted on the matter tomorrow, Jefferson knew that it would either be the greatest day in American history or the most tragic. It was not given him to know that, almost a half century from then, John Adams would recall how and why Thomas Jefferson was chosen to write this hallowed instrument of freedom:

The sub-committee met. Jefferson proposed to me to make the draught. I said "I will not." "You should do it." "Oh! No." "Why will you not? You ought to do it." "I will not." "Why?" "Reason enough." "What can be your reasons?" "Reason first—You are a Virginian and a Virginian ought to appear at the head of this business. Reason second—I am obnoxious, suspected and unpopular. You are very much otherwise. Reason third—you can write ten times better than I can."

"Well," said Jefferson, "if you are decided, I will do as well as I can." "Very well, when you have drawn it up, we will have a meeting."

A meeting we accordingly had, and I conned the paper over. I was delighted with its high tone and the flights of oratory with which it abounded, especially that concerning Negro slavery, which I knew his Southern brethren would never suffer to pass in Congress. I certainly would never oppose . . . I consented to report it, and I do not now remember that I made or suggested a single alteration.

We reported it to the committee of five. It was read, and I do not remember that Franklin or Sherman criticized anything. We were all in haste. Congress was impatient, and the instrument was reported, as I believe, in Jefferson's handwriting, as he drew it. . . .

Jefferson thought of it not as a personal instrument of liberty or an expression of an appeal for justice, but purely as a device to arouse world opinion in favor of the Colonies. The new America already had vituperative and venomous enemies from without and within; it was begging for a friend.

Far ahead, at the age of eighty-two, Jefferson decided to put his thoughts about the Declaration in a letter to Henry Lee dated May 8, 1825:

> . . . With respect to our rights, and the acts of the British Government contravening those rights, there was but one opinion on this side of the water. All American Whigs thought alike on these subjects. When forced, therefore, to resort to arms for redress, an appeal to the tribunal of the world was deemed proper for our justification. This was the object of the Declaration of Independence. Not to find out new principles, or new arguments, never before thought of, not merely to say things which had never been said before; but to place before mankind the common sense of the subject, in terms so plain as to command their assent, and to justify ourselves in the independent stand we are compelled to take. Neither aiming at originality of principle or sentiment, nor yet copied from any particular and previous writing, it was intended to be an expression of the American mind. . . .

It is possible that Jefferson, as an introverted intellectual, did not join any of his confreres for dinner. He probably had his supper with Bricklayer Graff, Mrs. Graff, and the mewling infant. It is a pity that Mr. Jefferson, poor speller, did not learn the letters of Graff's name. All his personal mail was addressed to:

> Mr. Thomas Jefferson, Esq.,
> c/o Graaf,
> Philadelphia, Pennsylvania

☆ July 2, 1776 ☆

MOST OF THE DELEGATES, WHILE IN THE CITY, kept "country" hours. They were abed by 10 P.M., up at 5:30 A.M., breakfasting at six. Fast was broken in many ways; the Congressmen knew that they would have nothing to eat until 4 P.M. supper, so they enjoyed ample morning meals. The most common was fruit in season, a cereal hot or cold, a thick slice of fried ham or beef, hot rolls and butter, and hot tea. It is known that John Adams and Thomas Jefferson utilized the breakfast hour as a time to read personal mail, and to respond. Benjamin Franklin, whose lifelong passion was knowledge, read New York and Philadelphia newspapers, mail from statesmen and friends, and whatever books, pamphlets, and tracts were in his house.

Hancock called the Congress at 9 A.M. Shortly after eight, Jefferson, splendid in a brown suit, brown buckled shoes, and brown silk stockings, locked his rooms and began the solitary walk. His hair was tied back with a gold ribbon and he wore no hat. As always, he attracted no more attention on the street than other well-dressed businessmen, although the portable desk caused some to stare at it. Others walked down Walnut or across on Market in twos. The freckled man had an upright, almost military stride, his eyes fastened on Philadelphia's tall landmark, the steeple of Christ Church.

The morning was clear. He had consulted his new three-pound, fifteen-shilling thermometer at 7 A.M. and noticed that it read 70 degrees Fahrenheit. He took this to mean that by early afternoon the room in State House would be eighty degrees or more. A hot, breathless day for liberty if the Pennsylvania and New York delegations did not ask for a postponement of the reading. The streets, some cobbled, some of clay, held pools of sparkling water from the night rain. The sun stared hard at the great city. Floating dumplings of clouds rimmed the horizon. Within an hour or two, those innocent ghosts could go dark and threatening with rain.

John Adams, walking from another direction, was in awe of this day. After a hundred and sixty years of colonial subservient life, over a century and a half of fighting a wilderness and taming it, of fighting Indians and driving them westward, of pleading and begging a motherland to treat the Colonies as adult dominions, of tearing the colonial conscience to shreds trying to decide whether to live in the shadow of the royal scepter or to die as free men, the future of the land was about to be brought into the present by a historic vote. Mr. Adams had no doubt about the vote or its outcome.

His ebullience was so boyish that he dashed a note off to Abigail in Boston: "The Second Day of July 1776, will be the most memorable Epocha in the history of America—I am apt to believe that it will be celebrated by succeeding Generations, as the Day of Deliverance by solemn Acts of Devotion to God Almighty. It ought to be solemnized with Pomp and Parade, with Shews, Games, Sports, Guns, Bells, Bonfires and Illuminations, from one End of this Continent to the other, from this Time forward, forevermore." Within the purview of John Adams, the caustic firebrand, there would not, could not, be a greater day for Americans than July 2, 1776. He was sure that it would be the day of birth of a new nation, a free land of free men, men who would show the pale scars of fetters on their wrists to the day of their death, bursting with pride about the day they shed all shackles.

At 9 A.M. John Hancock had been sitting at his desk a half hour. He was impatient to rap for order. However, he delayed, his eyes frisking faces in groups. John Dickinson and Robert Morris, the staunchest opponents of the Declaration of Independence, had not arrived. It was unlike them to delay the proceedings. Then, too, if there was to be articulate opposition on this day of destiny, the burden would naturally fall to Dickinson of Pennsylvania. If the gentlemen was ill, or was delayed by some misadventure, John Hancock knew that a messenger would arrive momentarily. In that event, a sportsmanlike gesture of goodwill would be expected from John Adams and Benjamin Franklin, who would ask a postponement of consideration of the Declaration.

Jefferson noticed the absence of his honorable opponents. At nine-thirty, Hancock rapped his hand on the desk for order and announced that the Second Continental Congress would proceed with the business at hand. There was some whispering among the delegates about the advisability of a motion to delay proceedings for an hour. Hancock waved the delegates down into their seats. He knew that Clerk Thomson had sufficient messages and letters to occupy the Congress through the morning.

Some anonymous person had named Pennsylvania "the Keystone Colony" many years ago. If the word "keystone" is taken to mean a wedge-shaped stone placed at the summit of an arch to hold the other pieces in place, then Pennsylvania was no more, no less of a keystone than the colony of New York. Both were large and prosperous, both were wedged between the northern and southern colonies. Neither had much influence in holding the colonies together.

No one can dispute that Pennsylvania was the richer of the two, a colony with good schools of higher education, rich tradesmen who used the Delaware River to good advantage. Pennsylvania also had a Philosophical Society and a Society of Astronomers. If it was reactionary, this was so because the Quakers controlled the province. They were one-third of the population and almost three-quarters of the trade. Another third was German Lutheran, fondly called "Pennsylvania Dutch." Mostly they were farmers who had settled in Pennsylvania looking for religious freedom.

The "Dutch" did not aspire to political control. The third third were Scotch-Irish Presbyterians, economically poorer than the Quakers and the "Dutch," but politically viable, a group which hungered for independence in the face of Quaker frowns. The rich group, Quakers, had the most to lose and argued hotly that they would not fight against their lawful king. The "Dutch" were new immigrants, too busy looking for rich black loamy land to make an issue of liberty. The Scotch-Irish, having the least to lose, were recruited into the Pennsylvania militia and stalked the Pennsylvania government by picketing State House with muskets.

It is an irony of history that on June 14, 1776, the Scotch-Irish won their fight to remove all restrictions from the votes of the Pennsylvania delegation. After that, Benjamin Franklin, Dickinson, and the others were free to tally their separate consciences. It is even more of a surprise that Dickinson and Sherman, who had a majority vote in the delegation of seven, chose to absent themselves on this day, tilting the delegation in favor of independence. Whether they did it because they thought that independence was the true will of the people or whether they did not relish risking Pennsylvania's position as the only colony to oppose the Declaration was not determined.

Benjamin Franklin left his delegation to sit beside Jefferson. He murmured, "*Jacta alea est; jacta alea est*"—the die is cast, the die is cast. It was obvious that the young patrician from Monticello required verbal support on this day because most of the delegates thought they had talent as writers, except that they seldom "had the time for it." This would lead to innumerable alterations and objections to Jefferson's draft. As a modest author who insisted that there was nothing personal or even original in the Declaration of Independence, he was prepared to writhe through the protests.

Hancock, however, had other ideas regarding the agenda for July 2. Instead of moving directly to Jefferson's document, he ordered Thomson to begin to read the advices and missives from the military. The room was hot; the windows tight against another oncoming thunderstorm. The voices within the room, sometimes weak and soft, were sometimes lost in muffled thunder. At other times, the shouting from the stable outside seemed louder than the delegates.

Washington asked for confirmation in the discipline of "two marine officers" who had offended the military code. He did not need the consent of Congress in minor military matters. However, some officers had friends and relatives in the Congress, and the Commander in Chief did not want to risk displeasure.

To the radicals, who sat squirming through the morning session, it seemed that Hancock was delaying a historic reading and vote. When the sun was high, he asked that the Committee of the Whole report to the Congress regarding the Lee resolution of yesterday. The delegations, which had assumed that the morning session would be taken up with dispensing of the three Lee resolutions, then getting on to a reading and perhaps a vote on the Declaration of Independence, regarded this as a delaying tactic.

No one would accuse John Hancock of being opposed to liberty. The popinjay of the Congress bowed to no one— not even Jefferson, Franklin, and Adams—in his ardent desire to be free of the British shackles. As a rich man, he had as much to lose as anyone. If anything, he felt, as president, that he had an almost proprietary right to keep the debates and voting of the Congress within "correct and well-defined" channels. Therefore, whether they were pleased or not, he proposed to force them today to resubmit the three Lee resolutions to the Committee of the Whole, in hopes of getting a unanimous vote before proceeding to consideration of Jefferson's epic.

It may not have occurred to him that the Congress had already been permitted—nay, urged—to go far afield in its duties and responsibilities. Certainly some of the provincial governments were dismayed to learn that the Second Continental Congress had not only built an army and was building a navy, it was also waging war against the mightiest nation in the world, even though the war had been imposed on the Colonies. It was requisitioning supplies for the army and several militias; it was establishing arms-and-munitions plants without authority anywhere it pleased; it was working mines, imposing taxes on citizens who had not authorized taxes; it had appointed an ambassador to France; it had printed money not backed by metal or good credit; it had even sent two messages to the King in the name of the local governments which it had not consulted—the two messages were no more than ultimatums designed to arouse His Majesty; the Congress had even told friendly Indian tribes where they could settle.

There was license in the assumptions of the delegates. There was deceit too. Richard Penn of the Colonies had appeared before the House of Lords. When he was asked about possible desires for freedom and sovereignty, he had said he had "never heard one of them breathe sentiments of that nature." The lords believed Penn. Benjamin Franklin, in an earlier aside to Lord Chatham, said that "having more than once traveled almost from one end of the continent to the other and kept a great variety of company, eating, drinking, and conversing with them freely, I never heard in any conversation, from any person drunk or sober, the least expression of a wish for a separation or a hint that such a thing would be advantageous to America." George Washington, en route to Boston to assume command of the Continental Army, declared that he "abhorred" the idea of independence.

The sky was at its darkest; the rain seemed to walk up Walnut Street in spangled sheets. A delegate sitting near a window heard hoofbeats on cobblestones. Curious, he opened a window with permission, stared out, closed it, and sat down grinning. Mr. Hancock asked that a Committee of the Whole be resolved to consider all three of the Lee resolutions, the first to be considered over again in the light of a nonunanimous vote.

The committee sat. The custodian unlocked the main door. A happy, bedraggled figure strode in, clanking spurs and leaving puddles as he reported to Benjamin Harrison, startled and openmouthed at the apparition. Caesar Rodney, fatigued by an all-day and all-night ride, was reporting in as the third delegate from Delaware. His garments were muddy; his face was soiled by rain and dirt. The kerchief he used to cover the cancer on his face was soaked and seemed plastered to his cheek. Still, his eyes were bright with flame; his mouth asked patiently if he was in time for a vote.

The delegates, or most of them, may have felt like cheering. John Hancock and his alter ego, Harrison, seldom permitted it. Demonstrations, either hisses or huzzahs, they felt, were unseemly, ungentlemanly. Rodney left his clothes on his horse in the stable. He shed a soaking jacket and shook hands with his fellow delegates, Thomas McKean and George Read. Read was cordial. He would vote against Jefferson; Read was certain that his vote would be buried in a vote for liberty; still, a man must maintain his integrity. Now, with the presence of Rodney and the vote of Tom McKean, Read knew that Delaware's unit vote would go to the majority.

One delegate, writing home, found it difficult to forget the valiant, forlorn figure of Caesar Rodney. "He is the oddest looking man in the world," he wrote. "He is tall, thin and slender as a reed, pale; his face is not bigger than a large apple, yet there is sense and fire, spirit, wit and humour in his countenance." Most of the delegates knew that when Rodney first detected cancer of the skin, he could have gone to England, there to command the attention of the finest physicians and surgeons. He was wealthy, a bachelor. If the doctors could not cure him, at least there would be palliatives for the wrenching pain he endured. But he could not go to England, knowing that he was opposed to King and Empire. To the contrary, he had risked his health further by riding eighty miles from Dover to Philadelphia in cold slashing rain to arrive in time to tip Delaware's slender vote toward freedom. The glances of admiration from the delegates were more eloquent than their unnatural silence. Had Adams and Franklin dared, they would have hugged Caesar Rodney to their bosoms.

As the delegates consulted each other for a unit vote on the first section of the Lee resolutions, the wall clock indicated that it was afternoon, and the members resolved that Dickinson and Morris would not be present. At home John Dickinson resolved, in good conscience, that he could not sign a declaration of independence. Robert Morris, a merchant with a Liverpool accent, decided that if the Declaration was passed, he would sign when the time came.

Thomson stood to read the Lee resolutions. Mr. Harrison said that the Committee of the Whole should consider the three resolutions as one—to be accepted or rejected by yeas and nays.

> Resolved, That these United Colonies are, and of right ought to be, free and independent States, that they are absolved of all allegiance to the British Crown, and that all political connection between them and the State of Great Britain is, and ought to be, totally dissolved.

That it is expedient forthwith to take the most effectual measures for forming foreign Alliances.

That a plan of confederation be prepared and transmitted to the respective Colonies for their consideration and approbation.

Thomson polled the Colonies, beginning with Georgia. Everyone was aware that as this vote went, so would go the Declaration. It would pass, of course, but no one would be content with a 9-to-2 vote, with two abstentions. The polling, therefore, was done in oppressive silence, except for the tremors felt in the room when lightning cracked and thunder rolled. Georgia voted aye; South Carolina surprised many by switching to the majority—aye; North Carolina—aye; Virginia—aye; Maryland—aye; Delaware (another breakthrough)—aye; New Jersey—aye; Pennsylvania (Benjamin Franklin's eyes sparkled as he announced the vote)—aye; New York (a delegate stood to announce that although it was the inclination of his group to vote for the Lee resolutions, they were still bound by an order from New York not to vote for independence; they hoped for a change of orders but it had not arrived)—abstained; Connecticut—aye; Rhode Island—aye; Massachusetts Bay Colony—aye; New Hampshire —aye.

The vote was 12 to 0, with one abstention. It was as close to unanimous as the Colonies could get. Overnight three votes had come to the radicals: South Carolina, Delaware, and Pennsylvania. The South Carolinians, in their gentlemanly manner, had indicated yesterday, "We may be with you tomorrow," but few had counted on an abrupt change. Delaware had been won by Caesar Rodney's presence. Pennsylvania had been the profound surprise.

The change in the Keystone Colony had been achieved by the absence of Dickinson and Morris, and the presence, and prescience, of Benjamin Franklin. As soon as it became apparent that the two reactionaries would not attend and vote, Franklin had worked his wiles on Judge John Morton of Ridley, Pennsylvania, and Judge James Wilson, a Scot. As they listened to Franklin's arguments, both men moved away from their conservative friends, Delegates Humphries and Willing. These two kept silence, but glanced frowning at Morton and Wilson, as though to warn them not to listen to the blandishments of Franklin. The old doctor needed both judges to achieve a 3-to-2 majority, and he got it.

The thing had been done. And well done. The fiery gentlemen had slammed the door on the King. There was no way for him to pass through it again, and there was no way back through that door for them. For good or evil, they were all revolutionaries now. Firebrands. It was, as John Adams maintained, a great day in history for freedom. It was also a dangerous day in which, symbolically, every delegate had placed his head in a British noose. The gentlemen knew they would be accountable for it. They were slow to disperse this afternoon. Some waited for the rain to abate. Others admitted that they would like to exchange thoughts about the future of the thirteen Colonies. Eighteen months ago, the First Continental Congress dared not discuss freedom and had denied entertaining the thought that they could exist and flourish without England. The sailors among them thought that they had cast off from a big ship in a small dory.

They were without guidance in government—without precedent indeed. There were no military strategists among them, and yet they sensed that a long and debilitating war lay ahead, one which might be won years from now, not in a smashing victory, but in the exhaustion of Great Britain or the Colonies. As a nation aborning, they needed friends badly. They must have proponents who would extend long-term credit and send arms, ammunition, perhaps even qualified army officers.

In sum, they needed everything. All they had was a

will to prevail. It was enough for today, but there was a serious question concerning the amount of suffering and despair a new country could endure. Even in military defeat—if that should happen to Great Britain—her navy would seal American ports against trade, stultifying growth and choking the Colonies on their own products.

Of the 2,500,000 persons dwelling in the Colonies, the Congress expected two-thirds to join it in the fight for freedom. The remainder were self-styled Loyalists, or, as the Yankees called them, Tories. This would create an enemy, a potent enemy, within the gates. This enemy would give sustenance to His Majesty's soldiers and intelligence, while surreptitiously trying to impede the Continental Army.

There was a repressed excitement—barely repressed— among the men who adjourned. If any saw the deep shadows ahead, they remained unmentioned. Almost everyone, it seemed, wanted to buy dinner and drink for other members. No one, with the exception of Thomas Jefferson and Benjamin Franklin, felt like retiring alone to dwell on the great and awful deed of the day. Nor would anyone remind others that if the population was 2,500,000, the Congress could count on no more than 1,600,000 men, women, and children to fight for the liberty they had proclaimed. They were ebullient schoolboys who had defied the proctor. They were men who had altered the history of the world in an hour of time. They were flaming revolutionaries who had scorched the earth between them and a rightful and righteous government. They had proclaimed themselves free, as though that was the end of the matter, instead of an agonizing beginning.

They would not speak of Tories or Redcoats or a parliament or king. They seemed not to have noticed that General Washington's letter this morning said that his spies had counted 140 ships in Lower New York Bay. It mattered not to them that the accurate count was four hundred transports convoyed by fifty-two ships of the line and twenty-seven armed sloops and cutters—the greatest war fleet ever assembled. The delegates had also heard General Washington's message to his nine thousand troops: "The time is near at hand which must probably determine whether Americans are to be free men or slaves. . . . The fate of unborn millions will now depend, under God, on the courage and conduct of this army. We have, therefore, to resolve to conquer or die. . . ."

Grave, shuddering words. They seemed not to have been heard, or, having been heard, left no more impression on the consciousness of the gentlemen than a plea for uniform brass buttons on military uniforms.

The paradox of the enthusiast is that he does not hear the deep toll of warning bells. John Alsop of New York, a man who feared the wrath of George III, went his lonely way late in the afternoon determined to return to New York and have no more of this business. He wanted it to be known that he had not voted for liberty. He would remain for the session tomorrow, but he would leave at once. If, by chance, the Redcoats threatened New York, Mr. Alsop would retreat to the woodlands of upper New York State.

If no one outside the New York delegation noticed his defection, it is equally true that those who rejoiced in freedom this evening remembered almost everything worth quoting that favored the cause. They would stand, tankards in hand, joyous sweat glistening on their brows, to shout:

"Britain is the parent country, some say. Then the more shame upon her conduct. Even brutes do not devour their young, nor savages make war on their own families."

"In England a king hath little more to do than make war and give away places; which, in plain terms, is to impoverish the nation and set it together by the ears. A pretty business indeed, for a man to be allowed eight hundred thousand sterling a year for, and worshiped in the bargain."

"Wherefore, since nothing but blows will do, for God's

sake let us come to a final separation, and not leave the next generation to be cutting throats, under the violated, unmeaning names of parent and child."

"There is ten times more to dread from a patched-up connection than from independence."

☆ The Road to ☆ Independence

IT SEEMS, IN RETROSPECT, AS THOUGH AMERICA was very young and naïve when it struck for independence. This is not true. Some colonies, such as Virginia and Massachusetts Bay, had 150 years of frontier and city life behind them. There were generations of Americans who had never seen England, whose allegiance was to one colony. Their forefathers had endured long and dismal voyages to the new land to find freedom—freedom of religion; freedom of expression; freedom from debtors' prison; freedom from an archaic caste system; freedom from the crushing burden of British taxes.

All of these freedoms constitute a rebellion against something. It is a matter of *reductio ad absurdum* that British citizens who were satisfied with the lawful constrictions of life in the British Isles remained there. By the same logic, those who departed for a new world were dissatisfied. It did not occur to the monarchy or to the American provincials that dissatisfaction might, after 150 years, flower to disloyalty and open rebellion.

The settlers of the seventeenth century were busy clearing land and fighting Indians. They had little time for politics. They had to grow food or die. All of the colonies were dotted

48

with coastal farms. There was a premium on hard work, clearing loamy bottomland of trees and scrub, tilling, seeding, waiting for spring rains and summer sun, thanking the Almighty for an autumn harvest. Colonial life was primitive and difficult.

It was not until the start of the eighteenth century that the farmers found themselves in a position to export food, tobacco, indigo dye, furs, and fish. The colonists, accustomed to struggling for life in the New World, were surprised to find that after satisfying their own needs, they could now export and sell to Mother England. New England made its living from fishing and shipping. The seas were rich in edibles; vast timberlands made the building of ships easy.

The Massachusetts Bay Colony also manufactured rum. This was placed in casks for something the provincial government called "the triangular trade." It was sent to Africa, there to be exchanged for slaves. The Blacks were shipped to the West Indies, which paid for them in molasses. The molasses was shipped to Massachusetts to be converted into rum. New England ships also exported foodstuffs to other colonies, the West Indies, and southern Europe.

The middle colonies exported grain, livestock, and furs. The farms of New York, New Jersey, Pennsylvania, and Delaware were larger and richer, unit for unit, than those on the rocky soil of Massachusetts. Tobacco almost ruined Virginia. The market was good for a while, but prices dropped and this large and affluent colony found itself in financial distress. Plantation owners, through necessity, sent slaves and overseers to the western part of the colony to clear suitable land for the growth of corn and cereals.

North Carolina grew tobacco as a mainstay, but also exported cattle and foodstuffs from the back country. Still, North Carolina and Maryland were called debtor colonies because they imported more than they sold abroad. At the turn of the eighteenth century, Georgia, the thirteenth colony, had not been organized.

The colonists who despised the caste system of the Old World brought it with them to the New. The aristocrats consisted of wealthy planters, clergymen, public officials, shipping merchants, and smugglers. Money begat power. The so-called middle class consisted of tradesmen, farmers, and artisans. The lowest class labored for the other two. The difference between unskilled labor in America and in Europe was that the colonial worker could move, if he chose, buy cheap land, and transfer himself to the middle class; or, if he became wealthy, be an aristocrat. As more joined the two upper classes, Americans found time for the arts, the sciences. Extensive libraries, known in 1700 to be found only in Harvard College and William and Mary, were imported to adorn the drawing rooms of the homes of the affluent.

Great Britain could not see and would not acknowledge the maturing of her colonies. Parliament—Commons and the House of Lords—and the monarchy looked down on America as one would a growing, brawling child. The Colonies were not regarded as a part of the British Empire, but rather as a distant and primitive appendage which required protection against itself and foreign enemies, for which it would have to pay. England looked upon America as a business investment, and the Mother Country had a right to expect that it would be profitable.

The Colonies would have English governors and English law. They would also house British soldiers in their homes. The Americans would pay for the British magistrates, courts, provincial governors, the army, and such navy frigates as were required to protect American ships from pirates. This was carefully computed by the Chancellor of the Exchequer; a government profit was added, in addition to Stamp Act taxes designed to help British industry to prosper. American shoulders bowed under this yoke, but the focus of attack in the early 1700s was not the taxes but rather the lack of a colonial voice in British government. The House of Commons told

America that it was insolent and presumptuous to demand representation in London.

On the colonial side, it seemed to be a madness for London to try to govern Boston, New York, Philadelphia, Williamsburg, and Charleston from a distance of over three thousand miles. When a colony had a problem, no matter how small, it had to be written out in the form of an appeal for redress, sanctioned by the colonial governor, sent to London by packet, which required six to eight weeks, heard and acted upon within two to four weeks, then it had to await a response which would be seaborne for almost two months more. The Americans usually waited four months for adjudication of any problem.

Two of the signs of American maturity were the establishment of John Campbell's *Boston News Letter,* which began circulation through the Colonies in 1704, and the establishment of post offices in 1710. These accomplishments guaranteed a fairly free exchange of information. As an accommodation the Crown permitted the Colonies to elect provincial assemblies. This was a mistake. The various assemblies arrogated to themselves the right to tax their peoples and thus to pay the royal governor. It is remarkable that London saw this as a blessing: the Colonies would be told how much to pay; their own representatives would collect the money.

Britain did not see the local assemblies as seed beds of insurrection. Overnight the apolitical colonists became professional agitators. When the royal and proprietary governors demanded funds, the assemblies insisted on freedom of debate, the right to pass on the qualifications of their own members, the right to adjourn when they pleased, the right to exclude officers of the Crown from their deliberations, the right to appoint customs and tax collectors, and lastly, the right to appoint and pay a representative to go to London and protect the rights of the colony concerned. If the royal

51

governor hesitated on any of these "rights," the assemblies refused to appropriate money for his use.

Sometimes colonial impudence went a step too far. Around 1725 there was considerable agitation for "written constitutions" and "territorial representatives in the House of Commons." If this was too much too soon, the response of Parliament was too little too late. The British government maintained that instructions given to royal governors were, in essence, "colonial constitutions." In addition, all members of Parliament represented all British subjects, not merely the constituencies which elected them.

The Colonies rejected both dicta out of hand. On one occasion, when the Crown disallowed ten laws passed by the Virginia House of Burgesses because the colonists forgot to include the provision that these statutes did not take effect until approved by the King, Virginia argued that any laws approved by the British governor were, in fact, approved laws. If this were not so, Virginia argued, then laws passed by Parliament were invalid until approved by the King.

Political activity led, in time, to political sophistication and the formation of political parties. There were four. One was the Court party; another was the Colony party. Two lesser ones were the Gentleman's Party and the Country party. The first and third were absorbed by the Conservative Gentleman's party. This became the party of the aristocrats, landowners who could protect their interests only by remaining loyal to the King. Within the span of two decades, they became known as Loyalists, and to the opposition as Tories.

The second and fourth parties evolved into the Liberal Country party. They demanded unlimited paper money, free land for all citizens, and strong defenses on the French-Canadian border and against Spanish-owned Florida. In time this group, as liberal as the other was conservative, was called Whigs. One of the rare ironies of history is that after the French were defeated in Canada, the British Crown permitted the formation of political parties, but these were not followed by imperial quarrels, nor did the majority of Englishmen in Canada strive for independence.

In the American Colonies, through the 1760s, both Whigs and Tories insisted that their quarrel was with Parliament; their loyalty to King George III was intact. The Americans did not realize that the King and his ministers were one; the contemptuous voices they heard from Parliament were, in the main, His Majesty's echoes. The more the Colonies bristled with resentment and tried to subvert the royal taxes, the more George III begged his ministers to punish the Americans.

All wars begin with a double lack of appreciation of intentions. So it was, long before America rebelled against the Mother Country, that the colonists misunderstood the outrage in England; and Great Britain failed to appreciate the stubborn resolve of indignant farmers. History and, most assuredly, historians have made little effort to understand London.

In the colonial press, for example, George III was dismissed as a "good family man" because he had fifteen children by an ugly wife. There was more to the King than this. He grew up indolent and opinionated. Informed or uninformed, he claimed to understand every complexity of government. With or without the assent of his ministers, he claimed to be able to solve any problem. He was a constitutional monarch, but expected abject fealty from everyone. When the Earl of Chatham wished to resign from the government, his letter to the monarch abridges time and distance and gives the reader a terse portrait of His Majesty as he saw himself:

> Sir—Penetrated with the high honour of Your Majesty's gracious commands, my affliction is infinite to be constrained . . . to lay myself again at Your Majesty's feet for compassion. My health is so broken that I feel all chance of recovery will be entirely precluded by continuing to hold the Privy Seal. . . . Under this load of unhappi-

ness, I will not despair of Your Majesty's pardon, while I again supplicate on my knees Your Majesty's mercy. . . .

Should it please God to restore me to health, every moment of my life will be at Your Majesty's devotion. . . . I am, Sir, with all submission and profound veneration Your Majesty's most dutiful and devoted servant . . .

The King was parsimonious to the point of pain. The royal family was sheltered in cold, drafty palaces and ate as meanly as commoners. The King would not pay a secretary and thus, when he found himself bound to untie small imperial knots, he did it at his desk, writing constantly, almost eternally, to explain and reexplain himself to the House of Lords, the colonial governors, and such others as were not beneath his dignity to address.

George regarded his interminable correspondence as public utterance and painfully portrayed himself as "moderate and firm," which, of course, was His Majesty's assessment of self. When Viscount Hillsborough proposed to punish the Massachusetts Bay Colony, the King wrote "highly proper"; "very right"; "not much objectionable." To counterbalance this, he said of the royal governors: "They ought to be instructed to avoid as much as possible giving occasion to the Assemblies again coming on the apple of discord." In truth, he was backing and filling almost constantly. When Hillsborough proposed outright confiscation of the charter of Massachusetts Bay, George moved in two directions; such a dire action might "from a continuation of their conduct become necessary; but till then ought to be avoided as the altering [of] Charters is at all time an odious measure."

The King's enemies portrayed him as a bulbous-eyed, addlepated monarch who, at royal levees, covered his ignorance in the presence of lords and ladies by cupping his ear and shouting: "What? What what?" Let it be said that George III was a conscientious king with a compulsion for enervating work. If he saw the American Colonies as vassals living off the sufferance of the Crown, it was because this reflected the astute thinking of all England. Each complaint about taxes or proper representation from the Colonies evoked fresh outrage from all London, with the exception of a few men in Lords and Commons. It was "impudence" and "insolence" on the part of ignorant colonists to protest to the Crown, whose benevolence permitted them to scratch out a living and to flourish in a far-off land owned and ruled by a just king.

His Majesty desired to love and protect America, but the children were fractious and self-centered. A sound spanking, as a result of each incoming mail, seemed to be in order two or three times each year. Much later, William Makepeace Thackeray would try to caricature the King with words of contempt, and would unwittingly come close to accuracy:

> [He] knew all about the family histories and genealogies of his gentry, and pretty histories he must have known. He knew the whole *Army List*; and all the facings and the exact number of buttons, and all the tags and laces, and the cut of all the cocked hats, pigtails and gaiters in his army. . . . He knew the *personnel* of the Universities; what doctors were inclined to Socinianism, and who were sound Churchmen; he knew the etiquette of his own and his grandfather's courts to a nicety, and the smallest particulars regarding the routine of ministers, secretaries, embassies, audiences; the smallest page in the ante-room or the meanest helper in the kitchen or stables. These parts of the Royal business he was capable of learning, and he learned.

He was not stupid. He was not ignorant. He was obsessive-compulsive in his concern with the minutiae of daily living. He studied Latin and did not master it. He studied German and French and was fairly fluent, though not scholarly. He was, at best, a master of the inconsequential.

He was conscious of being right and being correct.

And yet he ruled in good conscience. As a sedentary person, he was prone to overweight; the palace servants said that George III could read a newspaper for thirty minutes without falling asleep. No one has written that the King was known to laugh, or to tell an amusing story. He felt confined by the Parliamentary Act of 1688, within the bounds of which he ruled. This despite the fact that he had spent his youthful years studying how to rule within the scope of a constitution. If it is true that many monarchs ruled with shadowy men behind the throne, then George III confined himself to ruling Great Britain in the shadow of the House of Commons. It was his shield as he played the game of politics.

When the Colonies rebelled against the British Stamp Act in the 1760s, the King wrote in favor of an amendment to meet the "just grievances" of America, although there is a difference between "an amendment" and repeal. The contretemps made the King so angry that in later years he almost (but not quite) acknowledged that America was another nation: the enforcement of the Stamp Act in 1766, he wrote, "encouraged the Americans annually to increase in their pretensions" to the degree that the "thorough independency which one state has of another" was bound to be the abysmal result.

Repeal would amount to surrender to the Colonies. The King favored a sharp reduction of the Stamp Act tax to nullify criticism. When, first, the tax was instituted by the British government, he was opposed. Later, when it was repealed in the face of American insurrection, the King was opposed again. His mistake was in taking a public stand; no matter what the King's opinions, the powerful Whigs would pillory George III to sustain their positions. Nor was there any unity among those who looked with favor on Americans.

Lord Grenville defended the Stamp Act after the government was committed to its abolition. "Great Britain protects America!" he roared. "America is bound to yield obedience. If not, tell me when the Americans were emancipated. . . . This nation has run itself into an immense debt to give them protection; and now they are called upon to contribute a small share. . . ."

There was acrimony and personal hurt in the words. William Pitt the Elder stood to say that he was no "courtier of America," but he asked sarcastically, "The gentleman asks when were the Colonies emancipated? I desire to know when they were made slaves." He asserted that taxation was not a part of the governing or legislative power, although he risked traditional arguments to the contrary. "Americans are the sons, not the bastards of England," he said. The kingdom could "not take money out of their pockets without their consent. The gentleman tells us America is obstinate. America is in almost open rebellion. I rejoice that America has resisted."

This was January, 1766, when British merchants were staggering under a colonial boycott of English merchandise. They filled the corridors of Commons, shouting adulation at Pitt for wanting to repeal the Stamp Act, and hooting George Grenville, who became so angered that he tried to choke a spectator. After all the debates and a slaughtering of old friendships, the vote was 275 to 167 for repeal. The word reached America, and New York erected a statue of gilded lead to George III and set it on a stone pedestal at Bowling Green.

This was a mistake because the King was not their benefactor. To the contrary, George III sulked in silence through the great debates. Properly he found himself in agreement with Grenville, who saw the Americans as obstinate brigands who spent most of their time in illegal trading, smuggling, and general avoidance of laws enacted in England. Grenville had little faith in the British governors of the Colonies, claiming that they drew their salaries and emoluments from the Americans, and they hired Americans to do their work. He pointed out that American customs agents were worthless to England. On the infrequent occasions when they discovered smuggling, they taxed the smugglers a halfpenny per smuggled gallon, or a penny a carton for dry merchandise, and pocketed the money.

Political England was in convulsion. Landowners feared that the majority party, Whigs, would give the Empire away. The King wished heartily to be "rid of the Whigs." Governments and ministries came and went. One government reduced the colonial tax on molasses from threepence to one penny per gallon. The landed squires implored the government to notice that the repeal of the Stamp Act and the cider tax in America had cut revenues $650,000 a year. The only way in which the deficit could be nullified would be to raise land taxes to six shillings per British pound of value. They lamented that Englishmen would, in effect, be paying the American tax.

Something had to be done—but what? The King loathed George Grenville and did not want to call him to form a government. The Rockingham administration was tottering. His Majesty saw but one giant on the horizon—William Pitt the Elder. In August, 1766, he was summoned to the palace to form a government. As a reward, George III proposed to raise Pitt to become Lord Chatham. The news reached America and the colonists staged impromptu celebrations that "a friend at court" was to be head of the new government. In Wall Street, New York, a statue of Pitt in a toga was raised. He was referred to as "The American Moses." The joy in the New World was unbridled.

The Americans forgot that Pitt was first and last a loyal Englishman. He felt that Great Britain had more poignant problems than taming colonists to the royal whim. When the Americans entreated Lord Chatham to cancel the Mutiny Act of 1765, he turned away in irritation. He began to feel, as other Prime Ministers had, that the Americans could not be satisfied. The Mutiny Act, he felt, was of no concern to the Colonies. It had to do with British soldiers, who, once enlisted, were in service for life. As pay they received a few pence per day, and had to pay for food other than government rations, replace and repair uniforms and buttons, and pay for medical service.

The Americans opposed the Mutiny Act because one paragraph of it stated that British officers and soldiers in the Colonies would be quartered in private homes. The people of such cities as Charleston, Williamsburg, Philadelphia, and Boston did not want soldiers in their homes. The Americans exaggerated the criminal tendencies of soldiers, maintaining that they seduced and raped the women of the house, and stole anything portable. In a large standing force, there are bound to be abuses, but the colonists maintained that their women were revolted at the thought of Redcoats in the house.

Chatham pointed out that the "quartering of soldiers" in private homes was not the work of the government, but of the British Army. There was a shortage of barracks and public halls where soldiers could sleep. The "private homes" paragraph was struck from the Mutiny Act, but it embittered the Prime Minister. British officers, under the amendment, could quarter soldiers in "empty houses and barns," but the colonists kept writing polemics about "the Chastity of our Wives and Daughters" being exposed "to the insulting Arrogance of a rude and unpolished Soldiery."

The Mutiny Act was not new. The Americans did not protest it until they had achieved repeal of the Stamp Act. When the provision for quartering soldiers had been amended, the colonists noted that another part of the act made them responsible for furnishing barracks, fuel, vinegar, salt, and beer to the troops. A howl went up from America. The Stamp Act, the publicans proclaimed, was designed to force the Colonies to support the British Army in America. The Stamp Act had been replaced by provisions in the Mutiny Act which would compel Americans to raise money to support the army. In sum, Parliament had again violated the principle of no taxation without representation. What could be the difference between supporting the Redcoats under one act or another? The local assemblies went a step further. If they, as lawful bodies, were compelled to take orders from the "dictatorial mandates" of a British Parliament, then it was a waste of taxpayers' money to pay for colonial assemblies.

The customary outrage on both sides of the Atlantic was in full flower when an English warship with two companies of soldiers was driven by storm into Boston. The captain, under the Mutiny Act, asked the governor for barracks, fuel, and candles. Governor Francis Bernard sent the request, with some trepidation, to the Massachusetts Council. The councillors ordered the supplies sent to Castle William, where the soldiers were housed temporarily.

Overnight, Boston was in an uproar. Street gangs shouted that the Council needed purging. James Otis, addressing a church group, said that he would "as soon vote for the Devil as he would for Councillors who betrayed the liberty of their country by adhering to British law and placing it in the provincial law books." The British officials in America were astounded at the insolent use of the words "liberty" and "country." Massachusetts Bay, under law, had neither.

The public tirades caused the local House of Representatives to refuse supplies to the British ship and soldiers. Strangely, the British did not punish this act by disbanding the House of Representatives. Instead, British officers bought supplies for the storm-tossed men. The news spread south through the Colonies, and emboldened others to "tweak the tail of the lion." General Thomas Gage, British soldier and diplomat, sensed a distant danger when he wrote that the action of Massachusetts Bay "nearly annihilated all the authority of the British legislature over the Colonies."

The news reached New York, headquarters of the British Army in North America. This colony paid more in taxes under the Mutiny Act than any other. And yet New York was more prosperous under British law than any other, and it was the most loyal of all colonies. From Georgia—newly founded at Savannah in 1732—to New Hampshire, Americans watched New York. Within a few weeks the New York legislators declared the Mutiny Act "unconstitutional"—in effect, appointing itself as a court of appeals over the acts of Parliament. In the same breath, as though to temper its rashness, New York voted to honor "royal requisitions for Army supplies." No one pretended to understand whether this meant that "royal requisitions" would be paid for in British pounds or not.

In this instance, the twelve remaining colonies refused to follow New York. South Carolina retained a measure of independence by honoring the Mutiny Act but refusing to send beer and salt to English soldiers. Others tried to make their acts appear to be voluntary. New Jersey appointed commissioners who were ordered to treat each request from the army as an individual requisition, to be honored or dishonored, "according to the custom of this province." Pennsylvania stood alone in conceding that the Mutiny Act was a binding law.

The anger of the Colonies was reflected in the outrage of British citizens. Lord Chatham told Commons he thought that the original Stamp Act "had frightened those irritable people quite out of their senses." William Beckford, regarded as a friend of America, shook his head dolefully and said, "The Devil has possessed the minds of the North Americans." The common man in Great Britain complained that if the Colonies could nullify the Mutiny Act, they would nullify all acts of Parliament.

Lord Chatham saw a more personal danger in the American challenge. He might lose a vote of confidence, and the government might fall. He feared the sharp-tongued attack of George Grenville in the House of Commons. Grenville had been preaching armed subjugation of the Colonies for years. Benjamin Franklin, who had spent a lot of time in England, said that whenever London heard of rebellion in the Colonies, Parliament shouted, "Send over an army or a fleet, and reduce the dogs to reason."

So it was in 1767. The Chatham government could not afford to be outshouted by the opposition. In the House of Lords, the Duke of Bedford demanded bloody reprisals. He asked the government why it had not sent regiments to New York, and "let the Sons of Liberty fight if they dare." One member of Lord Chatham's government, Chancellor of the Exchequer Charles Townshend, had personal ambitions. He felt that Pitt's star was declining, while his was in the ascendancy. He made a speech in Commons in which he pointed out that America could not dictate to the Mother Country because "if we once lose the superintendency of the Colonies, this nation is undone."

This was precisely the point. Britain had won the French and Indian war in 1763, but at a terrific cost, estimated to be $500,000,000. Great Britain was in the awkward position of trying to reduce its debt by taxing the Colonies it had spawned and, at the same time, facing an economic revolt from its "children." Chatham saw the twin goals as irreconcilable and bemoaned the truth that he had inherited the Mutiny Act from Grenville. Admittedly, Chatham, or Pitt the Elder, was a great statesman, but his first mistake was to organize a government of all parties and factions—Whigs and Tories; patriots and the King's courtiers; friends and enemies. Grenville, eager to unhorse Chatham, said that there was a greater difference of opinion between the ministers than there was in the political factions of the House of Commons.

In this moment of crisis, the great Pitt's chronic gout made him so ill that he retired from embattled London to Bath. Rest and medication did not improve his condition. Within a few weeks body and mind appeared to deteriorate. Some of Lord Chatham's friends visited the statesman and said he verged on "insanity." Whatever his condition, it was certain that he could no longer hold the reins of government.

Charles Townshend required no greater encouragement to reflect the Crown's opinion in all phases of all problems. In Commons he was regarded as a wit who skated so lightly on several sides of a debate that he left no scars on any of the frozen faces around him; in fact, in any one speech, Townshend was often applauded by dissident groups of members. Parliament was so enamored of his speeches that most members did not notice that "Champagne Charlie" changed sides on public questions almost as frequently as he powdered his wig.

Now that Chatham was off in the shadows, Townshend, as Chancellor of the Exchequer, proposed to play the King's game of punishing the Colonies. As this was also the mood of the landed squires, it brought quick endorsement to his ambition to become Prime Minister. He threw oil on the fire of discontent when he announced that Major Farmer, who had been sent to America to take possession of the Illinois country in the name of the King, had drawn $150,000 in expenses from the British treasury. The squires denounced the land acquisition and argued that "the rich and overbearing Americans" would not pay a farthing of the total.

Townshend made a speech before Commons in which he made sport of the American distinction between external and internal taxes. A tax is a tax, inside or outside, he maintained. His opinions were running counter to the soft line of Chatham toward the Colonies, but no one remarked it. Parliament, he maintained, had all the legal and moral rights to tax its own colonies. It didn't matter whether the instruments were external or internal; Parliament should never abrogate its rights for fear they might grow rusty from disuse. The speech gave voice to precisely the thoughts of the majority and Townshend was drenched with applause.

George Grenville, who had been preaching this doctrine for a long time, got to his feet and demanded that

63

"Champagne Charlie" pledge himself publicly to a tax on the Colonies. Townshend told them what they wanted to hear: he would not only impose a tax on America, but he would legislate one that would reduce taxes in England. The benches shuddered with the thunder of approbation. Townshend's political popularity was at its peak.

Lord Chatham was pledged not to tax America for fear of additional alienation of affections between Colonies and Mother Country. His doctors said that he must rest; he must not discuss politics. The only politics he could discuss at this juncture would be the removal of Townshend. This was denied him, and the Chancellor of the Exchequer continued on his taxing scheme. In January, 1767, he said he was working on a plan.

In the same month, the Chancellor again opposed the will of Lord Chatham by defending the rights of the East India Company. This appears to be a great distance from American problems, but the common denominator was "profit for private interests." The subjugation of India was continuing, but, as in America, none of the profits accrued to the British government. The East India Company, which held a private charter, had, through corruption and oppression, drawn immense wealth from the subcontinent into the pockets of its agents and shareholders.

Chatham had demanded an investigation, with the possibility of revoking the charter. The East India Company, which had raped the economy of India and somehow bordered on bankruptcy, countered this threat by advancing its annual dividend from 6 percent to 10. Pitt, before becoming ill, had denounced the "Asiatic plunderers of Leadenhall Street." He proposed to stop the enrichment of the shareholders by turning all revenues to the Exchequer. This was popular with British merchants who held no shares, but Chatham became ill and "Champagne Charlie" stated that the government had no choice but to hold all charters as sacred instruments, not to be violated by any new government of a different political hue from the preceding one.

At once East India Company stock soared in price. The opposition, however, pointed to the inequity of a company which showed an annual profit of four million dollars and found itself backing up the wall of insolvency. Townshend won his point in a final vote, but it was expensive. The East India Company had to agree to pay the British government two million dollars each year and to restrict its profits to a reasonable return on investment. The great dissenter, Edmund Burke, said that the King was trying to confiscate the East India Company so that he could rule without Parliament.

This was an exaggeration, but the two-million-dollar tax only pointed up the desperate necessity of an American tax so that England would not be impoverished. In mid-January, 1767, the squires awaited Townshend's plan to tax the Colonies without, as he said, "offending them." Patience was running out when Townshend announced that the real estate valuation tax of four shillings per pound—a war measure—would have to be continued an additional year. Before the Chancellor could hear the howls of protest, he said the tax would stay on the books only to give room "for the most brilliant operation of finance which this country ever saw." The squires no longer believed him. The opposition of all political shades banded together, reducing the government majority in the House of Lords to three votes. George III grumbled that the minority groups coalesced "to storm my closet." The Commons reduced the four-shilling tax to three, presenting Townshend with an annual loss in revenue of three million dollars.

This brought Lord Chatham out of bed and down to London, determined to be rid of Charles Townshend for all time. At the capital his feverish mind worked to find opposition leaders, one by one, who would agree to accept Townshend's post. They declined because Chatham's government was in disfavor and would fall in any case. Pitt seemed close to death and was carried back to Bath. His physicians said that "only a good natural fit" would make him well and restore his mind to a natural balance.

Townshend maintained his pretensions to leadership, although his adversaries were convinced that he had been bluffing, not promising. Either way, "Champagne Charlie" and the Chatham ministry were in trouble. To save his political life, he made one more speech. This time he stole the preachment of Grenville that England needed "economy and taxation." Both would be necessary to survival. Economy could be established, he said, by withdrawing a large part of the British Army from North America. He would not countenance stripping the army of its protective duties in the Colonies—Townshend threatened to resign rather than face that —but the Redcoats could be reduced in number so that they could be quartered mainly in the coastal port cities.

"An American Army," he babbled, "and consequently an American revenue, are essentially necessary, but I am willing to have both in the manner most easy to the people, and will pursue the most moderate measures consistent with the attainment of these important objects." He told the ministers of the government that unless his suggestions were accepted, he would resign his office. This had the effect of rallying the leadership sheep around him. Overnight, the ministers swore to tax the American Colonies, no matter how dire the result.

When Townshend next appeared before Commons, the Rockinghams, Bedfords, and Grenvilles demanded to know his plan to "punish" the thirteen Colonies. He angered the opposition by declaring that to punish all the Colonies would unite them against England. He preferred to single out one colony at a time—New York first—and to punish in a civil rather than military manner. His way of doing things, he assured the back benches, would keep the colonies alien to each other.

Pennsylvania had already acknowledged the validity

of the Mutiny Act. The Chancellor proposed to pluck the big colony of New York from its stubborn stance and to suspend the New York Assembly as a law-giving body until it was ready to accept the Mutiny Act. When New York fell in line, smaller ones would surrender. He made it sound so moderate, so palatable, that Chatham sat in his sickbed and admitted that the measure was commendable.

Having won his point by a resounding vote, Townshend reverted at once to weathercock politics and decided to impose a tax on all the Colonies—a sure way of uniting the Americans. He asked Parliament to impose taxes on paper, lead, paint, glass, and tea. Amid deafening cheers, he said that such taxes would be appropriated by the British government and used to pay for "the charge of the administration of justice and the support of civil government in such provinces where it shall be found necessary," in addition to the cost of regiments used to defend the Colonies.

It sounded good to England. It wasn't until members of the House of Commons had the opportunity to review the proposed tax that it was called "minuscule." Englishmen had been paying a twelve-cents-per-pound tax on tea. Americans could pay as much. The whole tax structure would bring only $200,000 a year. Townshend, roaring like a lion, had spawned a political gnat.

The Chancellor entreated them one and all to bear in mind that once the precedent of taxation had been established, England could tax and tax and such revenue would "in time ease this country of a considerable burden." No one among the gentry wanted to tax while whispering on tiptoe, but if this was the only way to keep the Americans from uniting in rebellion, many members would vote for it.

Grenville opposed the Townshend "Tea Tax." So did Edmund Burke. Many feared that the irascible Americans would make no distinction between an external tax and an internal tax; also their umbrage would not be dissipated by the fact that it was a small tax. Still, it passed 180 to 89 and England was committed to confront the Colonies once more as mother to child. The King, writing about the Americans, stated: "the truth is that the too great leniency of this country increased their pride and encouraged them. I wish nothing but good, therefore everyone who does not agree with me is a traitor and a scoundrel."

The sense of Parliament was that it was forced to use its right to tax the Colonies; otherwise, Americans would be encouraged to embark on their "high and imperious ambition of being themselves a nation of independent states." Townshend's followers recalled the arguments of Dr. Benjamin Franklin, who referred to the Stamp Act as an "internal tax," unconstitutional for Parliament to levy. Now they had an "external tax," one which would be collected by customs inspectors at ports. Townshend's personal feelings, expressed to his friends, were that Americans were dolts with ironclad principles. If they could be made to think that one tax was "internal" and another "external," then Townshend was certain that in time he could levy a tax on them and convince them that it wasn't a tax.

American governments tried to limit the sovereignty of Great Britain by declaring that London could not impose an "internal" tax. The local assemblies arrogated to themselves the right to tax their citizens. On the other hand, some local governments acknowledged that the King could impose imposts and duty taxes on merchandise Britain shipped and sold in America.

Townshend's mistake in judgment was in assuming that he had America's word and bond on taxation.

Nine British warships sailed into Boston harbor and two regiments of young soldiers marched up the Long Wharf to pitch tents on the Commons. It was cold in October, 1768, and the recruits wanted to know why they weren't quartered in private homes. Captain John Preston explained that the people of the colony did not like British regulars and refused to help them in any way. When the weather became snowy, most of them would be housed in Castle William, the English fort on the bay.

The two regiments were present not to make war, but to enforce all the old, unenforceable laws and the new Townshend measures. They were an irritant. Boston was busy smuggling to evade payment of "external" taxes. John Hancock had been caught aboard his sloop *Liberty* with a cargo of Madeira wine. His friends rescued him, but not the wine.

American sailors, assisted by ships' chandlers and Boston rowdies, began to make fun of the Redcoats. They were called Lobsterbacks and Bloodybacks. When Bostonians saw squads of marching soldiers, they catcalled, "Lobsters for sale!" The ultimate humiliation occurred when the poorly paid soldiers sought odd jobs in the city. The hardworking merchants gave them menial work and paid them poorly.

The soldiers, needing a marching song, used "Yankee Doodle" to taunt Boston. Obviously, if Yankee Doodle went to town riding on a pony, stuck a feather in his hat and called it macaroni, he was an idiot. The song aroused the people, who devised ditties belittling the Lobsterbacks. Life for the two young regiments became so unbearable that the soldiers were drunk in most of their off hours.

March 2, 1770, was a day of fresh snow and blood. John Grey stood in front of his rope shop, squinting up at the lazy flakes still falling. He saw a soldier. "Hi, lobster!" he called. "You want work?" The soldier said he needed extra work. Mr. Grey told him he could earn a shilling or two by cleaning out the public toilet adjacent to the shop.

The soldier frowned. He stumbled in the snow, obviously partly intoxicated. He looked up at the warm faces behind cold windows and began shouting insults. A second rope maker listened, walked over, and knocked the soldier down. Windows were opened and raucous laughter heard. The soldier got up, his uniform covered with wet snow and mud. He shouted for help. A passing squad heard the call and tried to arrest the rope merchant. Men and boys emerged from buildings and beat the Redcoats back. An officer called for all hands to stand back. His face was smashed by a hard snowball.

Whatever feelings of animosity had been growing in the bosoms of Bostonians and soldiers, they became public property the next three days. The temperature dropped; the snow froze solid. Chunks of ice were thrown. Squads of soldiers, armed with bayonets and cutlasses, roamed the town shouting obscenities at citizens and pricking them with steel. Bands of young men quit work at dark, had their supper, and went looking for Lobsterbacks. The soldiers swore at the people; the people tossed chunks of ice at the soldiers.

Someone tolled a church bell. The people, thinking it warned of a big fire, hurried into the streets. All they saw were shouting soldiers and mobs of men. In front of the Customs House, a young boy teased an officer of the Horse Guards about paying his barber bill. A sentry emerged and clubbed the boy with a rifle. The crowd became ugly. The soldier ran back inside the Customs House and called for assistance. Captain Preston and eight soldiers responded.

The soldiers leveled their guns at the crowd. "Fire, damn you!" the crowd shouted. The people spat at the soldiers. "Fire, you lobsters!" A soldier named Montgomery became fearful of the crowd. He yanked the flint trigger and a little blot of blue lit the face of a Negro named Crispus Attucks. He fell face down in the snow. The other soldiers became unnerved and pulled the triggers. Several more people fell. The rest of the crowd stared, then fled. They had asked the soldiers to fire, but they weren't brave when the muskets exploded.

Acting Governor Thomas Hutchinson, sedate and

sedentary, put a greatcoat over his nightgown and hurried to Brattle Street to assure the people that justice would be done —that Captain Preston and his squad were under arrest. The people did not appear to hear. They were staring at the bodies bleeding in the snow. Five persons died.

Boston called it a "Bloody Massacre" and sent advices to the other colonies about it. Samuel Adams appeared before a Committee of Investigation and stated that unless the soldiers left Boston, he feared their presence would incite the people to civil riot. Hutchinson didn't want the soldiers to leave. Adams said that Boston would not be responsible for what might happen. Acting Governor Hutchinson sent the two regiments to Castle William. When the customs agents heard that they no longer had protection, they took their wives and children and hid inside Fort William.

Boston, which had tried to rid itself of soldiers and customs agents, accomplished both in one evening. It also had something else—five martyrs, and the onus of a "massacre" on British heads. John Adams and Josiah Quincy were so pleased that they offered to defend Captain Preston and his eight soldiers. The offer was accepted, even though Adams feared that Boston would misunderstand. As counselors for the wrong people at the wrong time, Quincy and Adams did well. They won acquittal for Captain Preston and six of his men. Two were found guilty of manslaughter—Privates Kilroy and Montgomery—and were publicly branded on the hand.

The Colonies gave off a surface aura of orderliness until June 9, 1772. It was a long warm evening and the people of Providence, Rhode Island, sat outdoors to catch a breeze. They heard the sound of a lonesome drummer. Usually, this was accompanied by some special news which the drummer shouted. This time he had good news. The British schooner *Gaspee* was hard aground off Namquit Point, seven miles south.

The merchants of Providence could hardly credit this

dispatch. The *Gaspee* had been chasing their smuggling ships for two years. They knew her commander, Lieutenant William Dudingston, and had often spat before his feet as he walked the streets of Providence and Newport. The boy who brought the news improved on it. He said that *Gaspee* had been chasing the sloop *Providence Packet,* a reliable smuggler. The *Gaspee* had followed the *Providence Packet* into shoal waters, firing her guns. The *Providence Packet* had fled, threading the sandbars, but the *Gaspee* was high and dry.

Most of this was untrue. Lieutenant Dudingston was sailing close to shore off Namquit Point, not chasing anyone, and had beached *Gaspee* on a bar. She would wait for a flood tide to free herself. The men of Providence began to smile. It was, they felt, a most interesting evening. Within an hour groups of them were at the wharf, muffling oars with shirts and rags. At dark, several of the boats, loaded with men and muskets, rowed for Namquit Point.

Two hours later, they approached *Gaspee* bow on. In this way no one aboard could depress her guns and fire on them. As they boarded, a sentry shouted. Dudingston came out of his cabin in his underwear, wearing a double-ender naval hat. He challenged the boarders; a musket ball hit him in the groin and he fell. The crew got out of bed. The men of Providence beat them with guns and sat on them.

The lieutenant and his crew were put in rowboats and taken to a rocky island. A physician was permitted to dress Dudingston's wound. The oarsmen returned to the *Gaspee* and set fire to her. They rowed out of range and watched. Some had brought jugs of liquor from John Sabin's tavern. They drank and watched the British ship burn all night. In the morning a blackened hull was visible. The respectable smugglers rowed back to Providence with another story. They told their women that the *Gaspee* was a "pirate ship."

The King was heartily sick of America and Americans by the spring of 1773. They were impossible to govern with any degree of majestic order. It was as though they waited in concert for Great Britain to assume a stance on any public question, at which point they ran off in the opposite direction. They were more than ingrates; they were infidels who despised their origins. George III saw himself as the personification of a benevolent father, and, in a sense, he was. He looked upon himself as the good example of husband, father, son, keeper of the faith and majesty.

The Americans had subverted the Townshend taxes with smuggling. The King could not believe that an entire people would stoop to wicked lawlessness when given a choice to obey the law. He had listened to their leaders five years ago when they defined internal taxes and external taxes. Since, he had been humiliated by their behavior; even their word was worthless.

Townshend had left the service. Lord North was now the principal minister. And North, in the privacy of the King's closet, had revealed some most distressing news. The East India Company was again on the edge of bankruptcy. It had eighteen million pounds of tea rotting in warehouses. The government owed the company twelve million dollars in exchange monies, but Great Britain was too poor to pay. What could be done?

North felt that the Townshend taxes should be nullified. The King squirmed in righteous anger. He did not, could not, agree to permit the Colonies to dictate to the Crown. North said the government would not appear to bow to colonial pressure—it would rescind the taxes as a gratuitous gesture to the rebellious Americans. He reminded the King of the huge cost of maintaining a fleet of warships off American ports to stop the smuggling. They had not stopped it. Taxes had not been collected to the amount of the cost of the warships.

Neither George nor North broached the subject of mismanagement of the East India Company. In the forty years between 1732 and 1772, gross profits had aggregated

120 percent per year. Officers of the company siphoned off millions for themselves. Huge bribes had been paid to members of Commons and the House of Lords to prevent government agencies from investigating East India's finances.

His Majesty appeared to be grudgingly satisfied when Lord North said that all taxes on British goods in America would be repealed except those on tea. East India had been paying twelve cents a pound to bring tea into Britain from India, then transshipping it to the Colonies. The new law would permit the company to send its tea directly to America from India, and sell it at a tax of but three cents a pound, making this American potable as cheap, or cheaper, than smuggled tea. Certainly the Americans would not quarrel with a good bargain.

The tea tax was enacted. The East India Company began to ship millions of pounds of tea to American port warehouses. The news reached Boston in early summer of 1773. John Hancock denounced the measure as another and rather adroit device for taxing Americans. British tea might be as cheap as or cheaper than Dutch tea, but the colonists would not buy it. They would not be taxed by England. Mr. Hancock, one of the most elegant smugglers, did not say that he had hidden warehouses full of Dutch tea, and perhaps that had no bearing on his outrage.

The articulate Americans had difficulty explaining why no one should buy the good cheap tea of Great Britain. Samuel Adams gave it a lot of thought. He decided that the low tax was a ruse. If the people bought British tea, the American smugglers would be bankrupt instead of the East India Company. American merchants would be out of business. If the tea tax worked for England, she would impose a small tax on another item, and another, until that day when the Colonies would have to assume the indebtedness of the Mother Country. America would be taxed to death.

It was a tenuous argument, but the colonists would

agree to any libel against Great Britain. They wanted to believe.

Three ships arrived in Boston harbor the first week of December, 1773. They carried seventy-five thousand dollars' worth of tea. They dropped their hooks in a gray fog. A call for wharfmen to unload the vessels was answered by silence. The radicals of Boston made speeches at the Customs House, on the Commons, and before State House (which the British governor said was a pretentious name indeed for a "towne house").

Darkness fell early on December 16. Thousands of Bostonians gathered at the Old South Meeting House to protest the presence of the three ships. The tea, their leaders vowed, would be returned to England without a thank-you, or the men of Boston would not be responsible for what happened to the ships. A man named Rotch, who owned one of the ships, asked permission to visit Governor Hutchinson and secure his assent for the sailing of the ships.

The Americans—some say there were seven thousand at the meeting—were easily goaded to anger. Rotch hurried to the governor, and hurried back. "The governor," he said, "has refused, sir." Boston refused to allow the presence of ships or tea in its harbor. Samuel Adams, short, round and almost apoplectic, stood with his arms waving until the crowd subsided. "This meeting," he shouted, "can do no more to save the country."

Most of the audience did not understand what he meant. If he intended that they disband peaceably, they would do so. At sea, an orange moon sat astride the horizon. Hancock and Adams stood at the edge of the wharf, watching fifty prominent Bostonians, dressed as Indians including war paint, embark in small boats carrying hatchets. They were gone three hours. The moon was high when they returned. The British merchant crew had not resisted when they boarded ship, smashed 342 boxes of tea, and threw them overboard.

The successful "Indians" emitted war whoops as they returned to Griffin's Wharf. Townspeople, hearing the strange sound, came out of doors to investigate. At water's edge they saw big half-opened crates of tea wallowing in the tide. December 16 was a long night for celebration.

Boston did not know that East India tea had been shipped to other ports. Nor did Boston know whether other colonies would resist or buy the tea. In Charleston the tea was taken ashore and buried in a dank cellar, never to come out. In New York wharfmen smashed many cases of tea and dumped the contents into ships' holds. In Philadelphia a British sea captain decided not to try to unload; he sailed back to England with his cargo.

One of the ironies of history is that the Americans thought that the British would back down; the British were certain that the rebellious colonists would back down. As each move was made to test the temper of the other, it was thought to be a final move. Hancock and Adams were sure that Parliament and Crown would rescind the tea tax, as they had so many others.

The news was in London at the end of January, 1774. Both Parliament and the King were shocked out of their senses. The destruction of private property, under English law, was punishable by death. The King resolved that if he had to haul a part of Boston back to London for hanging, he would do it.

On February 4, General Thomas Gage was summoned to the palace. Gage was a good-looking, good-tempered man who had fought beside Americans in the French and Indian Wars and had married a girl from New Jersey. Currently, he was Commander in Chief of British forces in America. His Majesty asked many questions about the colonists. That evening he wrote to Prime Minister North: "He says they will be lions whilst we are lambs, but if we take the resolute part they will undoubtedly prove very meek."

This was a perfect echo of what the King had been hearing for years—"a few rounds of musket shot, a few towns burned," and the Americans would flee before the Redcoats. General Gage said that if the King commanded, he could leave for the Colonies within a day. The Crown would not require Gage's services that quickly. First the King proposed to have a measure passed by Parliament closing the Port of Boston to all business until the tea was paid for. He asked Gage what numbers he would need in troops to crush "the rebellious faction."

The general said that four regiments—about fifteen hundred men—would be sufficient to restore order. The King stressed that he desired to have the general act as both diplomat and British officer. If he could come to terms with those who fomented rebellion, very well. However, it would be up to Gage to set the terms; the King could not bear to have Americans propose terms for the British. It would be pointless, His Majesty believed, to send royal commissioners to Boston to locate and hang the tea criminals. Last year, when eight boatloads of men from the colony of Rhode Island had burned the sloop *Gaspee* to the water's edge, a royal commission had sat in Providence for months without turning up a witness to the crime.

Parliament was aroused to a fury. The members could not believe that Great Britain, the mightiest of powers, a nation which had just achieved victories in wars over the French and Spanish, could be thwarted by bands of ignorant hayseeds who, it was said, could not and would not fight. The Earl of Sandwich, First Lord of the Admiralty, clenched his fist and stated that the colonists "would never meet our people in fair conflict." In truth, they could not fight anyone unless they were firing from behind trees and rocks, drinking their "poisonous rum."

He compared the Americans, as soldiers, to the Bengalese. They "are also fanatics, but it is well known that a few of our troops will rout the greatest number of them. Were I in General Gage's situation and heard that twenty thousand New England men were coming against me, I should wish that they were rather thirty or forty thousand."

Viscount Townshend stood to deplore the fate of Gage, who had no opportunity to gain glory by honest fighting, and would "have nothing to do but burn, sink and destroy." Lord Rigby added his opinion. "It is romantic," he said, "to think they will fight. It is an idea thrown out to frighten women and children. There is more military prowess in a militia drummer."

Lord Germain, who was accused of cowardice for refusing to advance his troops at the Battle of Minden in 1759, was the most scornful of all. He would treat the Americans as Rome treated her tempestuous provinces. He favored stripping the Colonies of any local government and turning the continent over to a British legate who would enforce his will from Rhode Island, which could be turned into a military base. He who had been declared unfit to serve the King, and a coward, shouted monstrous punishments for the colonists. His was the rage of the guilty.

Parliament had talked itself out in April, 1774. It passed what was called "the Coercive Act," officially closing Boston to all international traffic. The harbor was to be sealed by British warships. When the gentry of Boston paid for the tea they had destroyed, His Gracious Majesty was willing to listen to a plea that normal relations, and normal traffic, and normal taxes, be restored. The Coercive Act—or Boston Port Bill, as Parliament liked to call it—went a few steps further. The royal governor was ordered to move the capital city from Boston to Salem. The Governor's Council, the upper body of the Massachusetts Bay Colony legislature, would no longer have its members selected by the lower body; the governor would do it. The salaries of officials such as judges, sheriffs, and bailiffs would no longer be controlled by the colony; the governor would pay them and tax the colony at his whim. Any subject of Great Britain accused of a crime could be transferred to England or another colony for trial. And last and worst, the heartbeat of Massachusetts, the town meetings of elders, was abolished.

The summer and autumn of 1774 were a succession of parched days for Massachusetts. The colony appealed through the press and by letter for help from its twelve brothers. Mail on packet boats and by courier was intercepted by British forces, read, and often used as evidence for additional arrests.

In England, Dr. Benjamin Franklin, Deputy Postmaster General of the Colonies, was assailed. He was sixty-eight and had spent many years in Britain trying to improve relations between the Crown and the Colonies. His moderate stand won respect in Parliament, but he was now accused publicly of intercepting six letters written by Royal Governor Hutchinson to an English official. The fact appears to be that the official who received the letters displayed them to Franklin, who asked permission to copy them and send them on to Massachusetts.

Samuel Adams got the copies, read them to colonial officials, and, with Hutchinson's knowledge, had them published in the press. The missives did no more than put on the record the governor's lack of sympathy with the position of the colony. The men of Massachusetts had been aware of this, but they used the letters to petition the Crown for the removal of Hutchinson. In London, the Privy Council held a meeting on the subject, attended by Franklin. Attorney General Alexander Wedderburn noted the doctor's presence. Pointing at him dramatically, Wedderburn shouted, "There sits the common thief!" Franklin was not permitted to reply. The government brought him down in disgrace by removing him from office as Deputy Postmaster General.

Franklin's loyalties were ambivalent. He had been in

England for seven years, representing Pennsylvania and Massachusetts in their quarrels with Parliament. At dinners and public functions he reiterated colonial admiration of and loyalty to Great Britain. He had many friends in high places, and he wrote to Lord Kames: "I have long been of the opinion that the foundations of the future grandeur and stability of the British Empire lie in America, and though like other foundations they are low and little seen they are nevertheless broad and strong enough to support the greatest political structure human wisdom ever yet erected." His friend Charles Pratt said that in spite of Americans' loyalty to the King, they would one day strike for independence. Franklin pouted. "No such idea was ever entertained by the Americans nor will any such ever enter their heads unless you grossly abuse them."

In all the time he had spent defending the actions of the Colonies, he spent almost equal time defending King George III. He kept writing home that the enemy was Parliament, not the sovereign. The Americans believed him and professed fealty to the King. However, when the Coercive Act was passed, Benjamin Franklin altered his allegiance in a letter to his son, who was about to be appointed royal governor of New Jersey:

> Between you and I the late measures have been, I suspect, very much the King's own, and he has, in some cases a great share of what his friends call firmness. Yet by some painstaking and proper management the wrong impressions he has received may be removed, which is perhaps the only chance America has for obtaining soon the redress she aims at.

It amounted to a delicately shaded retreat from a lifetime of unreasoning loyalty to the Crown. Franklin hoped that an accurate recital of the mood of the Colonies could restore the King's benevolent mood toward America. The Pennsylvania doctor had no way of knowing that George III was a leader among those who believed that American aspirations made them appear to be perpetually insolent to the Crown, deserving nothing better than severe punishment. Most of the time the King was ahead of his ministers in devising strictures to ensure bringing the Colonies to heel. The King never claimed to see himself as a wise and benevolent father; he was, rather, a parent quick to anger, quick to punish.

Lord North was surely echoing his master when he said, "When [the Americans] are quiet and have respect for their mother country, the mother country will be good natured to them." The King wrote that he found it "unnatural" that a few members of the House of Commons should, by their leniency toward America, "encourage the American Colonies in their disputes with their mother country." When Lord Chatham learned that General Thomas Gage had been sent to Massachusetts at the head of four regiments, he urged that the soldiers be recalled at once. "We shall be forced ultimately to retract," he said. "Let us retract when we can, not when we must." The King called Chatham "a trumpet of sedition."

When the Coercive Act was passed, the King realized that he was forcing Englishmen and Americans to close ranks on one side or the other; the time for neutrals was past: "the die is now cast," he wrote, "the Colonies must either submit or triumph . . . by coolness and an unremitting pursuit of the measures that have been adopted, I trust they will come to submit; I have no objection afterwards to their seeing that there is no inclination for the present to lay fresh taxes on them."

It was a cool and sunny day—May 17, 1774—when Acting Governor and General Thomas Gage stepped ashore at Boston's Long Wharf. He had arrived before his troops and was without protection. On the wharf was a double row of smartly uniformed Boston cadets, led in solemn salute by John Hancock, the rich smuggler. Gage accepted the salute, and walked solemnly to the State House. He was armed with a parchment proclaiming the closing of the Port of Boston, and other attendant punishments including the abolition of all town-hall meetings.

Massachusetts Bay Colony was aware of this. But Boston acted as though it was honored to welcome so distinguished a governor. There was no disturbance; no street fighting; no shouts for liberty; no tavern disputes. General Gage was advised by Hancock that the colony planned a lavish banquet in his honor this night at Faneuil Hall. Could Gage refuse? Would he? No. He was puzzled, but he accepted.

He must have been surprised at the banquet to scan the faces of such revolutionary radicals as Samuel Adams, Benjamin Church, Dr. Joseph Warren, and others. They tendered eloquent toasts to Gage, to the King, to Great Britain. The general was so touched by the filial devotion that he stood and offered his glass of smuggled Madeira as a toast to his predecessor, Thomas Hutchinson. No one in the big room raised a glass. A low hiss was heard. It was a moment of embarrassment; nothing more. The best the general could hope was that his four regiments would arrive quickly, and spare him the enervating cordiality of the colonists.

Gage decided to remain at Boston, in spite of the fact that the new British capital was Salem. A fine house overlooking the harbor was made ready for him. He also contacted some Loyalists who would be the eyes and ears of the military. Their words shocked him. While the general was at the banquet, Hancock and Adams had sent a courier named Paul Revere, a local silversmith, riding south on his big gray horse to Rhode Island, Connecticut, New York, and Pennsylvania with an urgent appeal to support Massachusetts Bay with money, merchandise, and soldiers. Pennsylvania was asked to send the appeal south to the remaining colonies.

In the late morning, Samuel Adams convened a town meeting in the middle of busy Boston. Boston's port was now closed, he said, and men in shipbuilding, ship chandlering, and fishing were unemployed. What did Boston propose to do to help them? A few rich citizens stood to offer to pay part of the price of the tea dumped overboard. The rest could easily be paid by popular subscription. Adams said they were out of order. This was a town meeting, not a surrender. The affluent were urged to hire as many of the port workers as possible; many could be used on extensive farms in Lexington, Concord, Braintree, and Quincy. Those who had proposed paying for part of the tea agreed to spend the money on local salaries.

The Redcoats arrived. Some were quartered in the homes of Loyalists; others were sent to Castle William. Boston was abnormally quiet. So was Gage. He worried about Boston's secret plans for the British. There were no catcalls at marching Redcoats, no protests. He announced that the Coercive Act would be effective June 1, 1775. If Boston gave him nothing more than a polite ear and a closed mouth, Gage proposed to go beyond the city, and he called a meeting of the legislature for June 5. The members asked the purpose of the meeting. To pay for the tea, the general said. In that case, the members from all sections of Massachusetts said, the meeting would be pointless. No American would propose to pay for the tea and none would donate a farthing.

In the hot days of early June, General Gage felt a chill. The city was as cold as marble to the touch. On June 1, all thirteen colonies declared a day of mourning for Boston. Philadelphia closed the shutters on all homes and muffled its church bells with cloth. Christopher Gadsden of South Carolina sent two hundred barrels of rice to Boston with a promise of eight hundred more in two weeks. "Don't pay for an ounce of the damned tea," he wrote.

Wilmington, North Carolina, raised ten thousand dollars in a week. A ship's crew volunteered to take the money to Boston "free of any charge." Israel Putnam, who had fought with the British in the French and Indian Wars, drove a hundred of his sheep from his farm in Connecticut to Boston to feed the poor. His neighbors sent five hundred more sheep. The town of Marblehead, not far from Boston, sent "224 quintals of good eating fish; almost two casks of olive oil; and thirty-nine pounds, six shillings in cash." The citizens of French Quebec sent a thousand barrels of wheat. Salem, which competed with Boston as a port, vowed it would not take advantage of her sister city's distress, and offered the use of loading and unloading facilities, including warehouses, free.

In Boston all business was closed down. Bells tolled all day and people attended church services. Gage was told that the pulpits were fiery "pits of sedition." If there was sedition, it was spreading. Massachusetts Bay and other colonies were in receipt of letters asking all colonies to elect men of substance to something to be called a "Continental Congress" to meet in September in Philadelphia. The philosophy of the Congress would be to unite the thirteen into a semblance of unity so that an attack from outside on one would be regarded as an attack on all. They could also agree to help each other in times of stress. On June 17, Massachusetts voted 120 to 12 to send delegates to the Congress.

In one stroke the King had achieved the thing the thirteen colonies could not—unity and harmony. Each colony had proclaimed itself to be a separate province under the British Crown. Each also thought the word "state" meant a "nation." For the moment they were unified in the face of oppression from Parliament; they had a common heritage and common hardships. The ardent desire of all to go to the assistance of one was predicated on the notion that Parliament was determined to throw the yoke of economic slavery on the neck of America.

General Thomas Gage, far less optimistic in Boston than he had been sitting with the King in London, wrote a personal report to Lord North and His Majesty in which, through the use of massive colonial circumlocution, he seemed to advocate repeal of the Coercive Act. The Prime Minister was opposed. The King said it was "absurd. We must either master them or totally leave them to themselves and treat them as aliens." Gage's suggestion that a board of commissioners be sent to negotiate with Massachusetts Bay was greeted with royal scorn. "This looks so much like the mother country being more afraid of the continuance of the dispute than the Colonies and I cannot think it likely to make them reasonable." His Majesty said he did not wish to drive the Americans to despair; he favored "holding out the olive branch," but submission to British will must come first.

It was as though King and colonists lived in separate worlds—as, indeed, they did—and were studying each other through the wrong end of telescopes. Neither had an appreciation of the stubborn, unyielding attitude of the other. Neither saw the other in his true light; neither understood that the other could not and would not be pushed a step backward.

Perhaps William Prescott, a military officer, stated the case for the colonists succinctly in a letter that followed his sending of forty bushels of grain to Boston:

> Be not dismayed nor disheartened, in this great day of trials. We heartily sympathize with you and are always ready to do all in our power for your support, comfort and relief; knowing that Providence has placed you where you must stand the first shock. We consider that we are all embarked in one bottom and must sink or swim together.
>
> We think if we submit to these regulations all is gone. Our forefathers passed the great Atlantic, spent their blood and treasure, that they might enjoy their liberties, both civil and religious, and transmit them to their posterity. Their children have waded through seas of difficulty to leave us free and happy in the enjoyment of English privileges.
>
> Now, if we should give them up, can our children

rise up and call us blessed? Is not a glorious death in defense of our liberties better than a short, infamous life, and our memory to be had in detestation to the latest posterity? Let us all be of one heart, and stand fast in the liberties wherewith Christ has made us free.

On August 6, 1774, a British warship arrived in Boston harbor with the last provision of the Coercive Act, the one in which Parliament revised the charter of Massachusetts Bay and moved the capital to Salem. If this was designed to cow Massachusetts to obedience, it had the opposite effect. Within three days, men met in Worcester and drew up a resolution which declared that the people of Massachusetts owed no allegiance to British Parliament, that the Massachusetts Bay Charter was the basis of allegiance to the King. Any attempt to revise or vacate the charter would "have a tendency to dissolve the union between Great Britain and the Province."

Part of Gage's problem came from listening to the wrong people. He tried to stir up friends of the British government. He found some affluent Loyalists in Boston, but he mistook their undying hatred of the radical revolutionaries as the voice of reason. They had seen their friends kidnapped by mobs, to be tarred and feathered and sent home humiliated and beaten. Their loyalty to King and Mother Country had cost them dearly in the business world, in the social world, in public libel and calumny. Sometimes their women were spat upon; at others, servants begged permission to quit their jobs in the face of unbridled pressure. Because they were small in numbers, their loyalty amounted to bravery. They knew better than anyone else that if the protection of Crown and Redcoats was withdrawn, their homes would be burned or confiscated and they would have to flee to another world to start life anew. Being a Loyalist was not a simple road.

And yet, when Gage listened to these "Americans," he found they were a bloodthirsty lot anxious to put the

Liberty Boys to rout with musket fire. They were opposed to negotiation and conciliation. "Fire on them and they will disperse to the hills" was the word.

On one occasion, General Gage heeded advice. He received a confidential note from Major General William Brattle of the Massachusetts militia. Brattle was old and a Loyalist. He told Gage that the men of Massachusetts had for some weeks been removing gunpowder from the powder house in Charles Towne. They were storing it at home. What for, Brattle did not know. He did know, however, that there was no gunpowder elsewhere in Massachusetts and no means of getting it. One way of stopping a revolution before it started, the old general said, would be for the government to confiscate all gunpowder. Gage thought that this was sound advice. He sent 260 men in boats across to Charles Towne. They emptied the magazine of 250 half-barrels of powder. The same morning another detachment swept around the peninsula to Cambridge and returned with a half-dozen smoothbore cannon which Cambridge had recently purchased.

Gage had acted within his rights. However, alarms spread through New England that Boston was in flames; Cambridge had been the scene of raping and looting; British ships had launched a bombardment of the port from a point close to shore. Within a few days, twenty thousand men were marching from Connecticut and Rhode Island to make war on the Redcoats. This time Massachusetts had to preach temperance. General Israel Putnam, an old campaigner, was told that none of the story was true except the confiscation of gunpowder. Before he marched his men back to Connecticut, he advised Massachusetts: "Keep a strict guard over the remainder of your powder; for that must be the great means, under God, of the salvation of our country."

The presence of twenty thousand men alarmed General Gage. In his nervousness, while walking the street in Boston, he dropped the letter which Brattle had sent him. It was picked up by a patriot. That night, militiamen raided the home of the militia officer. He hid in a hayrick and was driven to Boston at top speed. He feared for his life. Gage sent him to Castle William.

Summer heat and thundershowers stirred the faces of the Colonies as fifty-four delegates from all the provinces except Georgia moved by many trails toward Philadelphia. George Washington noted in his diary of August 31, 1774: "After dinner in company with Patrick Henry and Mr. Pendleton, started to attend the General Congress at Philadelphia." He did not mention that, for the first time since the Indian Wars, he wore the uniform of an officer of the Virginia militia. It appeared to be a symbol of the poor chances for peace. And yet, when Colonel Washington dined and danced at Raleigh Tavern, he was known to close the evening pleasure with a toast to King George III.

In transit he was in excellent company. Virginia sent Richard Henry Lee, Patrick Henry, Benjamin Harrison, Richard Bland, and Peyton Randolph. None of the delegates was certain of what powers he had, or what the limitations might be. Massachusetts, begging assistance, had issued the first call for a body of men to represent each colony with a view toward Continental assistance and defense.

This was a vague and misty goal. The gentlemen decided, within two days of meetings in Carpenters Hall, that they would move cautiously, a half-step at a time. Samuel and John Adams of Massachusetts, who had the spirit of radical insurrectionists, decided that they would better serve Massachusetts Bay by remaining in the background, because it was their province which was seeking assistance.

They proposed that the stout and genial Peyton Randolph of Virginia be elected president of the body. This motion was carried unanimously. Some were in favor of calling the delegates a "General Congress"; others sought to set the body apart from provincial assemblies by referring to themselves as a "Continental Congress." The second suggestion won. The delegates were conscious that the term embraced all land from the Atlantic Ocean to the Pacific—gigantic tracts over which they had no control—but it had a solemn ring to it, and they appreciated the sound.

Charles Thomson of Philadelphia was chosen as secretary. He was active in Pennsylvania politics; he was also a member of Franklin's Philosophical Society; he was well regarded in the host city.

No one knew how far the delegates would go in defying Great Britain; the brave and the timorous waited side by side in a great room to explore the sense of the Colonies.

No one spoke of independence. It is doubtful that any delegate in September, 1774, permitted himself to dwell on a complete breach with the Mother County. The Congress, however, moved quickly to denounce all oppressive measures of Parliament from the year 1763 straight through the new Coercive Act. Without pause, it urged all colonies to raise and arm a local militia for self-defense. It then adopted an all-colony body called the "Continental Association"—a non-British importation, non-British exportation, non-British consumption agreement—a dagger to the heart of England.

They then elected a committee to address a placating petition to their sovereign King. They voted approval of an appeal which opened with subservient words:

As your Majesty enjoys the signal distinction of reigning over free men, the language of freedom cannot be displeasing. We ask for peace, liberty and safety. We wish not a diminution of the prerogative, nor do we solicit the grant of any new right in our favor. In the magnanimity and justice of your Majesty and Parliament, we confide for a redress of our grievances, trusting that when the causes of our apprehensions are removed, our future conduct will prove us not unworthy of the regard we have been accustomed, in our happier days, to enjoy. . . .

It is difficult to judge how much sincerity and how much hypocrisy went into the petition. Certainly most, if not all, of the delegates realized that the earlier acts of the Congress were seditious. The news of what transpired in Carpenters Hall could not be confined to the walls and solemn portraits staring down. It is possible that the reactionary and cautious delegates thought that the King might entertain the document and consider its contents as a modest appeal to the Crown. If this is so, they did not appreciate the temper of George III, who refused to accept the document and condemned it out of hand. On the other hand, it is certain that Lord North read it and acquainted His Majesty with its contents.

At the end of the year, George wrote: "I am sorry that the line of conduct now seems chalked out. . . . The New England Governments are in a state of rebellion; blows must decide whether they are to be subject to this country or independent." His Majesty was ahead of the most radical of colonial leaders in sensing that a war of independence was imminent. None was so radical that he did not fear the crushing might of the British Army and Navy. The Continental Congress had failed in its gambit to condemn the acts of Parliament while begging for the goodwill of the King.

George III was busy with army and navy lists at the end of the year. He was piqued to learn that his army numbered only 48,000 men, twelve thousand of them assigned to Ireland. Major General John Burgoyne suggested "supplies of arms for the Blacks to awe, in conjunction with the regulars, the southern provinces." The King visited ports to inspect warships and was chagrined to find that many of the Empire's proudest ships of war had worm-eaten keels, rusty, unused cannon, sailcloth torn in battle and not repaired.

Three thousand miles to the west, Thomas Gage decided that he and his four regiments were in danger. He began to fortify the city of Boston. It was more like an island than a peninsula. Behind it was a narrow strip of land called the Neck. The general would have to fortify this area to prevent the colonists from approaching his rear. Within the city he had most of his men quartered. In their spare time they fashioned longboats from timber. In the bay, Gage had ships of war but he asked the Crown for more.

His young officers had lost faith in the general and called him "the old woman." They wanted to dissipate all thought of rebellion by marching into any small Massachusetts town, firing a volley at the local militia, and setting fire to the homes of the seditious. Gage, perhaps, was overly conscious of his dual role and assumed that he must still offer an olive branch. When a Massachusetts committee of protest approached his headquarters, General Gage invited the men in and treated them cordially. They said that his new fortification was "a warlike act." No, he said, it was purely defensive. The visitors said that Gage must realize that the farmers could not attack the British regulars with any hope of success.

Gage said that the recruitment and marching of local militia in towns around Boston must have a militant objective. No, they said, they were defensive in character. A waste of time, Gage said, because he had no notion of attacking Americans. Throughout, Gage was warm and friendly. The committee had hardly left his presence when the general sent urgent messages to British army commands in New York, Quebec, and the southern colonies, demanding the presence of "every soldier who might be spared."

Within a few weeks he had four more regiments—not much of an offering. The Tenth and Fifty-second marched from Quebec; the Eighteenth and Forty-seventh from New

York. Four hundred British marines arrived aboard the warships *Asia and Boyne* from Newfoundland. Six months after General Gage's arrival in Boston, all he had learned was how to be frightened. He had promised his King to arouse the majority of citizens loyal to the Crown and he found a small, hateful minority. He had looked for mob violence so that he would have an excuse for massing his troops and firing muskets into the crowd, but there had been no unlawful assemblage. The rebellious people of Massachusetts had forced Gage to hole up inside Boston. No one had fired a shot. The calm within Massachusetts was deadly.

Unity cracked in the Colonies soon after calendars were turned to the year 1775. The adversarial role which the Continental Congress had assumed between the Americans and the British was spurned by New York. The landed gentry that controlled politics in the "big middle colony" denounced the Congress, formed a reactionary Committee of Fifty-one, and replaced such New York delegates as had voted with the Congress.

The political pendulum, which had been hanging in a hesitant dead center, swung wildly to the right. *Rivington's New York Gazeteer* propagated the Loyalist cause and said that New York, unlike New England, would "not permit a few rash men" to gain political power. The Committee of Fifty-one insisted that New York had the right to sell food and merchandise to General Thomas Gage, under silent siege in Boston. Almost overnight, the Whigs of New York, who had supported all the actions of the Congress, were intimidated by the Tories.

The break was severe. The Oglethorpe group in Georgia had sent no delegates to Philadelphia; now New York protested loyalty to King and Parliament. The cause of unity was reduced to eleven colonies, and not all of them were willing to bruise Parliament with reprisals as the gentlemen in Philadelphia had voted. Isaac Sears, a New York Whig leader, "became the laughing stock of the whole town." Tories who had been timid in public when the Whigs were in the ascendancy were now emboldened to speak as fervently—and as loudly— as the Adamses and Hancocks of Massachusetts.

British military officers in New York sent word to Lord North that the majority of New Yorkers considered that the "dispute with Great Britain is carried far enough, and abhor the thought of pushing it to desperate lengths." The Tories were ably led by rich merchants, clergymen, and Crown-appointed magistrates. The New York Assembly passed a measure dissociating the colony from the Continental Association. It was the sense of the Assembly that New York was determined to remain clear of the "treason" and "rebellion" fomented in Philadelphia.

The Assembly went further. Having divorced itself from the Continental Congress, it sent its own mild petition to the Crown. The political swing was so far to the right that the Tory party apologized to its constituents regarding the behavior of some of its delegates to the Congress. The gentlemen had been honest when they left New York, the disclaimed stated, but had been corrupted by the delegates they met in Philadelphia. "Let no honest man trust himself hereafter at a Philadelphia Congress," the Tories said. The political situation had degenerated into a battle of words, but the alarming truth was that those who feared New York would be the weakest link in the colonial chain were proved to be right.

Moving in disorder in the opposite direction, leading Whigs proposed that the Colonies stop trading with New York ("the assassins") as they already had with Great Britain and the West Indies. From New England threats were tossed at New York: "Take care of yourselves. We have more than enough Men to block up the Enemy at Boston; and if we are likely to fall by Treachery, by Heaven we will not fall un-avenged on the Traitors."

A Tory ditty swept the Colonies:

These hardy knaves and stupid fools,
Some apish and pragmatic mules,
Some servile acquiescing tools—
   These, these compose the Congress!
When Jove resolved to send a curse,
   And all the woes of life rehearse,
Not plague, not famine, but much worse—
   He cursed us with a Congress!

The new hero in Massachusetts was the handsome Dr. Joseph Warren, a dandy, a fop, above all a Boston patriot. The Assembly had selected him to deliver the "Massacre Day" oration at Old South Church. Warren, open of countenance and an articulate man, was chosen to mark the night when five citizens had been killed by Redcoats after throwing snowballs at a sentry.

Forty young officers of Gage's command asked for permission to attend the meeting. "The old woman" dared not refuse, though the request was couched in the most obsequious terms. Gage was aware that he was in disrepute among the young militants, as well as with the King and North. He asked the forty men to restrain their impulses no matter what the provocation.

When Warren heard about the uninvited guests, the physician passed the word that patriots should not be seduced into revealing their feelings, no matter how rude the forty might become. The original martyrdom of the slain five was still debatable, even within the ranks of the Assembly. And yet the observance of the Massacre became an annual bellows to the flagging fire of the Liberty Boys.

The night of March 5, 1775, was clear and cold. The people of Boston arrived early at Old South Church. The forty officers were a few minutes late, presenting themselves at the back door, pressing scabbards to their sides, crushed uniform hats under their arms. The ushers surprised the Redcoats with cordiality, showing them to three empty front pews. They bowed gravely and sat, some sitting on the altar steps, almost under the pulpit. The reservation of front pews expressed no warmth; if an untoward incident occurred, there was no way that the officers could hack their way through the entire congregation to escape through the back doors. They had heard the Boston rumor that friends of Dr. Warren swore that if the doctor was harmed—even slightly—blood would flow in the church aisle.

The doctor walked from the nave to the pulpit. He wore silk breeches, white stockings, an embroidered waistcoat, lace ruffles at throat and shirt cuffs, and a powdered wig. In the dim light of hundreds of candles, the moving shadows on his face made it appear to be more handsome, and, at other times, forbidding. He had no intention of thundering. He spread his hands across the pulpit, leaned forward, and announced his topic: "On the Dangers of Standing Armies in Time of Peace."

The people and the officers sat back. Warren reviewed the history of American relations with Great Britain, choosing words with the precise shading so as not to offend either side. In 1770, he submitted, five citizens would not have been shot if the Redcoats had not been present in "His Majesty's peaceable colony." There could be no confrontation between mob and military if the soldiers had not been seen as oppressors within the city. There had been no war then, he said. There was no war now. And yet Massachusetts was host to more and more regiments of Redcoats.

On the altar step, a youthful officer held the palm of one hand up and dropped five rounded lead bullets into it. Without hesitating in explicating his thoughts, Warren reached into his sleeve, found a lace-edge kerchief, and dropped it over the bullets and hand. The British, finding that they were unable to arouse Dr. Warren for possible arrest, began to make derisive remarks between his sentences. He ignored them. "An independence from Great Britain is not our aim," he said solemnly. "No. Our wish is that Britain and the Colonies may, like the oak and the ivy, grow and increase in strength together.

But whilst the infatuated plan of making one part of the empire slaves to the other is persisted in, the interest and safety of Britain as well as the Colonies require that the wise measures recommended by the Continental Congress be steadily pursued, whereby the unnatural contest between a parent honored and child beloved may probably be brought to such an issue as that the peace and the happiness of both may be established on a lasting basis. But if these pacific measures are ineffectual, and it appears that the only way to safety is through fields of blood, I know you will not turn your faces from our foes, but will undauntedly press forward until tyranny is trodden underfoot, and you have fixed your adored goddess, Liberty . . . on the American throne.

He had finished. There was no applause in the Old South Church. He had stated the case well, dangerously toward the conclusion, but with a patriot's determination to live a short time on his feet rather than a long time on his knees. The forty officers saw Warren bow and leave the pulpit. Several snorted with disgust. They had come to hear treasonable utterances, to make an arrest, start a fight. They returned to their private homes inside Boston Neck disappointed in Joseph Warren.

General Gage wasn't disappointed. He had quotations from the speech shortly after dawn. The general had set up a good intelligence system. It was not as numerous or as clever as the patriots had in Gage's camp, but the general had fewer sympathizers. Each found it difficult to keep a secret from the other camp. Gage assured his friends that he long knew that the Americans were building stores of powder and shot at the village of Concord, seventeen miles west of Boston. He boasted that he also knew every plan of the Committee of Safety, the executive branch of the Massachusetts Bay Assembly. In fact, the general (or members of his personal staff) knew precisely which measures had been voted on, and who proposed and who opposed.

It was thought, though never proved, that the general's most august spy was Dr. Benjamin Church. He was a stout man who in middle years had taken a mistress who said she would listen only to a man of means. Dr. Church was a man of means; his problem, after meeting the mistress, was remaining in that category. If Church was the spy most suspected in later years, he was ideal because he sold out, not for principles, but for money.

The position of Church as a patriot was unique. He and Dr. Warren were members of the Committee of Safety, privy to all the suspicions, actions, and counteractions of Massachusetts Bay Colony. Others who had been sent to the Continental Congress were not on the Committee of Safety and were concerned only with the political winds between the several colonies and their traffic and problems with Great Britain.

As Warren was making his "nonbelligerent" speech in the Old South Church, history was being made several hundred miles to the south in Old St. John's Church in Richmond. It was a startlingly white edifice with an ornate clock-and-chimes tower, the whole surrounded by a walled graveyard. There the young men of Virginia heard words counseling patience with Great Britain. They were angered. Patrick Henry stood, the long dark hair undulating as he scowled at his elders. "As for me," he said, pointing to his chest, "give me liberty or give me death."

A hush had fallen over the big room. The gauntlet had been flung. The men would, by these words, be forced to choose between ultimate war with Britain and ultimate reconciliation. Young Mr. Henry had chosen the path of independence, of war. Would he stand alone? No. Richard Henry Lee stood to endorse Patrick Henry's stand with considerable eloquence. The man who felt he had never made a good speech, Thomas Jefferson, followed Lee to remind the politicians and the members of the House of Burgesses that there was no other path. Great Britain and America had gone too far in their quarrels for conciliation. A move by either side to discuss differences would be taken by the other as a sign of weakness. He would not advocate immediate independence; what Jefferson wanted was unmistakable "resistance" to any tax or political device by which Britain wished to humiliate the Colonies.

In most colonies, the assemblies voted to take advantage of the wishes of the Continental Congress that each should draw up a provincial militia, armed, drilled, and prepared to defend its colony. In Massachusetts the local commanders advised the musketeers to be ready "at a moment's notice" for a call to action. They called themselves Minute Men. In Delaware a few regiments were drawn up and given beautiful uniforms by their rich sponsors. In Virginia the soldiers wore pale-gold uniforms with robin's-egg facings. British officers in the territories complained that most of the "sedition is flowing copiously from the pulpits." Some clergymen preached the love of the Prince of Peace, then handed out pikes and muskets to the young men in the congregation.

The word was passed from town to village, from colony to plantation that the militiamen everywhere must wait for General Gage to fire the first shot. A young British colonel watched a wagon loaded with hay leave Boston, and he remarked that it was strange because hay was usually brought into the city for horses. He and a guard stopped the wagon, searched, and found thirteen thousand musket balls. They were confiscated. The farmer who drove the hayrick angrily sought an interview with Gage and complained bitterly about the seizure. He was lucky that he wasn't shot.

General Gage was aware of the warlike preparations. His officers wrote complaining letters home to England that they were "cooped" inside Boston with "shivering cowardly magistrates" who, loyal to the Crown, sought refuge inside Boston. The British regiments should, these officers believed, burst out through Boston Neck and thrash the trash of New England, no matter what their numbers.

If there was anything worse than the cocky attitude of the colonists, it was the damage their rum was doing to the men in the ranks. Men off duty outside the city were plied with a liquor called Kill Devil. They were then reminded that their lot was indeed a hard one—eightpence a day, with deductions for torn uniforms and lost buttons—and they were enlisted for life. Why should such a private soldier risk his life fighting people who were of the same blood with the same aspirations for freedom? Some deserted. Some died of alcoholism ("It will destroy more of us," a British major said, "than the Yankees will"). Some took the risk of changing sides.

In England, Parliament had lost faith in General Gage and his four regiments. The expected confrontation between the British lion and the American turkey had not occurred. Lord North addressed the House of Commons in a speech of conciliation toward the Colonies which "amazed and confused" the members. It was obvious that North no longer wished to resort to arms; he said he was willing to forgo the tax on tea if the Americans would tax themselves and contribute to the welfare of Great Britain. There were shouts of "No! No!" and "Shame!" as he spoke. Privately he said that the members misunderstood his message; he believed that with New York loyalty he could drive a wedge between the northern and southern colonies, a wedge which would admit the British Army and Navy as a living threat to attack New England or the southern tier.

It required an impassioned plea by Sir Gilbert Eliot for

Commons to vote reluctant assent to anything labeled "conciliatory"; many members had first to be assured that the Americans would not accept such a gesture. Lord North, however, was a master of inconsistency. After the measure passed the House of Commons, North (in February, 1775) proclaimed that Massachusetts Bay was in a state of rebellion. This, under law, would require the British military to put down such rebellion, restore order, and hang the ringleaders.

Conversely, he insisted that the Conciliatory Act was in force, and that any colony that taxed itself for the use of the Empire would be exempt from all taxation. It was a complex, devious scheme, the purpose of which would appear to be to set New York against Massachusetts Bay. The focus of the frustration of the North government and the King was that they could not bend the Colonies to their will and they seemed unable to order Gage into action against the Americans.

North ordered Lord Dartmouth, a timid dilettante, to demand that General Gage do something at once. Of course, one of the most frustrating matters was the time lag between wishing something to be done and having it done. Dartmouth wrote to Gage in February. The message was not received by General Gage until April 14. "Force," the message said, "should be repelled by force." Dartmouth's words amounted to an entreaty. "A smaller force now, if put to the test, would be able to encounter them with greater probability of success than you might expect from a greater army. The only consideration that remains is, in what manner the force under your command may be exerted to defend the constitution and restore the vigor of the government. The King's servants also believe that the first and essential step toward reestablishing government would be to arrest the principal actors and abettors in the Provincial Congress."

Gage was a brave and able soldier. He knew what London didn't: that he had blockaded Boston, but was now a prisoner within the city; that if he arrested such leaders as Samuel Adams, John Hancock, Dr. Joseph Warren, and General Israel Putnam, it would light the torch of civil war; that he faced an ugly and armed group of Minute Men said to number about ten thousand men.

And yet all was not lost for Gage. He had received a secret advice that the colonists had amassed large caches of food, ammunition, and guns at Concord. In addition, the Continental Congress in Philadelphia had adjourned, so that no concerted action could be expected from that body. The Provincial Assembly of Massachusetts was to adjourn tomorrow—April 15—and thus the general would have time for a small limited offensive. Gage did not seem to realize that military intelligence, like a storm-tossed stream, runs in two directions. The colonists began to hide their military stores at Concord immediately after Gage called Colonel Francis Smith and Major John Pitcairn and ordered them to lead seven hundred British grenadiers to Concord. They knew his soldiers were coming before the lower-rank Redcoats had been told.

Close to midnight on April 17, Dr. Joseph Warren ordered two couriers, William Dawes and Paul Revere, to saddle their horses and to ride hard for Lexington and Concord, alerting the citizens that the Redcoats were coming. They would have to leave quickly, because General Gage would surely close the Neck of Boston at midnight, preventing citizens from moving out. Dawes and Revere were on their way two hours before Colonel Smith and Major Pitcairn, mounted on good horses, led seven hundred grenadiers on a long sweep through the villages of Massachusetts Bay.

It was to be a demonstration of strength, nothing more. Smith and Pitcairn had heard Gage repeat the order: "Destroy illegal stores of ammunition and military supplies; do not, in any case, fire on anyone unless you are fired upon." The colonel and the major had repeated the order to the soldiers, many of whom were scornful. They were expected to start a night march in the predawn hours of April 18, walk quietly through hostile country for twenty miles, endure the spitting insults of colonists, destroy some stores, and return quietly through the same country to Boston. There would be fifteen-minute rests, no sleep over a period of two nights.

They marched. To keep in step during the night, they whistled and sang endless refrains of the mocking "Yankee Doodle." Every village, every farm, it seems, was well lighted. The colonists were awake and waiting. Catcalls and hisses split the night air. The grenadiers, the tallest and strongest in General Gage's command, shuffled forward under the weight of their backpacks, their muskets and bayonets. Smith and Pitcairn sent a squad of skirmishers ahead of their horses.

At Lexington Green seventy Minute Men waited. In groups they sidled off in the darkness to Buckman's Tavern. They drank ale and whiskey and warmed their bones. They wore buckskins and beaver hats. They had no uniforms and they had not learned to march together. When they discussed the Redcoats, the farm militia made them more numerous, bigger, more ferocious than they were. No one doubted that the Minute Men felt fear. The remarkable feature of their trembling was that they would not run away. In darkness it would have been easy.

They were slouching and lounging against the stone buildings around the commons when they heard the lonesome sound of a drum. The men grabbed their muskets, put powder in the little metal pan and a round ball in the muzzle. They stood to attention in double ranks. Windows around the square flew up; pale-saffron beams framed the silhouetted figures inside. The Redcoats were at Lexington. The farmers braced themselves across the road leading to Concord.

The skirmishers came through the mist, followed by the officers on horses. Colonel Smith saw the "insolent, armed mob." He would not waste time. As the first company of Redcoats approached the Minute Men, he drew his sword and waved it forward. "March through the peasants!" he shouted. The Britishers kept step, disciplined soldiers, as though by weight they would continue straight through the opposing ranks. The Minute Men, almost in awe, began to fall back. They spread out a little, as though they might make room for the Redcoats.

A Minute Man, walking backward toward a low stone wall, fell over it. He sat up, almost in panic, and pulled the trigger of his musket. The flint clicked. The flashpan lit up. A crack ricocheted around the walls of the commons. Without order from officers, the Redcoats lowered their muskets. The front rank fired a volley into the Minute Men. Some of the farmers roared with pain. Some turned and ran. Eighteen men sank in varying forms of gracelessness to the ground. The uniform roar of sound, the haze of bluish smoke punctuated the uneasy peace between Britain and the Colonies; it closed an era throughout which men worried about consequences and thrust them into a historic confrontation. No statesman would ever undo the sound of the lone musket and the sound of a broadside.

Smith paused for a moment, glaring at the eight dying, the ten wounded, and urged his soldiers on to Concord. They had five miles more to march to get to Concord Bridge. Colonel Smith did not regard the salvo as a battle, or even a military engagement. He had met a disorderly mob; someone had fired on his men, and, quite correctly, they had fired back. He proceeded with his mission, standing his horse and looking backward as the seven hundred men marched across the bloody square. When he saw Major Pitcairn bringing up the last companies, he spurred his horse and trotted forward to take the lead of the column with the skirmishers.

At Concord the column continued its sedate march through farms and mills until it was deployed by Major Pitcairn. The soldiers began the search for munitions stores. They found little—some powder and a few hundred musket balls—but the men had not marched this far to be frustrated. They began to set fire to barns, claiming they had found guns inside. In the houses they were not gentle with farmers' wives or children. Those who answered questions with insolence were hurried outside to watch grim-lipped as the houses grew great with flame.

Colonel Smith felt that the mission was somewhat of a success. If the purpose was to prove the domination of Great Britain over Massachusetts Bay, he had proved it. He ordered Major Pitcairn to re-form the men into ranks. Old men and young boys stood silently on the small hills, watching the Lobsterbacks. The seven hundred men reversed their marching order and started back to Boston. They were near Concord Bridge before they saw the massed line of Minute Men. Some crouched, their muskets on their knees. Others stood, aiming dead at the red-coated line. Still others hid in fields and behind trees and low stone walls.

The colonel did not expect to march through this group. It was strong and it appeared ready to fire. He called Pitcairn to his side and ordered the leading ranks to charge with their bayonets. He would teach the Yankees the feel of cool steel. The Minute Men fired. Some Redcoats fell. The front ranks kept moving forward with their bayonets outstretched, gaps in their lines like a mouthful of old teeth. Steadily, the Americans reloaded. It required time. They fired again. Then the sheer weight of the British line went through them. Bayonets flashed with blood. A crackle of desultory fire came from behind trees and walls.

The British did not understand this type of battle. They were accustomed to facing the enemy in square standing ranks, firing when no more than forty paces apart. To the English, this was a cowardly type of battle, with musketry coming from God knows where. A bullet nicked Pitcairn's horse and he threw the major. The roughened balls whistled around him as he got to his feet, flicked the dust off his uniform, and grabbed the bridle and saddle to remount.

Colonel Smith, having dispersed the Americans, ordered the marching column to return to Boston. Still, shots were coming from the sides and the rear. The drummer boys beat their steady tattoo and watched with wonder as men kept falling out of line, some screaming with the agony of a fresh wound. There was nothing in the *Manual of Arms* to help Smith to fight this kind of battle, so he kept marching. He should have felt relief when he crested a hill and found Redcoats marching toward him. General Gage, as an afterthought, had sent Colonel Earl Percy with a thousand light infantry to relieve Smith.

Smith's seven hundred marched into the shadow of the larger unit and collapsed in grass. The men who had marched so well and so bravely were spent. They had marched into a wilderness of gunfire which was unexpected, and it was doubtful if the column could march back to Boston. Percy told Smith that when his men were rested, they would march back without going through Cambridge. This was a wise decision, because a regiment of Minute Men was waiting in Cambridge. Colonel Percy ordered his men, and Smith's, to march to Charles Towne. There, at water's edge, they would be under the protection of British warships. Longboats could take the Redcoats across the narrow inlet to Boston.

The Redcoats had sustained three hundred casualties. The colonists lost almost a hundred men. It was neither a battle nor a bloody declaration of war. The British looked upon the action as a seditious uprising of farmers. The colonists saw the fire fight as something they could use to portray Britain as a cruel bully while painting the Americans as God-fearing farmers whose only offense was in defending their homes and families. The crackle of musketry was no more than the snap of hickory nuts on a hearth compared to the cannonade of untruths emanating from Massachusetts to the Colonies, to Great Britain and European opinion.

On the morning of the twentieth, colonists described British troops as having "the ferocity of a mad wild beast," slaughtering "geese, hogs, cattle, and every living creature they came across" and "murdering women and children." At Lexington Common, British officers searched for Samuel Adams and John Hancock in a certain house. When it was ascertained that both men had left the province, "the barbarians killed the women of the house and all the children in cold blood, then set the house afire." Many homes in Concord were burned and "women in childbed were driven by the soldiery snakes into the streets; old men, peaceably in their houses, were shot dead."

By sundown of the next day, Dr. Joseph Warren assumed charge of all propaganda and reduced the charges against Colonel Smith and his Lobsterbacks to the written word. Warren wrote furiously, without let, sending copies of his outlandish indictments to all the colonies, and was waiting for a fast clipper ship to take his version of Lexington and Concord to Parliament in London. He stated that there were "depredations, ruins and butcheries hardly to be matched by the armies of any civilized nation on the globe"; the Iroquois tribe "would blush at such horrid murder, and worse than brutal rage." British soldiers moved through the smoke and the blood of innocents, ignoring "the cries of the wounded, killing without mercy and mangling their bodies in a most shocking manner."

All who could marshal thoughts into devastating words were requested to write, to send copies to far-off places. A Minute Man described England: "This pretended mother is a vile imposter—an old abandoned prostitute—a robber, a murderer—crimsoned o'er with every abominable crime shocking to humanity." The patriots (Whigs) pretended to see Lexington and Concord as an opening gambit of bloodletting by General Thomas Gage, to be followed as soon as possible with additional slaughtering and burning in Massachusetts Bay, before the British command moved to subdue the remaining colonies.

The leading Whigs knew, in truth, that Gage was a nervous prisoner in Boston, that he had been goaded by Lord North to assert his authority. Dr. Warren pretended to see the matter in quite another light. "They have begun it," he said, "that either party can do; and we will end it, that only one can do." The contradistinctions between the views of the Minute Men and the British are best seen in a condensation of General Gage's report to Lord North:

Lt.-Col. Smith embarked from the Common at Boston toward Concord where he was ordered to destroy a magazine of military stores deposited there for the use of an army to be assembled in order to act against His Majesty and His government. The Colonel gave orders that the Troops should not fire unless fired upon, and after marching a few miles, detached six companies under Major Pitcairn to take possession of two bridges on the other side of Concord.

Soon after they heard many signal guns and the ringing of alarm bells repeatedly, which convinced them that the Country was rising to oppose them and that it was a preconcerted scheme to oppose the King's Troops. About three o'clock the next morning, within two miles of Lexington, intelligence was received that about two hundred men in arms were assembled and determined to oppose the King's Troops: and on galloping up two officers informed him that a Man advanced from those assembled, had presented his Musquit and attempted to shoot them, but the piece flashed in the pan. The Major gave directions on no account fire without orders. At the end of the village they observed about 100 armed men drawn up on a green, and when the Troops came within a Hundred Yards of them they began to file off toward some Stone Walls. . . .

The Light Infantry ran after them. The major instantly called not to fire but to surround and disarm them. Some of them who had jumped over a Wall then fired 4 or 5 shot at the Troops, wounding a Man and the major's horse and at the same time several shots were fired from a Meeting House. . . . Without order or regularity the Light Infantry began a scattered fire and killed several of the Country People; but were silenced as soon as the Authority of their Officers could make them.

The whole body proceeded to Concord. . . . The people began to move towards the bridge in great numbers and fired upon the King's Troops, killed 3 Men, wounded 4 Officers, one sergeant and 4 Private Men. . . . Capt. Laurie thought it prudent to return towards the Main Body at Concord. . . . As soon as the Troops had got out of the town of Concord, they received a heavy fire from all sides, from Walls, Fences, Houses, Trees, Bars etc. The Troops had above Fifty killed and many more wounded. Reports are varied about the loss sustained by the Country People, some make it very considerable, others not too much. . . . The unfortunate affair has happened through the rashness and impudence of a few People who began firing on the troops at Lexington.

The disparity of views went even further. Warren, as an official of the Massachusetts Bay Committee of Safety, sent a message to each of the colonies: "The barbarous murders committed on our innocent brethren on Wednesday, the 19th instant, have made it absolutely necessary that we immediately raise an army to defend our wives and children from the butchering hands of an inhuman soldiery. . . . We conjure you, therefore, by all that is sacred, that you give assistance in forming an army. Our all is at stake. Death and devastation are the certain consequences of delay."

Later in the day, Warren penned another message, a masterpiece of hypocrisy, to Gage:

> Sir: The unhappy situation onto which this Colony is thrown gives the greatest uneasiness to every man who regards the welfare of the Empire or feels for the distresses of his fellow man. But even now much may be done to alleviate these misfortunes which cannot be entirely remedied, and I think it of the utmost importance to us that our conduct be such as that the contending parties may entirely rely upon the honor and integrity of each other for the punctual performance of any agreement that shall be made between them.
>
> Your Excellency I believe knows very well the part I have taken in public affairs. I ever scorned disguise. I think I have done my duty. Some will think otherwise. But be assured, sir, as far as my influence goes, everything which can reasonably be required of us shall be done and everything promised shall be religiously performed.

Having exonerated himself of all except the most peaceful of intentions, Dr. Warren suggested that Gage make arrangements for citizens who wished to leave Boston to be granted safe conduct, and all those "Loyalists" outside Boston be permitted to enjoy the protection of the British Army inside the gates. Obliquely, Warren suggested that Gage meet him to discuss "public affairs."

If the invitation to a peace talk was declined, Warren desired to have it in writing. Gage obliged. He sent a note by courier stating, in almost pontifical tones, that he could not meet Warren even if he wished because Warren was a member of the Committee of Safety, an illegal body. To receive its president in audience would amount to a tacit recognition of its legality. Gage suggested that the best way to communicate would be through the Selectmen of Boston. As Dr. Warren read the reply, it was already too late to discuss peace. The cry for military assistance was much more fervent than the self-serving appeal for peace to an unimaginative general.

Connecticut, Vermont, and New Hampshire were sending militiamen. General Artemas Ward—properly a colonel but promoted within a month—had been appointed commander-in-chief of the Massachusetts troops. He got up from a bed of pain—chronic kidney stones—donned his uniform, buckled his sword, and rode pell-mell to Cambridge, where he established headquarters for Continental forces. He was surprised to find that he had fifteen thousand men. Ward was an old Indian fighter and he had a chronic fear of idle soldiers. They were, he was sure, easily distracted by liquor and women. He ordered regiments to dig fortifications around Cambridge.

He sent Colonel John Thomas and his poorly equipped regiment to Roxbury, there to guard the approaches to Boston Neck. As staff colonels Ward had Captain William Prescott, a veteran, Captain William Heath, who had led the Minute Men at Concord, and Captain John Whitcomb. Ward drew a loop of soldiery on the landward side of Boston, running from Boston Neck almost to Charles Towne. He felt that the patriot irregulars were drawing a noose around Gage's throat. A journalist asked Ward how many men he would need to face Gage with his ten thousand regulars.

"Let me pick my officers," he said, "and I would not fear to meet them with half that number. Not in a pitched battle, not to stop them at once, for no troops are better than the British, but I would fight on the retreat and every stone wall we passed should be lined with their dead. Our men are lighter of foot, they understand our grounds and how to take advantage of them; and besides, we should only fall back on our reserve, while every step they advanced, the country would close in on their flanks and rear."

Gage was aware of the military preparations outside his door. He chose to ignore them with the contempt a mastiff might have for a solitary flea. His only public complaint was that the colonists were stopping the mails, opening and destroying official documents to keep the British version of Concord from reaching royal governors and the Loyalist press of the Colonies. Certainly General Gage had little understanding of the uses of propaganda as a hammer on the anvil of public consciousness. Warren did.

Spies told him that Gage's version of what happened had sailed at once on the warship *Sukey.* Warren had to wait two weeks for an American vessel sailing to England. It was the light, fast schooner *Quero,* outward bound from Salem. The physician urged the captain to put up all sail and to bend the masts to reach London before *Sukey.* The unknown captain sailed without cargo and reached London ten days before *Sukey.* The Warren story went directly to Benjamin Franklin, who was preparing to leave for Philadelphia. In an accompanying letter, Warren urged Dr. Franklin to have copies made of the story and to distribute them to members of Parliament, government ministers, captains of industry, even local lord mayors throughout Britain.

Warren did his work well. Before the Gage report arrived, John Horne, a loyal Englishman, had raised five hundred dollars for the widows and orphans of "our beloved American fellow subjects, who, faithful to the character of Englishmen, preferring death to slavery, were inhumanly murdered by the King's Troops at or near Lexington and Concord." In North Carolina, Warren's version arrived two months before the Gage story. The royal governor said that the delay was "fatal to the Loyalist cause." In Parliament, Lord George Germain, who had predicted that the colonists would run at the first sound of musketry, said he observed "with alarm the many jovial faces upon this event." No one, Tory or Whig, could design a British victory out of what had happened at Lexington and Concord. Nor had the peasants "ran for their lives."

Edmund Burke opted for an exercise of facetious tribute. "A most vigorous retreat," he said shaking his head, "twenty miles in three hours—scarce to be paralleled in history. The feeble Americans, who pelted them all the way, could scarce keep up with them." In Virginia, Thomas Jefferson noted that the news of Concord had agitated the people to a "phrensy of revenge." Virginia was prepared to send its best officers and finest regiments to assist Massachusetts Bay.

The military assistance sent to Boston raised a legal problem. The Committee of Safety could not appoint Artemas Ward commander of the combined forces. The industrious Joseph Warren realized this and, knowing that a Second Continental Congress would begin to sit in Philadelphia in late May or June, asked that body to appoint a man as Commander in Chief over all, responsible only to the Continental Congress. He also begged the Congress to adopt the Massachusetts Bay militia as part of the army. Warren knew that Adams, Hancock, Randolph, Lee, and others of the radical revolutionary wing of American politics would not countenance a general who would not be responsible to the civilian branch of government. They worried that a military hero could, in time of victory, become a king or a dictator. Whoever served, no matter what his attainments, would have to be subservient to the will of Congress.

In retrospect, it would appear that the handsome Dr. Warren thought of every contingency of war. In early May, 1775, with the first warm breezes covering Boston and the maples and oaks and poplars sprouting leaves too timid to seek the sun, he decided to cultivate General Gage through the Selectmen of Boston. Warren repeated his request that all in Boston who desired to leave the city be permitted to do so; all outside Boston who wanted to dwell in the safety of the British Army should be permitted entry.

Gage gave it thought. He seemed to have a personal fear that he was being outwitted by avaricious Yankees. At

112

last he announced, through the Selectmen, that all who wanted to leave could do so, but would have to surrender their weapons to him and then obtain a leave-taking pass. If Gage feared the Yankees outside, he had also harbored a cautious attitude about a public uprising within Boston. He could be rid of the patriots and their spying, and augment the number of citizens who were Loyalists.

Gage was dumbfounded when, within a few days, Bostonians had deposited 1,778 muskets, 634 pistols, 973 bayonets, and 38 blunderbusses on the floor of Faneuil Hall. The people within the gates had represented a real danger. Gage said that those people were free to leave, and would be issued passes. Warren announced that any people of Massachusetts who wanted to live under the protection of the "Ministerial Army" would be free to enter Boston at will. About four thousand Bostonians departed. The Tories within the city became alarmed. They entreated Gage to stop issuing passes, no matter what his promises. If Whigs continued to leave, there would be no one in the city except the army and Loyalists. "The rebels will burn it," the Tories protested.

The general could not deny his promise. To please the Tories he made it more difficult for anyone to secure a pass to leave Boston. Dr. Warren's fiancée, Miss Mercy Scollay, was not allowed to leave. The son of Samuel Adams was detained. On May 10, Warren protested in a May-it-please-Your-Excellency letter, but Gage did not respond. The doctor went on to other matters. Without publicity or public expression, he removed Dr. Benjamin Church, spy suspect, from the office of chairman of the Committee of Safety. Warren assumed the post. He continued to preach peace, but made ready for war.

He was stunned when a committee from the Connecticut Assembly appeared at Cambridge, stating that it would mediate all disputes between the Committee of Safety and General Gage. The radicals of Massachusetts had been aware for years that they ran the risk of being regarded as trouble-

113

makers by the remaining colonies. It was Massachusetts which resisted the taxes, defied the British Army and Navy, and cried the loudest with outrage when King George punished the colony. No one on the Committee of Safety wanted a mediator—especially from a neighboring colony which was supposed to endorse Massachusetts in its struggle against the Crown.

The doctor decided not to discuss the delicacy of mediation with the committee. Instead he wrote a hasty note directly to Governor John Trumbull of Connecticut. Trumbull was a Whig who had been elected by the colonists. "We fear that our brethren in Connecticut are not even yet convinced of the cruel designs of the Administration against America," he wrote, "nor thoroughly sensible of the miseries to which General Gage's Army have reduced this wretched Colony." Warren described the "miseries." There was an empty port; no shipping, no trade; deserted seaport towns; the treachery of Gage in attacking the defenseless. "No business but that of war is either done or thought of in this Colony. . . . Our relief must now arise from driving General Gage with his troops out of the country, which by the blessing of God, we are determined to accomplish or perish in the attempt. . . ."

Trumbull responded that Connecticut was beside Massachusetts in her struggle and would send regiments of militia. The Connecticut committee had met with Gage once; when the gentlemen appeared before Warren, he displayed Trumbull's letter. They departed for home.

This matter had hardly been settled to Warren's satisfaction when a Connecticut captain, Benedict Arnold, appeared with a plan to go north in New York and capture the British fort Ticonderoga. It was full of muskets, cannon, and gunpowder, Arnold said. Warren said he appreciated the plan but could not send armed militia into New York without the colony's approval. A letter was dispatched to New York, asking permission. The doctor did not wait for a reply. Three days after he sent the letter, Warren persuaded the Committee of Safety to brevet Arnold as a colonel with authority to enlist not more than four hundred men in "western Massachusetts for a secret service."

Benedict Arnold had little trouble getting the men and arms. Without permission he trudged off through Stockbridge. There he learned that a band of New Hampshire and Connecticut fighters calling themselves the Green Mountain Boys were ahead of him on the same mission. They were led by Ethan Allen. Arnold's group endured forced marches to overtake Allen's warriors. When they met, it was Arnold who persuaded Allen to share the command of both bodies of troops.

They attacked Fort Ticonderoga in stealth at dawn. The forty-five-man British garrison slept. The fort, which had successfully resisted an attack by eleven thousand men in 1758, surrendered without the firing of a shot. Both leaders were so enamored of the ease of victory that they planned to attack Quebec and reduce Montreal. The Green Mountain Boys were drunk on stores of rum, and resting, when word came from the Continental Congress to abandon Fort Ticonderoga and carry the captured stores to the south shore of Lake George.

They had seventy-eight cannon, six mortars, three howitzers, thousands of cannonballs, sixteen thousand pounds of musket balls, and thirty thousand musket flints. Ethan Allen and Benedict Arnold were ordered to keep a proper inventory of what they had seized so that, as the Congress explained, "they may be safely returned when the restoration of the former harmony between Great Britain and these Colonies, so ardently wished for by the latter, shall render it prudent." The two colonels were stunned and humiliated.

The order from Congress—obeyed with reluctance—points up the ambivalent attitude of Congress toward the Crown. The new body, which first sat at the State House in

115

Philadelphia on May 10, 1775, was sensitive to the wishes of the people back home. There was little unanimity in the thirteen Colonies. Some, such as New York, Pennsylvania, North and South Carolina, were certain that they could fight Parliament and, somehow, remain loyal to the King. Many Americans refused to entertain the notion that Parliament and His Majesty could be as one in their determination to punish rebellious America. The militant colonies, who saw a break with Parliament and King as inevitable—and perhaps to be desired—were Massachusetts and Virginia, followed by New Hampshire, Rhode Island, and Connecticut. The remainder—Delaware, Maryland, New Jersey, and Georgia—wavered between the two extremes, but looked upon a peaceful accommodation with the Crown as a holy grail, something that all men of goodwill would seek.

Figuratively, the Second Continental Congress found itself at a crossroads. All thirteen Colonies were increasing the strength of their militia. This was a warlike gesture, no matter how lofty and loud the disclaimers. None of the colonies allied their militia with the Redcoats. The King's generals protested that it was their function to protect the thirteen Colonies. The militia would have no purpose if not to fight the British Army. If this were so, then General Gage was correct in assuming that America was in rebellion against the Crown.

The new Congress planned to move further toward war. The delegates, including George Washington of Virginia and Benjamin Franklin of Pennsylvania, agreed to entertain the plea by Dr. Joseph Warren that the Congress adopt the Massachusetts militia as its own. If it did this, the Congress would have to "adopt" all such militia as crossed provincial boundaries to assist those who might be threatened. This, in turn, would constitute a Continental Army. And that, in turn, would require a national Commander in Chief.

In late May and June, Peyton Randolph of Virginia

sat as presiding officer of the Congress, watching as Massachusetts and Virginia deferred to each other in progressive legislation. It was Adams and Hancock who proposed Randolph as president of the Congress. In June, Lord Dunmore of Virginia called the House of Burgesses to order. Randolph realized that Virginia needed him more, at this moment, than the Congress. He asked permission to resign and proposed John Hancock of Massachusetts as his replacement. In Virginia, the electors proposed Thomas Jefferson to replace Randolph. The young philosopher arrived in Philadelphia for his first session with twenty-five servants and four horses. He sat with Patrick Henry, who was also a delegate.

The will of the Congress was to hesitate, to procrastinate, to withdraw from any measure that the Crown might regard as an affront. This attitude sickened John Adams, who wrote to Warren: "We find a great many Bundles of weak nerves. We are obliged to be as delicate and soft and modest and humble as possible." The Congress, for example, was appalled at the capture of Fort Ticonderoga. It ordered Benedict Arnold and Ethan Allen to withdraw with their spoils and to be accountable for every last musket ball. The Congress read depositions about who fired the first shot at Lexington and drew up an elaborate brief that it was the British. This was sent as a message to the King. The Congress happily abased itself to the throne, although George III refused to receive the message. It was entitled, "An Humble and Dutiful Petition to His Majesty."

The New York delegation announced that five thousand fresh Redcoats were expected in New York City. At once the Congress resolved itself into a Committee of the Whole and asked New York to receive the soldiers peaceably and to find housing for the troops, as required under the Quartering Act. Secretly, Dr. Benjamin Franklin had engaged in personal negotiations for peace with Admiral Lord Richard

117

Howe in London. This was almost traitorous to the Colonies because of its secrecy. Franklin told Howe at one point that he would have paid for the tea dumped in Boston harbor from his own pocket. Howe, after consultation with the home secretary, Lord Dartmouth, said that such payment would be a good gesture, but that the government was determined to insist on its new and restrictive charter on Massachusetts. Franklin withdrew his offer, stating that the charter related not to money but to liberty. In this he would be at the side of Massachusetts. He had spent his last day in London reading and weeping. Above all he hoped the Colonies would not resort to the "mad business of mixing soldiers and citizens."

By the time he reached Philadelphia the "mad business" had started at Lexington and Concord. At the age of sixty-nine, the inventive philosopher was shattered to learn that fifteen thousand Americans under arms were facing ten thousand Redcoats at Boston. The situation was potentially explosive. General Israel Putnam, who had served the British well in earlier wars, left a plow in Connecticut when he heard about the confrontation at Lexington, to join General Artemas Ward. In Connecticut, Putnam was known as an unlettered, semiliterate firebrand who had helped to organize the Minute Men. He arrived at Cambridge in farm attire and was given a new uniform and the command of regiments of light infantry.

Congress was fearful that someone at Boston would fire another first shot. It wanted a Commander in Chief, someone who was more cautious than the Putnams, Wards, Prescotts, and Warrens. The Massachusetts delegation, still courting Virginia, nominated George Washington for the post. The soldier-surveyor announced that he was a congressional delegate and should not be considered for the post. Adams and Hancock insisted, and their judgment was endorsed by other colonies. On an early day in June, Washington was persuaded to take command. He was told that at all times and for all purposes he would be under the direction of the Continental Congress, beholden to it in all that he did.

He was forty-three, tall, firm, and deliberate. He asked leave to recruit a retinue of officers before leaving for Massachusetts. A week later, he bade farewell to the Congress and started for Boston by way of New York. It became apparent, from his letters to the Congress, that he did not propose to hurry to Massachusetts. The trip was made in leisurely stages, too leisurely for the more excitable delegates. The reason for Washington's slow journey was that he required time to find out what kind of an army he had, how big and how disciplined, and the composition of the officer corps.

Recruits were paid less than seven dollars a month. The Congress decreed that uniforms should be brown, with different facings for each regiment. Most of the men had no uniforms. The Delawares and the Marylanders were exquisitely caparisoned by their wealthy officers, but the remainder were farm boys in loose shirts and suspenders. Most of these were adventurous, ready to shoot Redcoats but not ready to drill in a hot sun and certainly unprepared to stay beyond harvest time. They brought muskets or had them issued with long bayonets.

The weapons were accurate in firepower at a distance of eighty to one hundred yards. Beyond that, the round lead balls were spent and eccentric in flight. This was why the British command used its infantry for bayonet charges, or, if that was impractical, kept them out of range until they loaded, put a small amount of gunpowder in the flashpan, and closed the distance to fire a solid salvo. But then they stayed where they were to reload the powder, the lead ball inside a paper cartridge, and the flashpan powder before firing a second salvo. The bravery of the Redcoats was encompassed in the considerable time between salvos, when they stood in solid ranks loading as the enemy fired. It required enormous courage not to break ranks and flee.

The only other weapon of importance was the smoothbore cannon. It fired a lead or iron ball of large size a distance of four hundred yards. This fell and rolled through massed infantry in the manner of a modern bowling ball rolling through tenpins. At close range it could be devastating. At Lexington, when the British fired two of them, the Minute Men broke ranks and ran. The sound shattered their resolve. The men hid behind trees and low walls, which encouraged the British to state that the Americans were cowards and didn't know how to fight.

Weaponry dictated the order of battle. The British system, copied by all European armies, was to remain five hundred yards away from the enemy until loaded and ready. At this distance, even the biggest cannon were useless. When muskets were loaded, an order was given to charge. The Redcoat preferred to rely on his bayonet rather than his musket. However, by innumerable tests and drills, he was taught to fire two effective salvos in each charge.

George Washington found that he had some artillery. No one seemed to understand the use of big guns in battle, so he appointed Henry Knox "Chief of Artillery" with orders to read Muller's *Treatise of Artillery*. Foundries in Pennsylvania and Massachusetts began to cast iron cannon, although no one was sure how thick the muzzles would have to be to keep them from exploding. The largest ones tossed a twenty-four-pound ball and were hauled by oxen to the scene of battle. The Commander in Chief's first complaint was about provincial militia; he said it was his understanding that these constituted short-term enlistments. In sum, his army would be melting underfoot as fast as recruits arrived. Some tired of the adventure before their enlistments expired. These disappeared in the night and went home on foot. Washington determined to make a proper example of deserters by hanging a few outside Boston.

At the mouth of the Charles River, a beak of land narrowed the stream. On the south side stood staid Boston. A few hundred yards across the river stood Charles Towne, at the bottom of two hills—one called Bunker, and the nearer one had no name. To get from Boston to Charles Towne by land would necessitate a march through Boston Neck, Brookline, through Cambridge on the upper side of the beak through Bunker Hill, up the hill with no name, and down to the water's edge, where the homes, businesses, and cottages of Charles Towne could be seen in crooked hilly streets.

In the narrow estuary between Charles Towne and Boston, British warships rode at anchor. On May 13, General Putnam ordered all infantry regiments to report for a day march. They left headquarters at Cambridge in the morning, sang and whistled as they tried to keep step, carried their muskets and bayonets around the peninsula and up onto Bunker Hill. They moved forward to the no-name hill and down into the streets of Charles Towne. If exercise was the motive, or close-order drill instruction, Putnam could as easily have moved his thousands of troops westerly in the direction of Lexington.

His design could only have been to tantalize General Gage. Almost everyone in Boston could see the marching patriots. The whistling and singing carried across the water. British officers and soldiers paused in their rounds to stop and stare at the large body of troops. The captains of the men-of-war signaled the admiral that they had trained their big guns on the Minute Men, with sailors holding lighted tapers above the touchholes. Putnam, the wiry and fiery, could see the reaction. He purposely marched his men to the waterfront of Charles Towne, then led the long column back along the south shore road, in full view of the British fleet.

It was now a question of who would fire the first shot. Putnam had taunted the British, and they had not obliged him. Seldom were two adversaries in such proximity without resorting to blows. Two weeks later Israel Putnam decided on another adventure. He learned that the British Army and

121

Navy had been hoarding livestock on Hog Island. The forces had been running short of fresh meat. On May 27, Putnam sent a strong party of Minute Men wading through the shallows between Charles Towne and Hog Island with orders to drive the British livestock ashore inside Massachusetts lines. Admiral Samuel Graves saw the Minute Men and feared for his naval stores, cached on nearby Noddle's Island. Graves ordered the armed schooner *Diana* to protect navy property and, if necessary, to fire on the thieves.

The schooner hove to between Hog and Noddle's and fired a broadside. At the same time, British marines were sent wading ashore. As usual, the "cowardly" Americans hugged the marshes until the broadsides stopped, then fired a volley, killing two marines and wounding two. The Americans ran to Hog Island and rounded up three hundred sheep, cows, and horses and drove them through the shallows toward Bunker Hill. The British officers on *Diana* were helpless because the vessel was shearing on a sandbar.

General Gage could see the action from Boston's shore. He sent eighty marines and two cannon. Admiral Graves, alarmed to see *Diana* out of control and drifting toward the American forces, ordered the armed sloop *Britannia* and ten barges to get to *Diana* and tow the vessel to safety. The Americans asked Putnam for reinforcements, stating that they almost had a British prize. The general sent a thousand militiamen. He and Dr. Warren saddled their horses and rode to the scene. *Diana* drifted helplessly toward the Americans. When it was within range, Putnam yelled, "Surrender! Surrender!" The crew responded with blasts from their swivel cannon.

Both sides fired at will but the range was too great. In a brilliant burnt-orange dusk, *Diana* bumped ashore. The British crew, too close to the armed colonists, fled. Gage watched the entire action from his home at Province House. Beside him stood his recent reinforcements—General John

Burgoyne and General William Howe. They saw the farmers drive the animals ashore and watched them board *Diana*. The generals did not look upon the loss of livestock, the loss of *Diana*, the actions at Lexington and Concord as acts of revolution and war. It was, at best, an impudent and vengeful reaction to a tax. No more than that. They agreed that resistance was confined to the radical element of one colony.

At dawn Putnam's infantry stripped *Diana*. They could hear the taunting shouts of British officers in Boston as they went about the business of search and seizure. Her cannon were wrenched free and taken ashore. The sails were taken. Gunpowder went ashore in barrels. They took winches, a barge, furniture from the commander's cabin, and a hoard of British money. The fleet, under the command of Lord Howe, was helpless to stop the piracy and yet had no inclination to sink their own ship with their own guns. Putnam set fire to *Diana* and marched his troops back to Cambridge with their booty.

In the manner of a volcano, colonial resistance rose to flaming violence at times, then relapsed into hostile silence. General Artemas Ward decided to break the silence with a kind note to General Gage. He asked if the British had prisoners or wounded to trade. Gage sent a note to "Mr. Ward, Esq.," stating that he had eight Minute Men. The Americans had three British officers and five privates. Formally, both sides agreed to meet at the Charles Towne ferry for the exchange. Israel Putnam represented the militia; Major Moncrieff commanded the British party. It was a grim, no-nonsense moment until Putnam and Moncrieff identified each other. They emitted whoops of joy and fell into each other's arms. This bewildered the walking wounded, until both men, in tumbling speech, said that they had fought side by side in the assault on Havana in 1761.

Putnam hurried to a grogshop and returned with potables for both sides. The British sloop *Lively* maneuvered in

123

the narrow waters for two hours. Moncrieff and Putnam were both intoxicated, almost tearful, as the British left the ferry at "supper time." The animosity of old comrades-in-arms began to blur. Veterans in both commands regretted the unpredictable eruptions, and yet the officers on both sides felt an obligation to continue to "fight for the right."

Gage, for example, admired George Washington as a fighting officer. They had fought side by side in the disastrous battle near Fort Duquesne in 1755, and each remembered the other with fondness. They had maintained a personal correspondence for twenty years. Ten of General Gage's eleven children were born in the Colonies. The general, long ago, had bought nineteen thousand acres in upstate New York, a place he thought of using for retirement. Artemas Ward could run down a British list of general officers, ticking off the names of "proper officers" who were lieutenants and captains when he had served with them.

In the middle of June, Ward was still acting as commander-in-chief, and he decided to move the army into a defensive posture. For this the soldiers would need earthworks behind which they could hide. He said that he was prepared to attack, but that Boston still had "many friends." Besides, a frontal attack up Boston Neck and, simultaneously, across the ferry from Charles Towne to Boston was risky. They would have to burn Boston before chasing ten thousand British into the harbor. It would not do. Ward had an advice from a spy that General William Howe had advised Gage to fortify the peninsula of Dorchester, to the south of Boston, and Bunker Hill to the north. Thus the two prongs flanking the city would be invested with British troops.

Israel Putnam advised the generals in council that he had been advocating fortification works on the hill above Charles Towne for several weeks. General Thomas, in charge of the position outside Boston Neck, had warned against it as a "belligerent act." If Howe was allowed to place soldiers near Bunker Hill, Gage would have such a pronounced tactical advantage that he could threaten American headquarters at Cambridge from two directions—Boston and Bunker Hill. Besides, it was logical to assume that Gage was forced to make a move against the Americans; he could not remain a prisoner in Boston for long.

Dr. Warren misunderstood Putnam. Redoubts could not be used for a military advance on Boston, he said. General Ward agreed. "We have no powder to spare and no battering cannon," he said. "It would be idle to make approaches on the town." Putnam said he had no notion of approaching any town. He would like to build fortifications so that the British could see them from Boston. Sooner or later, they must attack the hill. The general would like to draw them out of Boston where the patriots could fight the British on equal terms, where the defenders could advance or retreat through interconnecting earthworks at their pleasure.

Putnam wasn't convinced that he could win such a battle. He hoped to inflict sufficient casualties on Gage's forces to make Boston untenable for him. Reliable spies, he pointed out, placed the British force at no more than five thousand fighting men; about fifteen hundred of these would continue to guard Boston Neck—ergo, Gage could field no more than 3,500 men. "We will risk only two thousand men of our force," he said. Ward said that the army had only nine rounds of powder and ball per man. When these were exhausted, men would have to fight with their hands or run for their lives. Seth Pomeroy, nearing his seventieth year, said that it was common for American hunters to go into a forest with but three charges of powder and return with a deer. The militia would not require nine charges to win or lose such an engagement.

Israel Putnam was a difficult man to deny. Which, he asked, was to be preferred? A battle on Howe's terms or one on Putnam's? Besides, he noted, the militia had been inactive for a long time. It was "rotting away with idleness." Artemas Ward remained unconvinced. If Putnam's plan was to succeed, he would have to negotiate a masterful line of retreat. Suppose Burgoyne or Howe cut him off on Bunker Hill?

Putnam smiled. "We will guard against that," he said, "and run when we can contend no longer with advantage; we can outrun them and behind every wall rally. But suppose the worst; suppose us hemmed in and no retreat; we know what we are contending for; we will set our country an example of which it shall not be ashamed and show those who seek to oppress us what men can do who are determined to live free or not live at all."

Dr. Warren cheered. Ward's frozen features began to glow. Stirring words, those. The phrase "our country" struck a spark. Warren was the highest civilian authority present. He was president of the Provincial Congress and president of the Committee of Safety, one with the power to stop any military action with an order, although powerless to start one. He admitted to the group that last night he had slipped into Boston to check with American spies. It was true—Howe had permission to fortify the Bunker Hill peninsula. A good part of Warren's charm was that he was handsome, a man given to lacy shirts and cuffs; one of such bravado and daring that he evoked both enthusiasm and fear—often together.

"Almost thou persuadest me, General Putnam," he said. "But I must still think of the project as a rash one. Nevertheless, if it should be adopted and the strife becomes hard, you must not be surprised to find me in the midst of it."

Putnam hoped not. "You are yet but a young man and our country has much to hope from you both in council and in war. It is only a little brush we have been contemplating; let some of us who are older and can well enough be spared begin the fray. There will be enough time for you hereafter, for it will not soon be ended." After further conversation, the council of war decided to fortify the Bunker Hill area and Dorchester Neck.

Artemas Ward learned, however, that he could not impose his military will on American officers. He galloped to Boston Neck to explain the double operation which, it was hoped, would divide Gage's army. It was acknowledged that General Thomas, at the Neck, would probably be the first to face the fury of a British attack. He felt that this gave him semi-independent status, and he called a council of war of his own and declined to send any of his seven thousand men to Dorchester. Ward returned to Cambridge and placed Captain William Prescott in charge of all Bunker Hill fortifications.

A measure of the mood of the men is seen in the words of Captain Thomas Knowlton. He was to lead two hundred men of Connecticut into the front lines overlooking Charles Towne. "I wholly disapprove of the project," he said to Putnam. "It will probably prove fatal to the American troops for the British, by landing at Charles Towne Neck under the protection of floating batteries and ships of war, will cut off from the hill all supplies of provision and ammunition. Besides it will render retreat extremely hazardous, if not impossible."

Putnam: "I am going. Will you come with me?"

Knowlton: "Yes, and every one of my men."

"Gentleman Johnny" Burgoyne raised his brass long glass to his eye and studied the heights above Charles Towne. What he saw appeared to be several hundred moles at work. Men were digging; pickaxes and shovels were arcing into the morning sunlight. They didn't seem to be soldiers—farmers, perhaps. He lowered his glass to Charles Towne and saw more wagons and hayricks than he had seen before. It must be that the town was being abandoned. All of which led the

British command to believe that, through some misunderstanding, the colonials were walking into Gage's trap. Anyone with a modicum of military sense could see that Howe and his forces could attack Charles Towne while Burgoyne led his regiments in longboats up the Mystic River and cut the colonials to ribbons from the rear. It was absurd to imagine so many farmers doing so much work merely to die on a hill which had no name.

On the hill the militia worked hard, digging a breastwork 160 feet long and half as wide. If they could not fight, they could dig. These were farmers and the sons and grandsons of farmers who had fought the granite soil for generations. They dug furiously, fully conscious that their life-span depended upon how quickly and how well this work was done. They wore leather trousers buckled at the knee; their long loose coats were on sod behind them; they wore heavy wool stockings dyed as rainbows; the cowhide shoes were thick and serviceable, and so were the round, broad-brimmed beaver hats.

Three men were in uniform. Gray-haired Israel Putnam was in brown and gold beside his horse. Captain William Prescott, tall, slender, a grim warrior who would rather fight than talk, was one of the few Americans who had been offered a commission in the British Army. He had declined tersely. Prescott wore a blue uniform with a flared jacket. When he was working his farm at Pepperell, Massachusetts, he spent his evenings reading European editions of books on military science. The third man was Colonel Richard Gridley, a superb engineer. It was said that if he had not found a way of getting William Howe's cannon up the perpendicular cliffs to the heights of Quebec, General Wolfe would surely have lost the battle. Gridley not only got the cannon to the heights of Abraham, he ordered their fire.

The British had pensioned Richard Gridley as an honored officer. In January an officer of the home secretary had written to Gridley to ask, considering the rebellious attitude of Massachusetts, where his sympathies lay. "I have never drawn my sword except on the side of justice," he had written, "and justice lies, I believe, with my countrymen." The pension stopped.

On this morning of June 16, 1775, Gridley was working as hard as his men. He held a huge schematic drawing in both hands. It called for earthworks stretching across the hill well above Charles Towne; on the side of the hill at Mystic River, it tapered downward almost to the water's edge. There were to be no fortifications on the side where the Charles River lay, closest to Boston. If they came in that direction, Putnam's men would race down the hill to meet the Lobsterbacks with bayonets. It would be a short fight and, for the British, a foolish adventure. No, Gridley was certain that they would come in two waves—up the hill from the direction of Charles Towne, and a big landing party from the Mystic River.

In Boston, Howe had ruined several maps of "The City of Boston and Surrounding Territory" with quill scratches. He asked for fresh ones. His battle plan, worked out with suggestions from General Burgoyne and General Henry Clinton, was almost complete. Carefully, he tracked in the final markings. It was to be a limited offensive with attainable goals if the British met with strong resistance. If the colonials broke and fled, as William Howe felt they would, this would activate a second contingency—an unlimited offensive including the capture of American headquarters at Cambridge, the shattering of their army, and the burning of stores and munitions, followed by an olive branch of peace to be offered by Howe.

The three generals marked off the whereabouts of the fifteen thousand militia, spread in a semicircle behind Boston from the Neck through Cambridge to a point east of Medford on the Mystic River. Howe worked hard on the final draft because the day was Friday and he planned to begin the assault on Sunday morning. In the night, the fleet guns would move close to Dorchester Point. Howe would send fifteen hundred men in an assault at dawn. He expected to find few Americans to resist the amphibious landing and would race through Dorchester, leaving a holding company of two hundred men. These would wheel to their right to attack General Thomas and his force at Boston Neck.

At that point, the blockade of Boston would be broken. In step with the attack on Dorchester, Henry Clinton would take a second amphibious force and move across Willis Creek between Cambridge and Bunker Hill. This group was expected to rout the colonials from the heights above Charles Towne. If all went well, Howe would sweep to Cambridge and join Clinton on one grand final assault on the Americans. As a reserve, General Burgoyne and his soldiers would remain in Boston at the call of either Howe or Clinton.

General Gage approved the final plan. Cadres of selected officers were told the field tactics and ordered to get their troops in a state of readiness without telling anyone that they would be moving out at dawn on Sunday. At that time enemies who spoke the same language, had the same customs and manner of worship, men who revered the same king, would begin to kill each other.

The newly appointed Commander in Chief of the Continental Army sat alone to write a letter to Martha Washington:

> My Dearest: I am now set down to write you on a subject which fills me with inexpressible concern, and this concern is greatly aggravated and increased when I reflect upon the uneasiness it will cause you. It has been determined in Congress that the whole army raised for the defense of the American cause shall be put under my care, and that it is necessary for me to proceed immediately to take upon me the command of it.

You may believe me, my dear Patsy, when I assure you in the most solemn manner that, so far from seeking this appointment, I have used every endeavor in my power to avoid it, not only from my unwillingness to part with you and the family, but from a consciousness of its being a trust too great for my capacity, and that I should enjoy more real happiness in one month with you at home than I have the most distant prospect of finding abroad, if my stay were to be seven times seven years. But as it has been a kind of destiny that has thrown me upon this service, I shall hope that my undertaking it is designed to answer some good service. . . . It was utterly out of my power to refuse this appointment without exposing my character to such censures as would have reflected dishonor upon myself and have given pain to my friends.

He asked her to attend her own comforts, whether it be on his estate at Alexandria or with her family. He said he had made out his will, and enclosed a copy. He hoped the terms would be agreeable to her.

I shall add nothing more at present as I have several letters to write, but to desire that you will remember me to Milly and all friends, and to assure you that I am, with the most unfeigned regard

My dear
Patcy Yr affecte
Go. Washington

The morning after the general sent his modest letter to Mrs. Washington, Captain Thomas Bishop of His Majesty's *Lively* stood on deck, staring up at the hills over Charles Towne. Bishop was stunned. He saw what he called "professional fortifications." The fresh scars of earth formed a big V aimed at his ship. He demanded his long glass and saw hundreds of men braiding branches of saplings into thickets, which were being placed as barriers in front of the fortifications. He stood, half dressed, in openmouthed amazement, as though between sunset and dawn he had seen a thousand hornets complete a nest.

Bishop ordered a spring to be placed on his anchor chain, so that the *Lively* would remain steady in the tide for gunfire. Gunners poured from companionways to load ten starboard guns. The captain donned his double-ender hat and roared, "Commence firing!" The roar of cannon and the diminishing thunder of echoes awakened most of Boston. The black balls hit the side of the hill, sending up gouts of fresh earth. Some bounded off rocks and rolled slowly downhill.

Admiral Samuel Graves, irritated, rolled out of bed. He ordered an aide to signal *Lively* and ask what in hell she was shooting at. This was Graves's first flag command and he did not trust his subordinates to do anything without his express command. He was told that Bishop replied he was firing at Americans who "are entrenching above Charles Towne." "He has no such orders," Graves snapped. "Tell him to cease fire immediately." A short time later, Admiral Graves, still grumpy, received a flag signal from Boston: "His Excellency would appreciate your examining the rebel fortifications on Charles Towne heights. They are reported to be substantial."

Graves grunted and asked for breakfast. He had been at pains to explain to General Gage that the navy was not responsible to him and would not obey his orders. Graves's orders were to seal Boston harbor and to use his command to patrol the outer harbors of the Colonies to stop all smuggling. A large number of British warships rode at anchor in Boston harbor, but Graves would insist that they were present for replenishment of stores. He realized, however, that if General Gage requested fleet support of a land action, he had better comply or face an inquiry by Parliament. Above all he would not concede that his animosity toward Gage was based on an old dispute between the fathers of both men. Nor would Gage reveal that his dislike of Graves was based on the presence of black-market meat in Boston at one guinea per pound. Army officers said that the admiral profited from this traffic.

After breakfast, Graves reconsidered his grunt. He studied the colonial fortifications from Boston. They were astonishingly complete. He ordered all ships of the line to close the distance on Charles Towne and to commence firing. The fleet maneuvered slowly so that the ships would not be subject to cannon fire from shore. When the guns boomed, there were 168 of them blasting at random. Many of the shots were short. Captains moved their ships closer.

The admiral watched them fire over the roofs of shops and houses in Charles Towne straight up the hill. Cannonballs smashed into the big V and, to the consternation of Graves, bounced harmlessly in air to roll back downhill. He and his brother officers could not believe that the impudent ones had built such a solid redoubt overnight. He also noted that while many of the colonists were crouching behind the earthen shield, many others continued to work amid the salvos. After an hour Graves ordered the fleet to cease fire but to maintain stations at anchor. He had done no damage except to alarm citizens all around the harbor.

The fleet had fired almost ten thousand rounds and had killed one man. He was Asa Pollard, who had led a daring party into Charles Towne to find water. A ball had decapitated him. The fear of cannon which always terrified the colonists now caused them to panic. They saw the surge of blood spout from Pollard's neck and they quavered, begging Prescott, "What shall we do now, sir? What shall we do?" He ordered them to start digging diagonally down the north side of the hill.

In Boston, General Gage handed his brass glass to Abijah Willard. "Do you recognize the tall man on the parapet?" he asked.

Willard squinted. "That is Colonel Prescott," he said, "my brother-in-law."

Gage was certain of Willard's loyalty. "Will he fight?"

Willard nodded emphatically. "I cannot answer for his men," he said, "but Prescott will fight you to the gates of hell."

Gage sighed. "Then the works must be carried," he said.

Events often fit into a scheme of natural progression. Gage chose this time to release his proclamation of amnesty. It was a bid for peace, forgiving all those who laid down their arms—except Samuel Adams and John Hancock. Thomas Gage, who verged on several well-intentioned but disastrous mistakes, asked General John Burgoyne to write it. Burgoyne had written several plays. This qualified him as a writer, but, given rein, he was inclined to be florid. The proclamation should have been simple and soothing. Burgoyne wrote:

> Whereas the infatuated multitudes who have long suffered themselves to be conducted by certain well-known incendiaries and traitors in a fatal progression of crimes against the constitutional authority of the state, have at length proceeded to avow rebellion, and the good effects which were expected to arise from the patience and lenity of the King's Government, have been often frustrated and are now rendered hopeless by the influence of the same evil councils, it only remains for those who are invested with the supreme rule as well as for the punishment of the guilty . . . to prove they do not bear the sword in vain.

The men of Massachusetts laughed when the bill was posted. On second reading, they scowled. Who was calling them "infatuated multitudes"? The bill posters were torn down. The crowds of citizens became angry. Abigail Adams read it and wrote to husband John in Philadelphia: "Gage's proclamation you will receive by this conveyance. Satan when driven from the regions of bliss exhibited not more malice. Surely the father of lies is superseded. Yet we think it is the best proclamation he could have issued."

The patriots also made mistakes. Artemas Ward was not willing to commit the bulk of his army to the defense of the Bunker Hill area. If the Minute Men were defeated—a likely possibility—he would have no force strong enough to defend Cambridge. If Cambridge fell, the cause was lost. The general entertained the idea that about two thousand men would be sufficient to fight an action. He had some cannon of considerable size, but Ward allocated only four four-pounders, taken from *Diana* and rebuilt with axles and wheels. No officer but Gridley had experience with cannon; he was exhausted ordering men to dig all over the hills.

Prescott, who had been advanced from captain to colonel, offered a reward for any of the diggers who recovered British cannonballs bouncing over the hard ground. Men left the trenches to retrieve them. Aaron Burr, a farm boy, ran toward a bounding iron ball and watched his right leg fly off and fall in grass nearby. The "reward" was canceled at once. The militia were fearful of the sound and effect of cannon fire in any case. Artemas Ward said that his soldiers were more fearful of their legs than their hearts. He was under pressure to send reinforcements to Prescott, and with obvious distaste Ward ordered two hundred men detached from New Hampshire forces at Medford.

Almost at once the general fell in a spasm of pain. Ward had been afflicted with "calculus," or bladder stones. The discomfort was so great that it was impossible to convey news or receive a reasoned order from the acting commander-in-chief. Israel Putnam, who desired to tell Ward that the British regiments were in marching order on the Boston Common, found Ward writhing, with aides trying to tie his arms to a bed. Putnam realized that he had lost more than a superior officer. Putnam expected to be in sole command of a battle, if a battle ensued. He was powerless to order other generals to send additional reinforcements—if they were required—to the hills above Charles Towne. He had four small

135

cannon, a superb earthworks, and over two thousand exhausted militiamen. It is a common thing, on the eve of battle, for generals to detect disastrous faults in their confreres. General Putnam was disturbed at the prospect of "no water, no more ammunition, no more men" at a crucial moment in colonial history.

It was as hot a day, and as miserable, in Boston. The people were on the flat roofs of their homes, or climbing Beacon Hill and Copp's Hill, as spectators to an impending drama which awaited its first curtain. In Province House, General Gage found himself opposed to the ebullience of General Henry Clinton. The subordinate general pointed gleefully to maps and insisted that the Americans had posted themselves in an untenable position on the hills. "They are now in a bag," he said, "and all we have to do is squeeze it."

Clinton would revise the tactics of the day. He told Gage that he would like five hundred men to land in longboats "under the guns of the fleet" across the Charles River in the neck of land between the hills and Cambridge. The colonials would then have but two choices—starve or surrender. Gage shook his head. "We must remember, gentlemen," he said, "the enemy has troops stationed at the Neck. How many we do not know. To place five hundred men between two enemy forces, each of whom may outnumber them, seems to be very dangerous tactics to me. It violates a fundamental military principle."

What Gage didn't know could hurt him. At the Neck was Colonel James Reed with a regiment. One mile away stood Colonel John Stark with eight hundred men. Howe, who had been sending letters to politicians in London damning Gage's tactics with the faintest of praise, found himself opposed to Clinton's daring plan. No one, he said, knew whether the south side of the hills was suitable for landings. No marine charts had been made of rocky shoals or strong tides. Of one thing he was certain: before the hills had been fortified, he had been rowed in a longboat to the north side of the peninsula. He found that there were two hundred yards of mud flats through which the amphibious force would have to wade—perhaps under murderous fire. He was opposed to a landing from the Mystic River because of what he knew, and opposed to a landing on the Charles River because of what he did not know.

Conversely, he went on, British troops had landed across Willis Creek behind Charles Towne for the march on Lexington and Concord. It had been good practice and a worthwhile venture. The approved plan called for Clinton to land his troops in the same place. Howe said he realized this would mean a frontal assault on the Americans high in the hills, but it held no unhappy surprises. Clinton said that a small army could not afford heavy casualties. He suggested that he might do well if he landed at Charles Towne and marched his men through the empty town before assaulting the hills. All of the officers opposed this. Gage asked Clinton if he had heard of Colonel Percy's experience at Cambridge, where he had learned of an American habit of placing six to eight snipers in each building, where they waited for British troops to pass. Clinton admitted that he had heard of this peculiar style of fighting, but doubted that the militia would try this nefarious device in Charles Towne.

Gage made a small speech. He did not underestimate the tactics of General Clinton, but there was a political consideration in the assault tomorrow. British troops had sustained exorbitant casualties at Concord. The Americans would have to be met and defeated on a battlefield of their choosing. This confrontation had to occur on the one small hill and two larger ones behind Charles Towne. It would be a stand-up bayonet charge followed by musket fire. The British generals in the field would be expected to do more than force the colonials back to Bunker Hill. They would "thrash them," scatter them to the fields and woods, and take Cambridge and

137

all the gunpowder and stores there. Thomas Gage was correct; it was much more than a military operation: the future of His Majesty's Colonies depended upon obliterating resistance to his will.

Henry Clinton was not convinced, but he fell silent. The man who continued to express doubt was General Timothy Ruggles. He was a general officer, a man without an army, an American. The others knew him to be sensitive. They listened when he said that General Gage had no proof that the fortifications on the hill amounted to a simple redan, an earthworks with one or two sides. He felt that when British soldiers arrived there, it might turn out to be a complete redoubt, with a stone wall connecting an outer fort with an inner fort. No one knew better than he the depth of bitterness in the hearts of colonial men. If captured, they knew that they could expect a hangman's noose—why then would they not fight to the death?

General Howe shrugged. "I do not see how the works could be more than a redan," he said patiently. "Never in my experience have I heard or seen even regular troops capable of building a complete redoubt in a single night's work." Ruggles snapped his uniform hat under his arm, bowed gravely to the generals, and left Province House. On the lawn he saw a Loyalist friend who asked what the generals were doing. "They don't think the Americans will fight," Ruggles said, shaking his head angrily. "They're going to attack them up there." He nodded toward the nearby hills.

Late in the morning, the British offensive began to move into position. The first order of business was for the ships of war to move closer to Charles Towne and to ease shallow draft vessels into the Mystic River, to fire their salvos between the hill with no name and Bunker Hill. Viewed from the side, the peninsula looked like a brown whale. The snout consisted of Charles Towne and the first hill. Then came the arched neck of the nameless place. Behind it was a road traversing the area between hills like a scarred band. This road was covered with bursting chain shot and ringshot. Behind it was Bunker Hill, the highest arch of the whale's back.

Israel Putnam felt that he was going mad. He was returning from nearby Cambridge after making little sense of General Ward's dismal howls of pain. At the top of Bunker Hill he saw the cannonading dead ahead and realized that Prescott had not provided for entrenchment for Bunker Hill. If the Minute Men were driven off the hill of no name they could be driven more easily off Bunker Hill and straight down into Cambridge. He swore and spurred his horse through the flying chain shot.

The soldiers were cowering in the big bunkers. "We must begin entrenchments on Bunker Hill immediately," Putnam shouted above the roar of big guns. "Have the men carry the entrenchment tools up there." Prescott tried to decline an order. His men were exhausted. They were frightened of the sound of battle. Headquarters had sent them no food, no water. Besides, he had lost too many through exertion. He had started with nine hundred, not counting Gridley's engineers; now he had five hundred. Putnam was adamant. He ordered the men sent back to Bunker Hill. "I promise," he said, "you will not lose a man."

Prescott ordered the soldiers back to Bunker Hill. He remarked that he had never been obeyed with such dispatch. The militia leaped and ran backward. Putnam showed them where to dig emplacements across the brow of the hill. He spurred his horse to head for Cambridge. Headquarters should know that if the men did not get food and water at once, and reinforcements, the army would lose the battle. On the point of the foremost hill, Gridley placed his cannon on wooden mounts. He discovered that they were aimed at a front wall of stone and earth. He had forgotten to ream out embrasures through which they could fire. Captain Ebenezer Bancroft saluted and said he could provide holes through which the cannon could be fired. Gridley, worn out, nodded permission. Bancroft put cannonballs in the cannon, plenty of black powder, then lit fuses. The men screamed with terror and ran out of the entrenchment. The four cannons fired, ripping big holes in the wall before them. "There," said Bancroft solemnly, "now you can fire them."

At 11:30 A.M. a signal hoist on Admiral Graves's flagship ordered the fleet to cease firing and alter their anchorages so that they could fire from the other side. For a half hour, there was silence. In it the men heard music. They lifted their heads timidly above the escarpments and looked across into Boston. Twenty companies of British grenadiers and the Fifth and Thirty-eighth regiments were marching to the tune of "Yankee Doodle" with fife and drum. The militia stared at the well-uniformed Redcoats with their tall pointed hats and their gleaming bayonets. Those, everyone agreed, were soldiers. The investment of Dorchester Heights had been completed; now, in the superior, almost supercilious manner of the British, they were marching to longboats at the wharf. A thousand men, infinitely disciplined, were about to embark for the Charles Towne peninsula. The bravest of the brave Yankee militia had to wonder which of these magnificently caparisoned men would kill him today.

Five hundred other men—some of them British marines—met the marchers at the Long Wharf. At noon the ships of war resumed their cannonade. Gridley's engineers were too busy, too fatigued to look. They were scarring the north side of the hills with a sloping trench down to the Mystic River. It was not until 1 P.M. that General Howe had most of his command boarded and seated for the half-mile trip. He left six companies on the wharf. *Spitfire, Lively,* and *Falcon* were firing broadsides. Calmly, energetically, two columns of longboats rowed under the gouts of blue-gray smoke from the warships. General Howe, in the lead boat with the Royal Welsh Fusiliers, paralleled the beach sufficiently far out to avoid musket fire. As he passed the town of Charles Towne, he brandished his sword. All boats turned at once toward shore, swiftly beached themselves, and landed Howe's complement before the admiring militia, up on the hill, could run down and shoot them.

Within twenty minutes his regiments were in proper ranks. To his left General Robert Pigot was ready with his royal marines. Pigot approached with a squad of men enclosing five disarmed marines. "They tried to desert, sir," said Pigot. "Ran for the American lines."

William Howe could not believe it. "The morning orders stated 'any man who shall quit his rank on any pretense will be executed without mercy.' I would like to hang the five of you," he said, "but I need men." He pointed to the two in the middle. "Hang those two," he said. The men fell to their knees begging for mercy, but Howe was off on a knoll with his long glass studying the American earthworks beyond the first small hill.

At this time General Putnam was riding through Cambridge at a dead gallop, shouting, "To arms! To arms! The British are landing at Charles Towne!" His son, Captain Israel Putnam, Jr., remained in the town to advise all able-bodied militia to hurry to Bunker Hill. Church bells were ringing. Farmers tending corn and beans hurried to their homes to don parts of uniforms and to fix bayonets on their muskets. Through the afternoon, reinforcements turned out to be a mass of walking, trotting, disorderly groups of men—a stream of all ranks and no rank at all.

Ward lifted himself from a bed of pain to insist that the strongest elements of the army remain at Cambridge. He sent his own regiment to battle. The acting commander-in-chief ordered the New Hampshire regiments, stationed east of Medford, to hurry into the line. However, the order was couched in so many words of caution and precaution that the New Hampshire group spent the afternoon marching aimlessly. A Colonel Porter arrived at General Ward's bed with a smart salute to announce that he had delivered two kegs of beer "through ye shot and shell of ye floating batteries to ye troops in Charles Towne." There were none but British troops there; the beer went to the exhausted militia on Bunker Hill.

Putnam was back on the hill in time to see a second landing of British longboats packed with troops. The fleet stopped cannonading as polished grenadiers stepped ashore with gleaming brass cannon. The point of both landings surprised Putnam. They were on the Mystic River side of the Charles Towne point. The choice gave Howe an option of marching up the north shore on the Mystic or swinging through Charles Towne to attack the south side of the hills along the Charles River. Putnam saw Captain Knowlton and two hundred Connecticut militia rushing downhill to attack Howe's pickets. "Stop!" he roared. "Here here! Man this fence. They will flank us fast!" He brought them back uphill behind a low fieldstone fence. The Connecticut men had been digging and fortifying for Prescott all night and all morning. Now they had to shake off dizzy fatigue and start to dig a trench behind the stone wall. "Stand fast, men," Putnam said as he whirled away on his horse. "There will be help on the way in half an hour or I'll know the reason why." He hurried back toward Cambridge, rounding up walking reinforcements to place them behind the fence.

Atop the hill of no name Captain Prescott moved among men sleeping on the grass as the British approached. Each had been issued fifteen rounds of ammunition the night before. Most of the men had fifteen additional rounds, used for hunting. To Prescott, the most important thing was to stop panic firing before it started. Over and over he told them to reserve their fire until the command was given. The fleet salvos began anew as Colonel Stark arrived with a regiment of New Hampshire men. Cannonballs were bouncing and rolling across the line of march. A nervous captain asked if the regiment could not double its pace—or perhaps run—to get the cannonballs behind them. Stark, who kept calling the steady stride, said, "One fresh man in action is worth ten fatigued ones." The march continued, somewhat sedately, through a heavy crossfire.

Stark and his men reached a point where they could see the Redcoats on the small hill above Charles Towne. He also saw Knowlton and his men digging at the farm fence. The colonel drew his sword, jumped up on rocks. Stark pointed to the British soldiers and reminded his New Hampshire men that these were the soldiers who said that all Americans were cowards. Within an hour, Stark said, his boys would have a chance to show the British how wrong they were. The men cheered and followed Stark down the slope to reinforce the Connecticut men. Other reinforcements followed. A Massachusetts regiment came on the field with fifes blowing and snare drums beating a tattoo.

A cheer from behind the main fort danced the length of the hills. The men from a Massachusetts regiment thought they saw a vision on horseback. It was Dr. Joseph Warren. He was to have been commissioned a major general, but the document had not arrived. He sat a black horse, smiling at the diggers, exhorting them to a great victory. He wore a waistcoat of summer-sky blue with lace cuffs, the whole laced in front with silver. His shirt was white ruffled lace. His riding breeches were blinding white, with silver flashing. To the delighted men he said he would not have missed this day, this fight for anything in the world. The doctor had been warned at Cambridge not to go. "You know the project is absolutely mad," Elbridge Gerry had said. "Every man on that hill is going to be killed or captured before evening. If you go, you will be certainly killed."

To Warren the panorama from Bunker Hill was intoxicating. He could see his student, Dr. William Eustis, setting up a field hospital; the men of New Hampshire were swinging picks and shovels in the rocky soil on the left; on the next hill he saw entire regiments loafing on sod; further ahead General Howe was drawing his regiments into glittering ranks of scarlet; ships of the line snorted blue smoke followed by the crack of cannon; in the clear air he could see Boston, its flat roofs and captain's walks polka-dotted with people. Boston, the largest prison in the world.

Among the niceties of battle was General Howe's decision to permit his troops to have lunch. His reasoning was sound: if his command of 2,500 troops was expecting to rout the farmers from the redoubts—an ugly, wasteful task—and chase them through Bunker Hill and down onto the plain at Cambridge, the battle could not be closed before sundown. At 2:30 P.M., he saw the second wave of British longboats coming his way and ordered all soldiers at ease to eat. He had a secondary motive. Howe felt that the quiet houses and shops of Charles Towne were full of snipers. He could not afford to have them in his rear.

He requested Admiral Graves to set fire to Charles Towne. The British Navy was equipped with hollowed-out cannonballs. These were filled with hot pitch and fired at close range into the buildings along the wharf. For a moment Charles Towne shimmered like a toy city in the hot sun. There was the sharp crack of cannon. Pale tongues of flame arched above the roofs. Redcoats lounging on Morton's Hill eating saw two depressing sights: an empty city burning and two soldiers twisting slowly on ropes. The church steeples caught fire. They looked like flaming haystacks. As the timber weakened, the bells began to toll. They fell clanging into the deserted streets, bouncing on the cobbles and setting up a final call for God.

Howe watched the fury of fire create its own furnace wind. He called his officers to a council. "Gentlemen," he said, "I am very happy in having the honor of commanding so fine a body of men. I do not in the least doubt that you will behave like Englishmen and as becomes good soldiers. If the enemy will not come out from their entrenchments, we must drive them out. At all events, the town of Boston will be set on fire by them. I shall not desire any one of you to go a step further than where I go myself at your head. . . ."

A black apostrophe of smoke stood over Charles Towne as Howe divided his command into two brigades. The first, under General Pigot, was to attack the main American redoubt; the second, under Howe, would file along the Mystic River edge, firing at extreme range to freeze Colonel Stark's men in their diagonal trench. A separate column of light infantry would run along the beach, out of sight of the Americans, to get behind the militia, so that, in effect, the Americans would be "boxed." The beach running column was not good field tactics, but Howe counted on the untrained colonists' firing too quickly—"after which our regiments would be upon them with the bayonet before they could reload."

Three streets of buildings on the south side of Charles Towne did not burn. Captain Benjamin Walker and three hundred Minute Men crouched and ran down the hill to occupy the nearest houses. Pigot's marines took station on the left of his line. They were fifty yards from Walker's men. The snipers began a sporadic fire. Marines began to drop in the ranks. Pigot had to pause, first to detail men to carry the wounded back to the boats; second, to turn part of his line toward Charles Towne to flush the snipers.

The second task was difficult. The Americans refused to come out, form a line, and fight a traditional battle. As the marines charged, the farmers retreated from house to house, always returning when the marines could not find targets. Colonel Pitcairn took a large part of his regiment and began a house-to-house search. The Americans, like ghosts, seemed to dissipate as they stole backward from house to house. When Pitcairn was finished, he re-formed ranks on Morton's

Hill. The Americans were back, picking off marines again. Pigot sent word to Howe that he could not proceed with the attack until what was left of Charles Towne was secured. "It alone will give us sufficient employment."

The hour was 3:30 P.M. Howe had not joined battle. The men in the ranks were shouting, "Push on! Let's get at the dogs!" This spirit encouraged the general to improvise. Pigot, on the hill, started forward deliberately. Howe, on the beach, moved his forces toward the American rail fence, a half-mile across flatland and up a rise of ground. The general, in white and red and gold, looked like a knight as he marched in the lead, his sword spangling in the sun. When he reached the first hollow behind a hill, he dispatched his light infantry as a flying column to run down to the beach again, hugging the high-water mark as the grenadiers tried to get behind the Americans, taking up a position between the hill of no name and Bunker. The fleet was bombarding this area to keep American reinforcements out. Howe had no artillery at his disposal except for the six-pounder brass cannon. They kept sinking in the soft earth.

In war the unexpected is seldom a good omen. The farmers whose livestock grazed these hills had departed two months ago. The grass and undergrowth were hip-high. Whole companies of soldiers were tripping over hidden farm walls. The heat was worse. Perspiration tickled the faces of His Majesty's finest. Two small ponds, hidden, created disorder for three regiments. The advance had to be stopped for several minutes as they re-formed on the other side of the water. The two most prominent targets were Howe and Putnam.

The fiery general rode his horse back and forth along the redoubt, warning the militia not to waste ammunition. "Do not fire," Putnam shouted, "until you see the whites of their eyes, then fire low. Take aim at their waistbands. You're all marksmen, men, and there's not a one of you that can't kill a squirrel at a hundred yards. Reserve your fire and we will destroy every one of them. Aim at the handsome coats. Pick off the commanders."

Near Mystic Beach, Colonel Stark sprang over the farm wall, a wooden stick in hand. He measured off forty yards and hammered the stake into the ground. "Not a man is to fire until the first regular crosses that stake," he said. "Watch their gaiters. When you can see their gaiters clear, that's when to shoot."

An uneasiness spread through the colonial lines. The strutting of the Redcoats took an emotional toll. Militiamen began to slink out of line, carrying muskets back to Bunker Hill. Israel Putnam saw an old comrade of the French and Indian Wars leave the line. "I am sick," the soldier said.

"I need you here to show these young fellows how to fight," Putnam shouted. The man shook his head. Putnam yanked his sword from its scabbard. "Get back into that line or I'll run you through on the spot." The man stood silent. Putnam jabbed his shoulder. The man hung his head. General Putnam swore a loud oath and sank the sword into the man's arm. Bleeding, the old soldier went back into the line. "If anyone else is thinking of leaving," Putnam shouted, "he'll get more than the tip of this sword."

At the edge of the beach, British grenadiers formed in ranks of twenty to a line, separated, and lowered their bayonets. The order was to run up through the tall grass in silence, leap the farm wall stuffed with hay and rails, and clear the area of Americans without firing a shot. These were the best in Howe's army, men accustomed to engage the enemy with the blade. Stark kept up a running commentary to his men not to fire; to keep their eyes on that stake. It was frightening not to fire, to watch those superb soldiers approach at a dog trot, the silence broken only by the thump of collective footfalls.

As they passed the stake, the British looked over the wall hopefully. Then the American line exploded in a hundred puffs of smoke. The first few rows of the Welsh Fusiliers, so close that the look of surprise was genuine, fell out of step, staggered, and disappeared in the grass. The remaining ranks re-formed behind the bodies of their comrades and began to press forward. This gave Stark's men sufficient time to reload and fire. The Fusiliers disappeared as though cut by a giant scythe.

A hundred yards behind came the King's Own. They raced up off the beach in perfect ranks. The colonials, most impressed and very nervous, barely had time to reload when the regiment was fifteen yards away from the wall. The Red-coats fell screaming with pain, the imperfectly rounded one-ounce lead balls tearing through stomachs, ripping thigh muscles loose, lodging in chests. And behind the fallen came the Tenth Regiment. These were the men who had cut down the colonials in the village square at Lexington. They had seen the Americans melt away from the scene. The militia, shaken by the successive waves of regiments, was barely able to hold its fire.

Pitcairn knew that one volley was possible. Even two. But in this year of 1775 he had not heard of three. He charged with the Tenth. Behind that low wall Stark had improvised. He had one long row of men on their bellies, firing through chinks in the wall. A second line behind them half crouched, saving their fire. A third stood tall behind the second. Stark ordered each to fire in turn while the other two reloaded. This permitted the almost continuous wall of fire which Major Pitcairn could not understand. Within minutes the Tenth Regiment was shattered. A score of soldiers stumbled back down the beach.

The Fifty-second regiment started forward and stopped. Their officers cursed them into motion, smashing the men with the flat edge of swords. The soldiers could hear the pitiful cries of brothers-in-arms dying in the tall grass. Hesitantly, they stepped forward and stopped, stepped forward again. When the first row was inside that small stake, the militia fired. Soldiers fell groaning. The remainder of the regiment turned and ran. Their officers ordered a retreat after the men had fled.

One small phase of the attack was over. John Stark stood in the trench and looked on the dead and dying. "I never saw sheep lie as thick in the fold," he said. An officer of the King's Own, his tunic splashed with blood, hurried all the way to General Howe on Morton's Hill. He explained the carnage, the stunning retreat.

Howe had been robbed of a chance to cut the Americans off at the rear. He had but one tactic left—a frontal attack on the redoubt. "Pass the word," he said. "Attack all along the line." Within fifteen minutes the British regiments were moving toward the Continentals. When the mass of men was within seventy yards of the earthen fort, Lieutenant James Dana of the Connecticut militia fired his musket—even though the distance made the shot ineffective—"to draw their fire." The grenadiers paused to fire a salvo. In the rear, the Fifth and Fifty-second regiments stumbled into the grenadiers. Dana was right; the grenadiers would not have time to reload.

It is possible that General Howe thought that the regiments attacking Stark behind the stone fence were inept. It is a certainty that he did not attribute the defeat to the marksmanship or bravery of the provincials. They were, in his eyes, military clods. If this were not so, Howe would not be sending a double row consisting of nine hundred soldiers against entrenched militia numbering fifteen hundred. At a distance of sixty yards, the grenadiers stumbled over a low rail fence. The soldiers kicked at it as they pressed the big lip of stone and earth.

At thirty yards, Israel Putnam roared, "Fire! Fire!" There was a sporadic, uneven wall of smoke. The grenadiers fell in massive groups. The uninjured stared down in shock at their writhing comrades. The second line tried to stumble forward. The militia fired at random. Many were firing at flitting ghosts through the blue smoke. One British regiment lost all but a half-dozen men; the Fifty-second counted eight able soldiers left; five officers stood, out of forty-nine in the line. Colonel James Abercromby fell with a mortal wound. He had been quoted as calling all Americans "cowards." As soldiers picked him up, some Americans recognized him and called out, "Colonel Abercromby, are the Americans cowards now?"

The proud General Howe saw his regiments melt in the blazing sun. As he turned with chin up to regroup on the beach, he watched his aides melt too as they were hit by musket balls. Lieutenant Jourdain, his naval aide, fell with a bullet in his head. Howe stooped to attend his personal aide, Captain Sherwin, but the man was beyond assistance with a bullet in his chest. Howe made a striking target, but he was leaving the area, conscious only of the fact that his forces had sustained 80 percent casualties. He seemed dazed as the musket fire stopped. General Pigot and his men, held in reserve off the brow of the hill, concluded that the Americans were retreating. They ran through the smoke, cheering. This time, Colonel Prescott ordered the men to hold their fire until the Lobsterbacks were twenty yards away. "Fire!" he shouted. Big gaps were torn in the British lines. Pigot shouted the order to retreat. The Americans had not left their posts.

The British re-formed in thin ranks three hundred yards away. At the rear, pipers wailed a march tune for the drummers. The Redcoats marched forward. Colonel Prescott crouched inside the line, moving from group to group. "You drove them back once. You can do it again. Hold your fire until you get the order and do not shoot until you have a target." Some were short of musket balls. They jammed nails and small stones down the barrels of their guns. The temperature was 90 degrees.

The British were indomitable. One more time they breasted the hill. One more time they closed ranks until they numbered six hundred men. One more time they moved over their own dead and dying, ignoring the pitiful cries for help, staring straight at that wall with the muskets sticking out. Once more they would not ask mercy or accord it. The march music, the snap of the snare drums, kept them marching in tempo. They scaled the broken farm fence. In a moment they were thirty yards from the redoubt. Up and down the line, Yankee officers yelled, "Fire!" The blast again tore huge holes in the British lines. Captain Evelyn's company was decimated as he shouted, "Charge!"

William Howe had splotches of darkening blood on his white trousers. "Once more, men—!" he shouted, but no one heard him in the din of fire flashes. The whole men turned and ran. Howe walked after them. Exultant, the Minute Men leaped over the stone and logs, shouting and chasing the British. Officers commanded that they cease fire and return to the redoubt. On the left side of the line, Israel Putnam was yelling like a happy boy.

The haze cleared. The Americans shouted, "There's an officer. Let's get him!" The officer, standing dazed and alone, turned to face the muskets. Putnam recognized an old friend, John Small.

"Don't!" Putnam shouted, jumping off his horse, knocking musket barrels straight up. "For God's sake spare that man! I love him like a brother." Major Small made a correct bow of gratitude, turned, and marched downhill.

Beyond the hot ashes of Charles Towne, Howe counted 450 soldiers. It was not enough. Henry Clinton, whose function was to send reserves if necessary, marshaled eight hundred soldiers in Boston and led them across the narrow waters. General Clinton and his men disembarked at the bottom of Morton's Hill. The longboats were sent to Charles Towne wharf, where two hundred British wounded bled in silence, half suffocated by the smoke from burning buildings.

The citizen soldiers up in the fort were spent. Putnam's

officers and men had worked all night making the big redoubt; they had spent a hot morning finishing the trenches leading down to the Mystic River. They had been promised water and food. Neither had arrived from Cambridge. The men drank the last of the rum. Their eyes were red and caked with pale powder. They tried to eat salt pork, but couldn't swallow. Their ammunition was practically gone. Prescott ran the length of the fort and counted 150 men. Every time a militia soldier was wounded, four or five of his comrades volunteered to help him back to Bunker Hill. None, it seems, had returned. Whether the men could continue to stand much longer, without facing another attack, was a formidable question. A hoarse voice croaked, "If the generals in Cambridge can't send water, why not send beer?" Prescott did not answer. Dr. Warren, still cheerful, said, "Lick them once more, boys, and they'll never come back. We will drink tea in peace for the rest of our lives."

The British artillery had at last been hauled out of the mud. Howe had the pieces hauled up from the Mystic River to a point where the brass cannon could fire almost the length of the redoubt, enfilading the militia. He addressed the men he had left, and the men Clinton brought from Boston. Quietly, he ordered the men to drop their heavy packs. The light infantry, the royal grenadiers, the Fifth and Fifty-second would proceed up the Mystic side, as though to attack the farm fence. Pigot and his men would attack from the Charles River side. When they were within sixty yards of their objective, both attacks would turn to the center of the redoubt and join forces to breach it and send the militia in flying retreat.

It was the third attack. Howe knew that there would be no fourth. His reputation, his future as a general officer depended on this final chance. He repeated the plan of battle—a feint on both sides of the American position, a sudden wheeling motion to join forces at the center. He ordered all men to load muskets. The grenadiers, who would lead the

152

operation, were to fire when they were within ten yards of the colonists. This would keep the Americans from firing on other British units. The brass cannon would be dropping grape, chains, and cannonballs the length of the American line.

Up on the hill, Putnam wondered what had become of his reinforcements. Prescott had but 150 weary campaigners left. He rode his fat horse back to Bunker Hill. Putnam was shocked to find that almost two thousand men were crouching behind trees and rocks as the British fleet bombarded the area. He was amazed and ashamed in the presence of men who quailed and moaned at cannon fire, but could hold their own in the face of a musket charge. He cursed and shouted for them to move forward. A colonel said he couldn't move, he was exhausted. Other officers said the battle was almost lost, why risk more men on that hill? Putnam lost his temper. He swore and tried to beat the crouching men with his sword. They would not move.

At Boston Neck, Lord Percy maintained a heavy barrage of cannon and musketry. General Thomas, in charge of seven thousand militia, was certain that an attack was imminent. He had the men fell trees, and placed cannon in a cemetery, waiting for the British to charge. No charge came because the effective reserves had been taken from Lord Percy to send to Howe. In a tumult of noise all day, there was but one known casualty. The daughter of Connecticut governor John Trumbull, Mrs. Jedediah Huntington, had come to the Neck to join her husband. The shouts, the cannonading, the fear on so many faces caused the young lady to lose her mind. She died a week later.

Thomas Gage, his eye to a long glass, crouched in the North Church steeple to watch the battle. He did not record his thoughts until much later. Surely he was crushed, watching William Howe push strong red waves up the hills, only to be dashed on rocks of provincial determination. And yet he suspected that Howe had been sent to America to succeed him, to be forthright where he had temporized, to teach a lesson to colonists with steel, a lesson he had tried to impart with a quill.

Howe again led his men. He swept his sword forward as though it would pull the men faster. He was nine hundred feet from the colonial breastworks when the brass cannon enfiladed it. Howe did not know, nor could he guess, that cannon fire induced terror in the militia. The black iron balls and grape tore the center of the redoubt. Howe was three hundred feet away when Doolittle's regiment of militia bolted. Their officer, Captain Willard Moore, was dying, his bones shattered by a cannonball. The men dropped their muskets and ran. Companies to the left and right began to waver.

Captain Samuel Trevett arrived with two four-pounders and manned the gap in the line. He fired as fast as he could load. Heavy shot caused holes in the British line. Still the Redcoats came on. Colonel Gridley took command of the guns. A British shot blew one of his guns to chunks of smoky metal. Howe's men paused to fire muskets. A ball tore Gridley's thigh. Two cannoneers were detached to assist him to the rear. Trevett ordered the remaining men to fire at Howe. They hesitated. They broke and ran. The two advancing lines of British soldiers swung smartly inward and attacked the empty center of the redoubt.

Howe turned to look at Pigot's marines coming up the hill. They paused to fire a volley. Most of the bullets went into the backs of the regiment ahead of them. The general screamed, "Cease fire! Cease fire!" He was horrified. "Your one hope is your bayonets!" he roared. "Men, your bayonets!" Up behind the center of the redoubt, Colonel Prescott solved the field tactic. The British were killing each other, but they would turn in at the broken center of the Continental line. He looked down into the redoubt. He had possibly four hundred men left.

Prescott took a forlorn look down at the rail fence,

edging down to the river. One thousand five hundred men were there, but they were firing at British artillery. They would be too late to help now, even if they left their positions; even if they swung wide and came up behind General Howe's men. Putnam, far behind on Bunker Hill, was still trying to cow the relief column into digging trenches. They moaned a refusal as shells from the British fleet bounded on the hill. He saw Colonel Thomas Gardner bringing a fresh and smartly attired regiment up from Cambridge. Putnam made the mistake of his life. He ordered Gardner's men to dig trenches. Prescott would have given his life for those replacements.

Inside the redoubt, Prescott rearranged his men so that they closed the empty spaces. "Get down," he ordered. "Cock your muskets, men, and do not fire until I give the word." The British thrust their bayonets forward at chest level. They were outside the earthworks. Some were grinning in triumph. Prescott peeked. "Now!" he shouted. The muskets came up, were leveled, and belched eight hundred feet of flame. Panicked, the militiamen hurried to reload. They did not look over the top to see the grenadiers fall out of line. To Howe, it was the first and second charge over again. The British general shrieked as he entreated his men to continue the charge, to carry the breastworks.

Major Williams fell. So did Major Spendlove. Captain Harris and Lieutenant Rawdon jumped down into the ditch in front of the redoubt and urged their men to follow. Both knew that, in classical war, the defenders left a redoubt when a charge was this close. None of the militia had read the books. Twice Rawdon hooked one leg over the mouth of the redoubt and twice it was beaten away by muskets used as clubs. A militia musket fired about a foot from Captain Harris's head and cut a furrow in his scalp. Rawdon tried to drag him off so that he would be out of the way. "For God's sake!" Harris moaned. "Let me die in peace!"

Howe was limping in the rear. A musket ball had

bounced off his foot. Major Pitcairn was killed while shouting orders to an officer. An unknown American stood on high ground behind the redoubt and fired muskets in the manner of a machine. The grenadiers figured that several men must have been loading for him as he stood exposed. In five minutes he shot a minimum of twenty British officers. A grenadier paused in the ditch, raised himself on his toes, and fired one deliberate shot. The sharpshooter disappeared.

The militia, out of ammunition, could find no more nails or small stones to fit their muskets. "Suddenly," an adjutant said, "their fire went out like a spent candle." Prescott ripped an artillery cartridge and divided the gunpowder among a few men. Somewhere back on the hill, American officers lay dead. "Man your bayonets," Prescott said. Less than fifty men had bayonets. The red wave came over the top. The few met the many. Prescott could have ordered a retreat, except that the colonel and General Putnam had never discussed how it could be carried out. "Twitch their guns away," he yelled. The broad trench was full of men struggling, grunting, and moaning. "Let them have rocks in the face."

A British officer roared, "Surrender, you rebels!"

Prescott was outraged. "We are not rebels!" The colonel saw his farmers twisting on foot-and-a-half-long blades. "Give way, men. Save yourselves. Run quick." It would be known in military annals as the most poorly phrased order to retreat uttered by a man who didn't understand the word.

Prescott fought with his sword. His long coat hung in tatters. British soldiers saw the fierce fight in his face and turned away. The colonel watched his men leave. "Spread out," he begged. "Don't be a target!" At last Prescott jumped out of the trench, whirled around to defend himself, and backed away. Alkali dust swirled up from the pounding feet of many men. The blood of colonists and Redcoats ran across the bottom of the trench and dampened the dust. Dr. Warren, on the hill behind the earthworks, called to Prescott and his

156

men to follow. To the remnants of Prescott's command, he looked like an apparition, something out of a painting of a wealthy gentleman.

Pigot's soldiers came up and hemmed the Americans in on two sides. Howe's men—those who were alive—followed out of the trench. All raised their muskets. They didn't fire because they would hit the King's Own. Dr. Warren held his arm. He had a bayonet wound. The colonials backed down the hill away from the British. They were glaring and spitting dust. Warren walked serenely, almost sedately. He said he would never be caught running before "Bloodybacks." A group of soldiers surrounded the doctor. They would protect him. The British thought that the Americans were making a stand around someone who looked like a dandy. They hesitated.

A British officer commanded the grenadiers to take aim. Warren was still walking proudly. "Fire!" the officer said. An entire group of Americans fell. Warren stumbled. He fell dead with a bullet in his head. Down the side of the hill, Ward's regiment was stunned to find that it was alone. Looking up, they could see their comrades retreating in a roiling cloud of smoke. The Redcoats could attack the men behind the fence from two sides. Colonel Stark gave the order to file slowly backward toward Bunker Hill. A fresh company of men from Charles Towne was in the line. They insisted on revenge for the burning of their homes. Colonel Knowlton begged them to leave the line. As they started back, British regulars saw them and charged. The men from Charles Towne stood their ground and waited for the Redcoats. They fired one salvo and counted the men who dropped. Then they departed. British artillery caught Connecticut and New Hampshire regiments in an open field. They decimated both.

Eight hundred fresh British troops had landed in longboats. They were now trotting up the hills trying to catch the colonists. The Americans did not hurry. Nor did they tarry.

They kept walking. On Bunker Hill, Israel Putnam welcomed the warriors with orders to defend it. Few paid attention. He shouted, he cursed. They continued to walk. It was the slowness of retreat which cost many casualties. Cannonballs from the fleet decapitated one officer, ripped the chest of another. The brow of the hill was thick with American dead.

Prescott met Putnam. "General," said the colonel, fatigued beyond caring, "why did you not support me with reinforcements as we agreed?"

Putnam was hurt. "I could not drive the dogs up."

Prescott looked up at the man on the horse. "You might have led them up," he said.

On the hill of the redoubt, General Clinton met General Howe. Clinton was shocked by Howe's appearance. The commanding officer was disheveled, his white trousers were flecked with blood and blades of grass, his hair was askew, he seemed dazed. Howe murmured, "My left was gone. Totally." Clinton ordered some officers to restore order in the ranks. He left his superior on the hill and led the remaining regiments toward Bunker Hill. He did not want to permit the colonists to make a stand there.

The sun was still high and hot. It was 4 P.M. when Clinton, emboldened by success, asked permission of General Howe to drive the Americans from Bunker Hill and move on to take Cambridge. Howe was a man emerging from an indistinct horror. He looked down the hill and saw a carpet of British uniforms. Some stirred. Some were still. Some cried out. Some maintained the silence of eternity. No, he said. No. He could not grant such permission. He could see no reason why the obstinate rebels would not defend Bunker Hill in the same bloody way that they had fought the best infantry in the world.

General Clinton was ordered to bring all artillery up to the vale closest to Bunker Hill. The guns fired for an hour. The fleet guns moved up the Charles River and the Mystic to provide a crashing crescendo to the battle. Slowly, the militia retreated down the neck leading to Cambridge. Slowly, Prescott and Israel Putnam followed the men. At 5:30 P.M. Clinton's infantry edged up onto Bunker Hill and hoisted the British banner in triumph. The day was done.

Or was it? It is rare for both sides to feel defeated. Both Howe and Putnam felt that they had failed. The fate of battles is usually decided in favor of the party ultimately occupying the disputed area. In that case, the British were victorious. They occupied the scene of battle. And yet, when General Gage sent Howe with strong well-disciplined forces to Charles Towne, he had two objectives. One was to break the siege of Boston; the other was to roll up two wings of the Continental Army at Charles Towne and at Boston Neck, and to occupy Cambridge and destroy armed resistance to the Crown.

Neither objective was attained. Throughout the night the British buried their dead and carried their wounded to the longboats. Howe lost almost a thousand effectives in dead and wounded. Putnam sustained 450 casualties. The most poignant unsung scene occurred on Prince Street in Boston. There the women waited all night, keeping a pathway clear for the wounded, hoping not to see a beloved face. Some of the women carried pitchers of water and shirts torn into strips. The muffled roar of cannon was replaced by the sobs and shrieks of the next of kin. In the first litter ashore was Major Williams, nodding his head absentmindedly as he bled to death. Behind him were three dead captains, who had been alive when they left Charles Towne.

A drummer boy, surely not more than fourteen years of age, was carried through the streets with his instrument on his stomach. Lieutenant Dutton's wife and two children remained inside their house, praying that he had been spared. He had not. Some of the Loyalists in Boston were so moved by the parade of blood that they offered their services to carry litters

159

or to bind wounds. The Loyalists were frightened for them-selves. If Howe won the battle, as they had heard, he won at a fearful price. He had not broken the siege of Boston, and those who remained loyal to the King realized that if the British left Boston, they would be at the mercy of the colonists. Their homes would be burned in time; their businesses and savings confiscated; the lives of their men would be forfeit. The Loyalists had the most to lose.

Most of the wounded were doomed to die in the days ahead. British army surgeons understood the use of a tourni-quet, how to bleed a soldier, spread a bread-and-milk potion on a wound, and how to drill holes in a skull to "remove pressure on the brain." Probing a wound, the doctors were advised to dig with their fingers "for the ball." The talking wounded had a choice of opiates: one grain of opium or a beaker of rum. The British Army *Medical Book* advised: "You should act in all respects as if you were entirely un-affected by their groans and complaints." The most common operation was amputation. All arm and leg wounds in which a bone was splintered were corrected by removing the limb. That night the doctors probed wounds and removed nails, stones, and bits of glass. They did not ascribe this to a shortage of ammunition, but rather considered it as proof that the colo-nists were "barbarians."

Two days later, Surgeon Grant sent a letter home. "Their muskets were charged with old nails and angular pieces of iron; and from most of our men being wounded in the legs, we are inclined to believe it was their design, not wishing to kill the men, but leave them as burdens on us, to exhaust our provisions and engage our attention, as well as to intimidate the rest of the soldiery."

A week later, General George Washington was in New York with his newly appointed major generals, Philip

Schuyler and Charles Lee. It seemed to some as though all of New York—22,000 persons—turned out to welcome the new Continental Commander in Chief. He understood that he was in strong Tory territory and he tempered his public remarks to hopes for peace and an agreeable accommodation with the Crown. It was the general's custom each night to drink a toast to His Majesty King George. The ruling families of the city took to Washington kindly, certain that the tall, dignified Virginian would not be a firebrand seeking war.

He attended a few parties, spending a few nights in late dancing; on others he played cards for stakes. While he was in the city the general intercepted a courier who was bringing news of Bunker Hill to the Continental Congress. He read the reports of the battle and continued his leisurely trip to Boston. It seemed, to those around him, as though George Washington held no fears that the ragtag army would be defeated before his arrival. After his appointment, he had tarried in several colonies to pay his respects and, perhaps, to be appraised or assessed by local leaders.

When he arrived at Cambridge, the people of Massachusetts had arranged a tumultuous welcome under an old elm tree. Some thought that Artemas Ward and Israel Putnam were qualified to lead the army; but the thing had been done by the Congress, and Massachusetts was going to make the alien welcome in the warmest sense. If the new commander had any handicap, it was that the people knew he was an Episcopalian; they were Puritans. The few Episcopalians they had known were staunch Tories.

Washington accepted the honors with unsmiling dignity, perhaps because he was wearing a set of wooden teeth. By late afternoon he was conferring with Ward, Putnam, Prescott, Thomas, and Lee. He had left General Schuyler in New York as commandant of the colony. If the New Englanders harbored any notion that Washington might be a dilettante,

161

he altered their thinking by morning. On July 4, 1775, he ordered published a list of orders for the Continental Army. There was nothing polite or hesitant about them:

Headquarters July 4th, 1775.

Parole Abingdon. Countersign Bedford.

Exact returns to be made by the proper officers of all the Provisions, Ordnance, Ordnance Stores, Powder, Lead, Working tools of all kinds, Tents, Camp Kettles and all other Stores under their respective care, belonging to the Armies at Roxbury and Cambridge. The commanding officer of each Regiment to make a return of the number of blankets wanted to compleat every Man with one at least.

The Hon: Artemus Ward, Charles Lee, Philip Schuyler and Israel Putnam Esquires, are appointed Major Generals of the American Army, and due obedience is to be paid to them as such. The Continental Congress, not having compleated the appointments of the other officers in said army nor had sufficient time to prepare and forward their Commissions; any officer is to continue to do duty in the Rank and Station he at present holds, until further orders. . . .

The Continental Congress having now taken all the Troops of the several Colonies, which have been raised or which may be hereafter raised for the support and defense of the Liberties of America, into their pay and service. They are now the troops of the UNITED PROVINCES of North America; and it is hoped that all Distinctions of Colonies will be laid aside; so that one and the same spirit may animate the whole, and the only contest shall be who shall render, on this great and trying occasion, the most essential service to the great and common cause in which we are all engaged. . . .

The General most earnestly requires and expects a due observance of those articles of war, established for a government of the army, which forbid profane cursing, swearing and drunkenness; And in like manner requires & expects, of all Officers and Soldiers not engaged on actual duty, a punctual attendance on divine Service, to implore the blessings of heaven upon the means used for our safety and defense.

All Officers are required and expected to pay diligent Attention to keep their Men neat and clean—to visit them often at their quarters, and inculcate upon them the necessity of cleanliness as essential to their health and service. They are particularly to see that they have straw to lay on, if it to be had, and to make it known if they are destitute of this article. They are also to take care that Necessarys be provided in the Camps and frequently filled up to prevent their being offensive and unhealthy. Proper Notice will be taken of such Officers and Men as distinguish themselves by their attention to these necessary duties.

The commanding Officer of each regiment is to take particular care that not more than two Men of a company be absent on furlough at the same time, unless in very extraordinary cases.

No person is to be allowed to go to Fresh-water pond a fishing or on any other occasion as there may be danger of introducing the small pox into the army.

It is strictly required and commanded that there be no firing of Cannon or small arms from any of the lines or elsewhere, except in case of necessary, immediate defense, or special order given for that purpose.

All prisoners taken, Deserters coming in, Persons coming out of Boston who can give any intelligence; any captures of any kind from the enemy are to be immediately reported and brought up to Head Quarters in Cambridge.

The guard for the security of the stores at Watertown is to be increased to thirty men immediately.

A sergeant and six men to be set as a guard to the Hospital, and are to apply to Doctor Rand.

Complaint having been made against John White,

Quarter Master of Col. Nixon's Regmt. for misdemeanors in drawing out Provisions for more Men than the Regmt consisted of; a court martial consisting of one captain and four subalterns is ordered to be held on said White, who are to enquire, determine and report.

The General desires that some carpenters be immediately set to work at Brattle's Stables, to fix up stalls for eight Horses, and more if the room will admit, with suitable racks, mangers, &c.

These general orders, published and read to the army within twenty-four hours of George Washington's arrival, did several things for him and for the troops. It established him as a wise and stern father-figure, one prepared to appreciate a disciplined soldiery, one who would accept nothing less than a brave and obedient officer corps. For the men in ranks, it established that Washington was not a remote overseer, but one who cared for the health of men's bodies and spirits. He would not countenance laxness or running home. He would want to know the stores, the ammunition, even the amount of straw bedding of each unit under his command. Nor was he above telling them that he expected clean latrines, to be covered frequently. Above all, they were to understand that George Washington was the new and permanent Commander in Chief and they were no longer units of colonial militia, but units of a one-piece army called the Troops of the United Provinces of North America.

Within three days Washington addressed himself to the question of cowardice in a second general order. It was a serious problem among the volunteers, and the general instructed that the following should be posted at every regiment and read aloud to the troops:

Head Quarters, Camrbidge July 7, 1775
Parole, Dorchester. CSign Exeter.
It is with inexpressible Concern that the General,

upon his first Arrival in the army, should find an officer sentenced by a General Court-Martial to be cashier'd for Cowardice. A Crime of all others, the most infamous in a Soldier, the most injurious to an Army, and the last to be forgiven; inasmuch as it may, and often does happen, that the Cowardice of a single Officer may prove the Destruction of the whole Army: The General therefore (tho' with great concern, and, more especially as the Transaction happened before he had Command of the Troops) thinks himself obliged, for the good for the service, to approve the Judgment of the Court-Martial with respect to Captain John Callender, who is hereby sentenced to be cashier'd. Capt. John Callender is accordingly cashier'd and dismissed from all further service in the Continental Army as an Officer.

The General, having made all due inquiries, and maturely consider'd this matter, is led to the above determination not only from the particular Guilt of Capt. Callender, but the fatal consequences of such conduct to the army and the cause of America.

He now therefore most earnestly exhorts Officers of all ranks to shew an Example of Bravery and Courage to their men; assuring them that such as do their duty in the day of Battle, as brave and good Officers, shall be honored with every mark of distinction and regard; their names and merits made known to the General Congress and all America: while on the other hand he positively declares that every Officer, be his rank what it may, who shall betray his Country, dishonour the Army and his General, by basely keeping back and shrinking from his duty in any engagement; shall be held up as an infamous Coward and punish'd as such, with the utmost martial severity; and no connections, interest or intercessions in his behalf will avail to prevent the swift execution of justice.

G. Washington
Commander-in-Chief.

Within ninety-six hours of his arrival at Cambridge the general had hammered together an army from several militia with local loyalties, established himself as the Commander in Chief, and inaugurated a system of rewards and punishments for all ranks. His greatest achievement in four days was something Washington could not see or weigh. Morale in the ranks crested to a new high. Even his coded heading was primly militaristic; the "Parole Dorchester" was a password given only to officers of the guard and inspectors of the guard. The second note, "CSign Exeter," was the countersign which all soldiers would have to give to sentries before being permitted to enter Continental Army lines.

The government of Lord North was still trying to digest the shocking news of Lexington and Concord when in early August of 1775 the first reports of the Battle of Bunker Hill reached London. Their lordships realized, for the first time, that the Colonies would fight and were fighting. The gentlemen blamed each other for the situation; special abuse was heaped upon those who espoused "peace commissioners." The King was distressed because, to lower taxes, the army had been reduced to 48,000 effectives, of which twelve thousand were stationed in Ireland and could not be released. In his compulsion for detail, he had itemized every ship of war used by the British Navy and found that, in this year of peace, he had less than half the capital ships he would require to blockade American ports.

Everyone of prominence had a panacea. General Gage wanted 32,000 soldiers—an impossible number unless the King could hire mercenaries from the German states. Major General John Burgoyne wrote that "supplies of arms for the Blacks will awe, in conjunction with the regulars, the southern provinces." Lord George Germain, who had been cashiered for cowardice sixteen years earlier, proposed that the British Army burn the cities of Boston and Philadelphia.

General James Grant favored arming the Indians: "A few scalps taken by Indians and Canadians would operate more on the mind of these deluded, distracted people than any other loss they might sustain."

The Duke of Grafton read the first reports of Bunker Hill, asked permission to see his King, told him that His Majesty was being deceived with optimistic reports from America. He resigned as Lord Privy Seal. Royal governors in America added to the confusion, painting the resistance to Great Britain as superficial and transitory. Dunmore said he could restore submission to the Crown in Virginia if he had two or three hundred men. Martin of North Carolina could bring that colony back to cheerful acceptance of King and Parliament if he were "properly supported and encouraged." Lord William Campbell of South Carolina stated that the presence of two thousand armed men "will be sufficient to set matters right within his government." Oglethorpe's Georgia "will return to her duty as soon as South Carolina is brought to a submission." The King asked the government to send General Henry Clinton from Boston to South Carolina with two thousand men. It was a poor appreciation of the extent of American defection, but, as George III wrote to the Earl of Sandwich, "The English lion, when 'rouzed, must match the vigor of the rebels and show that it possesses also the swiftness of the race horse."

It was a popular pastime in London to caricature the King as a dolt given to writing interminable letters, many of them to himself. And yet it must be said that George III was the first person to see the inevitability of conflict in America. He was not soothed by the military reporters who minimized the effectiveness of farmers in revolt. He was anxious to get on with the war before successive governments were ready to concede that there would be a war. He was ready to give up peace talks and prepare to fight a rebellious uprising in 1773. The King knew, in August, 1775, that a war was being

167

imposed on Great Britain. It arrived unbidden, and, unless the Colonies could be cowed quickly, it would be a dreary, interminable affair, something of incalculable cost to England in blood and treasure.

On the other side of the Atlantic some men prepared for war and others were of a mind to think beyond it. In the summer of 1775, John Adams dwelled upon the form of government the thirteen Colonies should choose:

> These efforts could not be made without government and, as I supposed no man would think of consolidating this vast continent under one national government, we should probably, after the example of the Greeks, the Dutch and the Swiss, form a confederacy of states, each of which must have a separate government. . . . That this could be done only by conventions of representatives chosen by the people in the several Colonies in the most exact proportions. That it was my opinion that Congress ought now to recommend to the people of every Colony to call such conventions immediately and set up governments of their own, under their authority; for the people were the source of all authority and the origin of all power.

By implication John Adams seemed to endorse the sentiments of other Americans that the logical result of a war of independence would lead to the establishment of thirteen coequal nations, confederated only for purposes of a common defense and for trade. The word "state" in the eighteenth century was a common synonym for "nation." Each state would expect to send delegates to a "Continental Congress," but their powers and duties would be limited to the solution of problems common to all. Five months later, Adams would be asked what plan of government he would advise.

> A plan as nearly resembling the government under which we were born, and have lived, as the circumstances of the country will admit. Kings we never had among us. Nobles we have never had. Nothing hereditary ever existed

in this country; nor will the country require or admit of any such thing. But governors and councils we have always had, as well as representatives. A legislature in three branches ought to be preserved, and independent judges.

In this case, his use of the word "country" to describe a unification of thirteen colonies suggests that John Adams had moved closer to the notion of a central government. He rejected kings and nobles, but endorsed thirteen governors and a tricameral form of legislature as necessary to the well-being of the Colonies, or states. And yet, even in this second statement on government, he left empty the space for a president or a congress superimposed over the provinces. The politic atmosphere in the Colonies, it should be noted, was so stringently opposed to a king, a prime minister, or a president that the delegates from New England and Virginia—the most militant—would not discuss the topic in public. The central, or ruling, figure, as embodied in a king, chafed their sensibilities and wounded their sense of justice. Had a king or prime minister or president—one person over all others—been proposed in 1775 or 1776, it is possible that some colonies would have broken away from others and pursued their own lives and government.

And yet, on October 26, 1775, the figure so despised in America, rotund, popeyed King George III, stood to address the opening session of Parliament. Under normal circumstances, the King would enunciate a well-rounded speech on the disparate problems of empire. This time, however, he decided to incite the lords and members of Parliament against the Colonies.

My Lords and Gentlemen: . . . .Those who have too long successfully labored to inflame my people in America by gross misrepresentations, and to infuse into their minds a system of opinions repugnant to the true constitution of the colonies, and to their subordinate relation

169

to Great Britain, now openly avow their revolt, hostility and rebellion. They have raised troops, and are collecting a naval force; they have seized the public revenue and assumed to themselves legislative, executive and judicial powers, which they already exercise in the most arbitrary manner over the persons and properties of their fellow subjects.

The rebellious war now levied is become more general, and is manifestly carried on for the purpose of establishing an independent empire. I need not dwell on the fatal effects of the success of such a plan. The object is too important, the spirit of the British nation too high, the resources with which God hath blessed her too numerous, to give up so many colonies which she has planted with great industry, nursed with great tenderness, encouraged with many commercial advantages, and protected and defended at much expense of blood and treasure. . . . When the unhappy and deluded multitude, against whom force will be directed, shall become sensible of their error, I shall be ready to receive the misled with tenderness and mercy. . . .

The Adamses of Boston and Franklin of Pennsylvania and Jefferson of Virginia—four who understood the use of propaganda without knowing the word—would use that speech to arouse the colonists further. "Against whom force will be directed" would be called a declaration of war against the innocent and oppressed Colonies. There was no word, no act that these gentlemen could not turn to their advantage. Later Benjamin Franklin would be asked to support his charges that British soldiers were "barbarians who slit the stomachs of pregnant women." His response was that it was important to the cause of liberty to defile its enemies in every way possible, that perhaps he had exaggerated the conduct of Redcoats. He might also have said, with truth, that the Continental Army feared the enemy within its gates—at least 20 percent of Americans were Loyalists.

170

In Boston, General Howe tried to put the Loyalists to good use. He published a proclamation on October 28, 1775, asking all "loyal and faithful citizens" to form themselves into companies and join the British Army. The Battle of Bunker Hill had depleted his ranks; he sent an urgent request to England for army and navy reinforcements; it was no more than just that if Howe was to protect the Tories of Boston and their property, they, in turn, should give their young men to him to augment that protection.

The colonial propagandists would use Howe's appeal as an indication of British weakness. Great Britain, they would trumpet, could not find enough Englishmen to fight its wars; it was now trying to enlist warriors from the ranks of American Tories.

The King was in the marketplace trying to hire Hessians to fight his war. Between June, 1775, and June, 1776, the focus of American anger would switch from Parliament to George III. He would become, in cartoon and song, the swollen drooling toad trying to devour and digest the thirteen Colonies.

Some, like Thomas Jefferson, thought the issue would be decided with one more major engagement. He was in Philadelphia, writing to Edmund Randolph of Virginia on November 29, 1775, when he stated: "One bloody campaign will probably decide, everlastingly, our future course; I am sorry a bloody campaign is decided on. If our winds and waters should not combine to rescue these shores from slavery, and General Howe's reinforcement should arrive in safety, we have hopes he will be inspirited to come out of Boston and take another drubbing; and we must drub him soundly, before the sceptered tyrant will know we are not mere brutes, to crouch under his hand and kiss the rod with which he deigns to scourge us."

In this Jefferson was a far more radical revolutionary than George Washington. In Cambridge the general wrote that he could not bring himself to think of Howe's army "as the King's troops." He thought of the Redcoats as "the ministerial army." John Rutledge of Charleston burst into tears when he saw a South Carolina resolution instructing its congressional delegates to use their own judgment if Congress voted for independence. Another delegate felt chilled when he heard the word; he said, "I feel like a child being thrust violently out of his father's house." Carter Braxton of Virginia warned that independence was "in truth a delusive bait which men inconsiderately snatch at, without knowing the hook to which it is affixed." This proved what every colonial politician knew: that patriots and patriotism came in several shades of color, some wild and radical, others in hues of caution. New Hampshire, for example, drew up a state constitution calculated to endure only "during the present unhappy and unnatural contest with Great Britain." On January 6, 1776, the Continental Congress adopted a resolution stating that the thirteen Colonies "had no design to set up as an independent nation." This, ironically, was rebuttal to the constant charge in Parliament that the colonists would not fire on English troops unless their goal was independence.

Between January, 1776, and June the political aspects of the Colonies would swing, almost violently, from Crown conservatism to radical revolutionary. The change would be effected by two unrelated forces: Howe's army, which was seen as an instrument of revenge; and Thomas Paine's tract *Common Sense,* published in January, 1776. The first created fear; the second, hope.

No cannon has ever reverberated across a land as loudly as Paine's quill. No lonely bugle has called such diverse men to common arms. The drumbeat of Paine's 22,000 words was so thunderous in the Colonies that sixty days after it was published the Congress feared that its delegates were not as militant as the people.

Thomas Paine was, under assessment, a majestic failure. He was born and raised in Thetford, England, the son of a Quaker corset maker. He could not or would not complete his elementary school education and at the age of thirteen was apprenticed to his father. He failed at that and ran off to sea. He married twice. Paine's first wife died a year after the nuptials. His second wife paid him $165 to permit her to get a divorce.

He was fired from or quit most of his jobs in England. His spare time was spent studying government, books, lectures, science. His most ardent desire was to build an iron bridge; no government was interested. Someone introduced Paine to Benjamin Franklin in the spring of 1774. It was the high point in Paine's life. Armed with letters of introduction from Franklin, the thirty-seven-year-old failure sailed to Philadelphia. The letters got him a job as a contributing journalist to Robert Aiken's *Pennsylvania Magazine*. He admired the colonists beyond words, although he refused to join the Quakers at worship because, he said, certain parts of Christian history were replete with cruelty.

In 1775, he wrote publishable articles about inventions, "Cupid & Hymen," and the abolition of slavery. In spite of being almost a professional bankrupt, Thomas Paine was bright-eyed and cheerful. He powdered his hair white, with double rows of curls over his ears. His eyes were large and dark, his brows broad and black, his mouth was turned upward at the corners, as though he were inwardly amused.

In a bookshop he captured the interest of Dr. Benjamin Rush. The physician, only thirty years old, was already the best-known doctor in the Colonies, an associate at Pennsylvania Hospital, a teacher at the University of Pennsylvania, a leader in the American Philosophical Society. Rush was also allied with Benjamin Franklin in political purpose, even though freedom and liberty were unpopular causes in Philadelphia. Dr. Rush invited Paine to his house for tea and political chats. The physician seemed to be impressed with the views of the young journalist because they coincided with his own. Further, Paine appeared to be bold where Rush was timid. Also, Paine seemed to marshal his arguments with such inarguable simplicity that Rush decided to drop a project of writing of the necessity of freedom to the colonists and instead asked Paine to do it.

Paine was so pleased—even though Rush remained silent and contributed nothing except minor criticism as sections were completed—that he spent all of his time preparing a text which he entitled

COMMON SENSE
addressed to the
INHABITANTS
of
AMERICA

The document was published January 10, 1776. It was sold by R. Bell of Philadelphia. The agreement was that printer and author should share the profits equally. Paine insisted on two conditions: one, that the author be listed as "Anonymous"; the second, that Paine's half of the profits be used to buy mittens for the northern wing of the Continental Army. The booklet sold at two shillings. Within sixty days it became the all-time best seller in the Colonies, second only to the Holy Bible. Bell disposed of 110,000 copies by mid-March. "It is sound doctrine and unanswerable reasoning," said George Washington. "By private letters which I have lately received from Virginia, I find *Common Sense* is working a wonderful change there in the minds of men." General Charles Lee wrote to his family: "A masterly, irresistible performance. I own myself convinced, by the arguments, of the necessity of a separation."

The long-term failure, the unlettered journalist, wrote in part:

> Some writers have so confounded society with government as to leave little or no distinction between them; whereas they are not only different, but have dif-

ferent origins. Society is produced by our wants and government by our wickedness; the former promotes our happiness *positively* by uniting our affections, the latter *negatively* by restraining our vices. The one encourages intercourse, the other creates distinctions. The first is a patron, the last a punisher.

Society in every state is a blessing, but government, even in its best state, is but a necessary evil; in its worst state an intolerable one; for when we suffer or are exposed to the same miseries *by a government,* which we might expect in a country *without government,* our calamity is heightened by reflecting that we furnish the means by which we suffer. Government, like dress, is the badge of lost innocence; the palaces of kings are built upon the ruins of the bowers of paradise. For were the impulses of conscience clear, uniform, and irresistibly obeyed, man would need no other lawgiver; but that not being the case, he finds it necessary to surrender up a part of his property to furnish means for the protection of the rest; and this he is induced to do by the same prudence which in every other case advises him out of two evils to choose the least. *Wherefore,* security being the true design and end of government, it unanswerably follows that whatever *form* thereof appears most likely to ensure it to us, with the least expense and greatest benefit, is preferable to all others.

In order to gain a clear and just idea of the design and end of government, let us suppose a small number of persons settled in some sequestered part of the earth, unconnected with the rest; they will then represent the first peopling of any country, or of the world. In this state of natural liberty, society will be their first thought. A thousand motives will excite them thereto; the strength of one man is so unequal to his wants, and his mind so unfitted for perpetual solitude, that he is soon obliged to seek assistance and relief of another, who in his turn requires the same. Four or five united would be able to raise a tolerable dwelling in the midst of a wilderness, but *one* man might labor out the common period of his life without accomplishing anything; when he had felled his timber he could not remove it, nor erect it after it was removed; hunger in the meantime would urge him to quit his work, and every different want would call him a different way. Disease, nay even misfortune, would be death; for though neither might be mortal, yet either would disable him from living, and reduce him to a state in which he might rather be said to perish than to die.

Thus necessity, like a gravitating power, would soon form our newly arrived emigrants into society, the reciprocal blessings of which would supersede and render the obligations of law and government unnecessary while they remained perfectly just to each other; but as nothing but heaven is impregnable to vice, it will unavoidably happen that in proportion as they surmount the first difficulties of emigration, which bound them together in a common cause, they will begin to relax in their duty and attachment to each other; and this remissness will point out the necessity of establishing some form of government to supply the defect of moral virtue.

Some convenient tree will afford them a statehouse, under the branches of which the whole colony may assemble to deliberate on public matters. It is more than probable that their first laws will have the title only of REGULATIONS and be enforced by no other penalty than public disesteem. In this first parliament every man by natural right will have a seat.

But as the colony increases, the public concerns will increase likewise, and the distance at which the members may be separated will render it too inconvenient for all of them to meet on every occasion as at first, when their number was small, their habitations near, and the public concerns few and trifling. This will point out the convenience of their consenting to leave the legislative part to be managed by a select number chosen from the whole body, who are supposed to have the same concerns at stake which those have who appointed them, and who will act in the same manner as the whole body would act were they present. If the colony continue increasing, it will become necessary to augment the number of representatives, and that the interest of every part of the colony may be attended to, it will be found best to divide the whole into convenient parts, each part sending its proper number: and that the *elected* might never form to themselves an interest separate from the *electors,* prudence will point out the propriety of having elections often. . . .

I draw my idea of the form of government from a principle in nature which no art can overturn, viz. that the more simple anything is, the less liable it is to be disordered, and the easier repaired when disordered; and with this maxim in view, I offer a few remarks on the so much boasted constitution of England. That it was noble for the dark and slavish times in which it was erected, is granted. When the world was overrun with tyranny, the least remove therefrom was a glorious rescue. But that it is imperfect, subject to convulsions, and incapable of producing what it seems to promise, is easily demonstrated.

Absolute governments (though the disgrace of human nature) have this advantage with them, they are simple; if the people suffer, they know the head from which their suffering springs; know likewise the remedy; and are not bewildered by a variety of causes and cures. But the constitution of England is so exceedingly complex that the nation may suffer for years together without being able to discover in which part the fault lies; some will say in one and some in another, and every political physician will advise a different medicine.

I know it is difficult to get over local or long standing prejudices, yet if we will suffer ourselves to examine the component parts of the English constitution, we shall find them to be the base remains of two ancient tyrannies, compounded with some new republican materials.

First.—The remains of monarchical tyranny in the person of the King.

Secondly.—The remains of aristocratical tyranny in the persons of the Peers.

Thirdly.—The new republican materials, in the persons of the Commons, on whose virtue depends the freedom of England.

The two first, by being hereditary, are independent of the people; wherefore in a *constitutional sense* they contribute nothing towards the freedom of the state.

To say that the constitution of England is a *union* of three powers, reciprocally *checking* each other, is farcical; either the words have no meaning, or they are flat contradictions.

To say that the commons is a check upon the king, presupposes two things.

First.—That the king is not to be trusted without being looked after; or in other words, that a thirst for absolute power is the natural disease of monarchy.

Secondly.—That the commons, by being appointed for that purpose, are either wiser or more worthy of confidence than the crown.

But as the same constitution which gives the commons a power to check the king by withholding the supplies, gives afterwards the king a power to check the commons, by empowering him to reject their other bills; it again supposes that the king is wiser than those whom it has already supposed to be wiser than him. A mere absurdity!

There is something exceedingly ridiculous in the composition of monarchy; it first excludes a man from the means of information, yet empowers him to act in cases where the highest judgment is required. The state of a king shuts him from the world, yet the business of a king requires him to know it thoroughly; wherefore the different parts, by unnaturally opposing and destroying each other, prove the whole character to be absurd and useless.

Some writers have explained the English constitution thus: the king, say they, is one, the people another; the peers are a house in behalf of the king, the commons in behalf of the people; but this hath all the distinctions of a house divided against itself; and though the expressions be pleasantly arranged, yet when examined they appear idle and ambiguous; and it will always happen that the nicest construction that words are capable of, when applied to the description of something which either cannot exist or is too incomprehensible to be within the compass of description, will be words of sound only, and though they may amuse the ear, they cannot inform the mind; for this explanation includes a previous question, viz. *how came the king by a power which the people are afraid to trust, and always obliged to check?* Such a power could not be the gift of a wise people, neither can any power, *which needs checking,* be from God; yet the provision which the constitution makes supposes such a power to exist. . . .

That the crown is this overbearing part in the English constitution needs not be mentioned, and that it derives its whole consequence merely from being the giver of places and pensions is self-evident; wherefore, though we have been wise enough to shut and lock a door against absolute monarchy, we at the same time have been foolish enough to put the crown in possession of the key. . . .

An inquiry into the *constitutional errors* in the English form of government is at this time highly necessary; for as we are never in a proper condition of doing justice to others while we continue under the influence of some leading partiality, so neither are we capable of doing it to ourselves while we remain fettered by any obstinate prejudice. And as a man who is attached to a prostitute is unfitted to choose or judge of a wife, so any prepossession in favor of a rotten constitution of government will disable us from discerning a good one.

* * *

Mankind being originally equals in the order of creation, the equality could only be destroyed by some subsequent circumstance: the distinctions of rich and poor may in a great measure be accounted for, and that without having recourse to the harsh ill-sounding names of oppression and avarice. Oppression is often the *consequence,* but seldom or never the *means* of riches; and though avarice will preserve a man from being necessitously poor, it generally makes him too timorous to be wealthy.

But there is another and greater distinction for which no truly natural or religious reason can be assigned, and that is the distinction of men into *kings* and *subjects.* Male and female are the distinctions of nature, good and bad the distinctions of heaven; but how a race of men came into the world so exalted above the rest, and distinguished like some new species, is worth inquiring into, and whether they are the means of happiness or of misery to mankind.

In the early ages of the world, according to the Scripture chronology there were no kings; the consequence of which was there were no wars; it is the pride of kings which throws mankind into confusion. Holland without a king hath enjoyed more peace for this last century than any of the monarchical governments in Europe. Antiquity favors the same remark; for the quiet and rural lives of the first patriarchs have a happy something in them, which vanishes when we come to the history of Jewish royalty.

Government by kings was first introduced into the world by the heathens, from whom the children of Israel copied the custom. It was the most prosperous invention the Devil ever set on foot for the promotion of idolatry. The heathens paid divine honors to their deceased kings, and the Christian world hath improved on the plan by doing the same to their living ones. How impious is the title of sacred Majesty applied to a worm, who in the midst of his splendor is crumbling into dust!

As the exalting one man so greatly above the rest cannot be justified on the equal rights of nature, so neither can it be defended on the authority of Scripture; for the will of the Almighty, as declared by Gideon and the prophet Samuel, expressly disapproves of government by kings. All anti-monarchical parts of Scripture have been very smoothly glossed over in monarchical governments, but they undoubtedly merit the attention of countries which have their governments yet to form. *"Render unto Caesar the things which are Caesar's,"* is the scripture doctrine of courts, yet it is no support of monarchical government, for the Jews at that time were without a king, and in a state of vassalage to the Romans.

Near three thousands years passed away, from the Mosaic account of the creation, till the Jews under a national delusion requested a king. Till then their form of government (except in extraordinary cases where the Almighty interposed) was a kind of republic, administered by a judge and the elders of the tribes. Kings they had none, and it was held sinful to acknowledge any being under that title but the Lord of Hosts. And when a man seriously reflects on the idolatrous homage which is paid to the persons of kings, he need not wonder that the Almighty, ever jealous of his honor, should disapprove a form of government which so impiously invades the prerogative of heaven.

Monarchy is ranked in scripture as one of the sins of the Jews, for which a course in reserve is denounced against them. The history of that transaction is worth attending to.

The children of Israel being oppressed by the Midianites, Gideon marched against them with a small army, and victory through the Divine interposition decided in his favor. The Jews elate with success and attributing it to the generalship of Gideon, proposed making him a king, saying, *Rule thou over us, thou and thy son, and thy son's son.* Here was temptation in its fullest extent; not a kingdom only, but an hereditary one; but Gideon in the piety of his soul replied, *I will not rule over you, neither shall my son*

181

rule over you. THE LORD SHALL RULE OVER YOU. Words need not be more explicit; Gideon doth not *decline* the honor, but denieth their right to give it; neither doth he compliment them with invented declarations of his thanks, but in the positive style of a prophet charges them with disaffection to their proper sovereign, the King of Heaven. . .

To the evil of monarchy we have added that of hereditary succession; and as the first is a degradation and lessening of ourselves, so the second, claimed as a matter of right, is an insult and imposition on posterity. For all men being originally equals, no *one* by *birth* could have a right to set up his own family in perpetual preference to all others forever, and though himself might deserve *some* decent degree of honors of his contemporaries, yet his descendants might be far too unworthy to inherit them. One of the strongest *natural* proofs of the folly of hereditary right in kings, is that nature disapproves it, otherwise she would not so frequently turn it into ridicule by giving mankind an *ass* for a *lion*.

Secondly, as no man at first could possess any other public honors than were bestowed upon him, so the givers of those honors could have no power to give away the right of posterity, and though they might say "we choose you for our head," they could not without manifest injustice to their children say "that your children and your children's children shall reign over ours forever." Because such an unwise, unjust, unnatural compact might (perhaps) in the next succession put them under the government of a rogue or a fool. Most wise men in their private sentiments have ever treated hereditary right with contempt; yet it is one of those evils which when once established is not easily removed; many submit from fear, others from superstition, and the more powerful part shares with the king the plunder of the rest.

This is supposing the present race of kings in the world to have had an honorable origin; whereas it is more than probable that, could we take off the dark covering of antiquity and trace them to their first rise, we should find the first of them nothing better than the principal ruffian of some restless gang, whose savage manners of pre-eminence in subtility obtained him the title of chief among plunderers; and who by increasing in power, and extending his depredations, overawed the quiet and defenseless to purchase their safety by frequent contributions. . . .

But it is not so much the absurdity as the evil of hereditary succession which concerns mankind. Did it insure a race of good and wise men it would have the seal of divine authority, but as it opens a door to the *foolish,* the *wicked,* and the *improper,* it hath in it the nature of oppression. Men who look upon themselves born to reign, and others to obey, soon grow insolent. Selected from the rest of mankind, their minds are early poisoned by importance; and the world they act in differs so materially from the world at large that they have but little opportunity of knowing its true interests, and when they succeed in the government are frequently the most ignorant and unfit of any throughout the dominions.

Another evil which attends hereditary succession is, that the throne is subject to be possessed by a minor at any age; at which time the regency, acting under the cover of a king, have every opportunity and inducement to betray their trust. The same national misfortune happens when a king, worn out with age and infirmity, enters the last stage of human weakness. In both these cases the public becomes a prey to every miscreant who can temper successfully with the follies either of age or infancy. . . .

In England a king hath little more to do than to make war and give away places; which in plain terms is to impoverish the nation and set it together by the ears. A pretty business indeed for a man to be allowed eight hundred thousand sterling a year for, and worshipped into the bargain! Of more worth is one honest man to society,

183

and in the sight of God, than all the crowned ruffians that ever lived. . . .

Volumes have been written on the subject of the struggle between England and America. Men of all ranks have embarked in the controversy, from different motives, and with various designs; but all have been ineffectual, and the period of debate is closed. Arms as the last resource decide the contest; the appeal was the choice of the king, and the continent has accepted the challenge. . . .

The sun never shined on a cause of greater worth. 'Tis not the affair of a city, a county, a province, or a kingdom; but of a continent—of at least one-eighth part of the habitable globe. 'Tis not the concern of a day, a year, or an age; posterity are virtually involved in the contest, and will be more or less affected even to the end of time by the proceedings now. Now is the seedtime of continental union, faith, and honor. The least fracture now will be like a name engraved with the point of a pin on the tender rind of a young oak; the wound would enlarge with the tree, and posterity read in it full grown characters.

By referring the matter from argument to arms . . . a new method of thinking has arisen. All plans, proposals, &c. prior to the nineteenth of April, i.e. to the commencement of hostilities, are like the almanacks of the last year; which though proper then, are superseded and useless now. Whatever was advanced by the advocates on either side of the question then, terminated in one and the same point, viz. a union with Great Britain; the only difference between the parties was the method of effecting it; the one proposing force, the other friendship; but it has so far happened that the first has failed, and the second withdrawn her influence.

As much has been said of the advantages of reconciliation, which, like an agreeable dream, has passed away and left us as we were, it is but right that we should examine the contrary side of the argument, and inquire into some of the many material injuries which these colonies sustain, and always will sustain, by being connected with and dependent on Great Britain. To examine that connection and dependence on the principles of nature and common sense; to see what we have to trust to, if separated, and what we are to expect, if dependent.

I have heard it asserted by some, that as America has flourished under her former connection with Great Britain, the same connection is necessary towards her future happiness, and will always have the same effect. Nothing can be more fallacious than this kind of argument. We may as well assert . . . that the first twenty years of our lives is to become a precedent for the next twenty. But even this is admitting more than is true; for I answer roundly that America would have flourished as much, and probably much more, had no European power taken any notice of her. The commerce by which she hath enriched herself are the necessaries of life, and will always have a market while eating is the custom of Europe.

But she has protected us, say some. That she hath engrossed us is true, and defended the continent at our expense as well as her own is admitted; and she would have defended Turkey from the same motive, viz. for the sake of trade and dominion.

Alas! we have been long led away by ancient prejudices and made large sacrifices to superstition. We have boasted the protection of Great Britain without considering that her motive was *interest,* not *attachment;* and that she did not protect us from *our enemies* on *our account,* but from her enemies on her own account, from those who had no quarrel with us on any *other account,* and who will always be our enemies on the *same account.* Let Britain waive her pretensions to the continent, or the continent throw off the dependence, and we should be at peace with France and Spain were they at war with Britain. . . .

But Britain is the parent country, say some. Then the more shame upon her conduct. Even brutes do not devour their young, nor savages make war upon their families; wherefore, the assertion, if true, turns to her reproach; but it happens not to be true, or only partly so, and the phrase *parent* or *mother country* hath been jesuitically adopted by the king and his parasites, with a low papistical design of gaining an unfair bias on the credulous weakness of our minds. Europe, and not England, is the parent country of America. This new world hath been the asylum for the persecuted lovers of civil and religious liberty from *every part* of Europe. Hither have they fled, not from the tender embraces of the mother, but from the cruelty of the monster; and it is so far true of England, that the same tyranny which drove the first emigrants from home pursues their descendants still.

In this extensive quarter of the globe, we forget the narrow limits of three hundred and sixty miles (the extent of England) and carry our friendship on a larger scale; we claim brotherhood with every European Christian, and triumph in the generosity of the sentiment.

It is pleasant to observe by what regular gradations we surmount the force of local prejudices as we enlarge our acquaintance with the world. A man born in any town in England divided into parishes, will naturally associate most with his fellow parishioners (because their interests in many cases will be common) and distinguish him by the name of *neighbor;* if he meet him but a few miles from home, he drops the narrow idea of a street, and salutes him by the name of *townsman;* if he travel out of the county and meet him in any other, he forgets the minor divisions of street and town, and calls him *country-man, i.e. county-man;* but if in their foreign excursions they should associate in France, or any other part of *Europe,* their local remembrance would be enlarged into that of *Englishman.* And by a just parity of reasoning, all Europeans meeting in America, or any other quarter of the globe, are *countrymen;* for England, Holland, Germany, or Sweden, when compared with the whole, stand in the same places on the larger scale, which the divisions of street, town, and county do on the smaller ones; distinctions too limited for continental minds. Not one third of the inhabitants, even of this province [Pennsylvania], are of English descent. Wherefore, I reprobate the phrase of parent or mother country applied to England only, as being false, selfish, narrow, and ungenerous.

But, admitting that we were all of English descent, what does it amount to? Nothing. Britain, being now an open enemy, extinguishes every other name and title: and to say that reconciliation is our duty, is truly farcical. The first king of England, of the present line (William the Conqueror) was a Frenchman, and half the peers of England are descendants from the same country; wherefore, by the same method of reasoning, England ought to be governed by France. . . .

I challenge the warmest advocate for reconciliation to show a single advantage that this continent can reap, by being connected with Great Britain. I repeat the challenge, not a single advantage is derived. Our corn will fetch its price in any market in Europe, and our imported goods must be paid for, buy them where we will.

But the injuries and disadvantages which we sustain by that connection are without number; and our duty to mankind at large, as well as to ourselves, instruct us to renounce the alliance: because, any submission to, or dependence on, Great Britain, tends directly to involve this continent in European wars and quarrels, and set us at variance with nations who would otherwise seek our friendship, and against whom we have neither anger nor complaint. As Europe is our market for trade, we ought to form no partial connection with any part of it. 'Tis the true interest of America to steer clear of European contentions, which she never can do while by her dependence on Britain she is made the makeweight in the scale of British politics.

Europe is too thickly planted with kingdoms to be

long at peace, and whenever a war breaks out between England and any foreign power, the trade of America goes to ruin, *because of her connection with Britain.* . . . Everything that is right or reasonable pleads for separation. The blood of the slain, the weeping voice of nature cries, 'TIS TIME TO PART. Even the distance at which the Almighty hath placed England and America is a strong and natural proof that the authority of the one over the other, was never the design of heaven. The time likewise at which the continent was discovered, adds weight to the argument, and the manner in which it was peopled, increases the force of it. The Reformation was preceded by the discovery of America; as if the Almighty graciously meant to open a sanctuary to the persecuted in future years, when home should afford neither friendship nor safety.

The authority of Great Britain over this continent is a form of government which sooner or later must have an end. And a serious mind can draw no true pleasure by looking forward, under the painful and positive conviction that what he calls "the present constitution" is merely temporary. As parents, we can have no joy, knowing that *this government* is not sufficiently lasting to insure anything which we may bequeath to posterity; and by a plain method of argument, as we are running the next generation into debt, we ought to do the work of it, otherwise we use them meanly and pitifully. In order to discover the line of our duty rightly, we should take our children in our hand, and fix our station a few years farther into life; that eminence will present a prospect which a few present fears and prejudices conceal from our sight.

Though I would carefully avoid giving unnecessary offense, yet I am inclined to believe that all those who espouse the doctrine of reconciliation may be included within the following descriptions: Interested men, who are not to be trusted, weak men who *cannot* see, prejudiced men who *will not* see, and a certain set of moderate men who think better of the European world than it deserves; and this last class, by an ill-judged deliberation, will be the cause of more calamities to this continent than all the other three.

It is the good fortune of many to live distant from the scene of present sorrow; the evil is not sufficiently brought to *their* doors to make *them* feel the precariousness with which all American property is possessed. But let our imaginations transport us a few moments to Boston; that seat of wretchedness will teach us wisdom, and instruct us forever to renounce a power in whom we can have no trust. The inhabitants [Tories] of that unfortunate city, who but a few months ago were in ease and affluence, have now no other alternative than to stay and starve, or turn out to beg. Endangered by the fire of their friends if they continue within the city, and plundered by the soldiery if they leave it, in their present situation they are prisoners without the hope of redemption, and in a general attack for their relief they would be exposed to the fury of both armies.

Men of passive tempers look somewhat lightly over the offenses of Great Britain, and, still hoping for the best, are apt to call out, *Come, come, we shall be friends again for all this.* But examine the passions and feelings of mankind; bring the doctrine of reconciliation to the touchstone of nature, and then tell me whether you can hereafter love, honor, and faithfully serve the power that hath carried fire and sword into your land? If you cannot do all these, then are you only deceiving yourselves, and by your delay bringing ruin upon posterity. Your future connection with Britain, whom you can neither love nor honor, will be forced and unnatural, and being formed only on the plan of present convenience, will in a little time fall into a relapse more wretched than the first. But if you say you can still pass the violations over, then I ask, Hath your house been burnt? Hath your property been destroyed before your face? Are your wife and children destitute of a bed to lie on, or bread to live on? Have you lost a parent or a child by their hands, and yourself the ruined and wretched survivor? If you have not, then are you not a judge of those who have. But if you have, and can still shake hands with the murderers, then are you unworthy the name of husband, father, friend, or lover; and whatever may be your rank or title in life, you have the heart of a coward, and the spirit of a sycophant.

This is not inflaming or exaggerating matters, but trying them by those feelings and affections which nature justifies, and without which we should be incapable of discharging the social duties of life, or enjoying the felicities of it. I mean not to exhibit horror for the purpose of provoking revenge, but to awaken us from fatal and unmanly slumbers, that we may pursue determinately some fixed object. 'Tis not in the power of Britain or of Europe to conquer America, if she doth not conquer herself by *delay* and *timidity*. The present winter is worth an age if rightly employed, but if lost or neglected the whole continent will partake of the misfortune; and there is no punishment which that man doth not deserve, be he who, or what, or where he will, that may be the means of sacrificing a season so precious and useful.

It is repugnant to reason, to the universal order of things, to all examples from former ages, to suppose that this continent can long remain subject to any external power. The most sanguine in Britain doth not think so. The utmost stretch of human wisdom cannot, at this time, compass a plan, short of separation, which can promise the continent even a year's security. Reconciliation is *now* a fallacious dream. Nature has deserted the connection, and art cannot supply her place. For, as Milton wisely expresses, "Never can true reconcilement grow where wounds of deadly hate have pierced so deep."

Every quiet method for peace hath been ineffectual. Our prayers have been rejected with disdain; and have tended to convince us that nothing flatters vanity or confirms obstinacy in kings more than repeated petitioning—and nothing hath contributed more than that very measure to make the kings of Europe absolute. Witness Denmark and Sweden. Wherefore, since nothing but blows will do, for God's sake let us come to a final separation, and not leave the next generation to be cutting throats under the violated unmeaning names of parent and child.

To say they will never attempt it again is idle and visionary; we thought so at the repeal of the stamp act, yet a year or two undeceived us; as well may we suppose that nations which have been once defeated will never renew the quarrel.

As to government matters, it is not in the power of Britain to do this continent justice: the business of it will soon be too weighty and intricate to be managed with any tolerable degree of convenience, by a power so distant from us, and so very ignorant of us; for if they cannot conquer us they cannot govern us. To be always running three or four thousand miles with a tale or petition, waiting for four or five months for an answer, which, when obtained, requires five or six more to explain it in, will in a few years be looked upon as folly and childishness. There was a time when it was proper, and there is a proper time for it to cease.

Small islands not capable of protecting themselves are the proper objects for government to take under their care; but there is something absurd in supposing a continent to be perpetually governed by an island. In no instance hath nature made the satellite larger than its primary planet; and as England and America, with respect to each other, reverse the common order of nature, it is evident that they belong to different systems. England to Europe: America to itself.

I am not induced by motives of pride, party, or resentment to espouse the doctrine of separation and independence; I am clearly, positively, and conscientiously persuaded that 'tis the true interest of this continent to be

191

so; that everything short of *that* is mere patchwork, that it can afford no lasting felicity—that it is leaving the sword to our children, and shrinking back at a time when a little more, a little further, would have rendered this continent the glory of the earth.

. . . No man was a warmer wisher for a reconciliation than myself, before the fatal nineteenth of April, 1775, but the moment the event of that day was made known, I rejected the hardened, sullen-tempered Pharaoh of England forever; and disdain the wretch, that with the pretended title of FATHER OF HIS PEOPLE can unfeelingly hear of their slaughter, and composedly sleep with their blood upon his soul.

But admitting that matters were now made up, what would be the event? I answer, the ruin of the continent. And that for several reasons.

First. The powers of governing still remaining in the hands of the king, he will have a negative over the whole legislation of this continent. And as he hath shown himself such an inveterate enemy to liberty, and discovered such a thirst for arbitrary powers, is he, or is he not, a proper person to say to these colonies, *You shall make no laws but what I please!* . . .

But the most powerful of all arguments is, that nothing but independence, i.e. a continental form of government, can keep the peace of the continent and preserve it inviolate from civil wars. I dread the event of a reconciliation with Britain *now,* as it is more probable that it will be followed by a revolt somewhere or other, the consequences of which may be far more fatal than all the malice of Britain. . . .

The colonies have manifested such a spirit of good order and obedience to continental government as is sufficient to make every reasonable person easy and happy on that head. No man can assign the least pretense for his fears on other grounds than such as are truly childish and ridiculous, viz., that one colony will be striving for superiority over another.

Where there are no distinctions there can be no superiority: perfect equality affords no temptation. . . .

If there is any true cause of fear respecting independence, it is because no plan is yet laid down. Men do not see their way out. Wherefore, as an opening into that business I offer the following hints; at the same time modestly affirming that I have no other opinion of them myself than that they may be the means of giving rise to something better. Could the straggling thoughts of individuals be collected, they would frequently form materials for wise and able men to improve into useful matter. . . .

But where, say some, is the king of America? I'll tell you, friend, he reigns above, and doth not make havoc of mankind like the Royal Brute of Great Britain. Yet that we may not appear to be defective even in earthly honors, let a day be solemnly set apart for proclaiming the charter; let it be brought forth placed on the divine law, the Word of God; let a crown be placed thereon, by which the world may know, that so far as we approve of monarchy, that in America THE LAW IS KING. For as in absolute governments the king is law, so in free countries the law *ought* to BE king, and there ought to be no other. But lest any ill use should afterwards arise, let the crown at the conclusion of the ceremony be demolished, and scattered among the people whose right it is. . . .

Ye that tell us of harmony and reconciliation, can ye restore to us the time that is past? Can ye give to prostitution its former innocence? Neither can ye reconcile Britain and America. The last cord now is broken, the people of England are presenting addresses against us. There are injuries which nature cannot forgive; she would cease to be nature if she did. . . .

O ye that love mankind! Ye that dare oppose not only the tyranny but the tyrant, stand forth! Every spot of the old world is overrun with oppression. Freedom hath been hunted round the globe. Asia and Africa have long expelled her. Europe regards her like a stranger, and England hath given her warning to depart. O receive the fugitive, and prepare in time an asylum for mankind. . . .

Were the continent crowded with inhabitants, her sufferings under the present circumstances would be intolerable. The more seaport-towns we had, the more should we have both to defend and to lose. Our present numbers are so happily proportioned to our wants that no man need be idle. The diminution of trade affords an army, and the necessities of an army create a new trade.

Debts we have none; and whatever we may contract on this account will serve as a glorious memento of our virtue. Can we but leave posterity with a settled form of government, an independent constitution of its own, the purchase at any price will be cheap. . . .

The debt we may contract doth not deserve our regard, if the work be but accomplished. No nation ought to be without a debt. A national debt is a national bond; and when it bears no interest, it is in no case a grievance. Britain is oppressed with a debt of upwards of one hundred and forty millions sterling, for which she pays upwards of four millions interest. And as a compensation for her debt, she has a large navy. America is without a debt, and without a navy; yet for a twentieth part of the English national debt, could have a navy as large again. The navy of England is not worth at this time more than three millions and a half sterling. . . .

In almost every article of defense we abound. Hemp flourishes even to rankness, so that we need not want cordage. Our iron is superior to that of other countries. Our small arms equal to any in the world. Cannon we can cast at pleasure. Saltpeter and gunpowder we are every day producing. Our knowledge is hourly improving. Resolution is our inherent character, and courage has never yet forsaken us. Wherefore, what is it that we want? Why is it that we hesitate? From Britain we can expect nothing but ruin. If she is once admitted to the government of America again, this continent will not be worth living in. Jealousies will be always arising; insurrections will be constantly happening; and who will go forth to quell them? . . .

TO CONCLUDE. However strange it may appear to some, or however unwilling they may be to think so, matters not, but many strong and striking reasons may be given to show that nothing can settle our affairs so expeditiously as an open and determined DECLARATION FOR INDEPENDENCE. Some of which are:

First. It is in the custom of nations, when any two are at war, for some other powers not engaged in the quarrel to step in as mediators, and bring about the preliminaries of a peace; but while America calls herself the Subject of Great Britain, no power, however well disposed she may be, can offer her mediation. Wherefore, in our present state we may quarrel on forever.

Secondly. It is unreasonable to suppose that France or Spain will give us any kind of assistance if we mean only to make use of that assistance for the purpose of repairing the breach and strengthening the connection between Britain and America; because those powers would be sufferers by the consequences.

Thirdly. While we profess ourselves the subjects of Britain, we must, in the eyes of foreign nations, be considered as rebels. The precedent is somewhat dangerous to *their peace,* for men to be in arms under the name of subjects; we, on the spot, can solve the paradox; but to unite resistance and subjection requires an idea much too refined for common understanding.

Fourthly. Were a manifesto to be published and despatched to foreign courts, setting forth the miseries we have endured and the peaceful methods which we have ineffectually used for redress; declaring at the same time that,

195

not being able any longer to live happily or safely under the cruel disposition of the British court, we have been driven to the necessity of breaking off all connections with her; at the same time assuring all such courts of our peaceable disposition towards them, and of our desire of entering into trade with them: such a memorial would produce more good effects to this continent, than if a ship were freighted with petitions to Britain.

Under our present denomination of British subjects, we can neither be received nor heard abroad; the custom of all courts is against us, and will be so until by an independence we take rank with other nations.

These proceedings may at first seem strange and difficult, but like all other steps which we have already passed over, will in a little time become familiar and agreeable; and until an Independence is declared, the continent will feel itself like a man who continues putting off some unpleasant business from day to day, yet knows it must be done, hates to set about it, wishes it over, and is continually haunted with the thoughts of its necessity.

No call to arms, no freedom bell, no spell-binding oratory nourished the courage of the colonies as the iron-clad logic of Thomas Paine's *Common Sense*. Neither Franklin nor Jefferson nor Adams could match the marching words which commanded the colonists to commit themselves to a war against the mightiest nation in the world. *Common Sense*, verbose and repetitive, was the instrument which made militants of Americans everywhere. As many delegates to the Congress pointed out, the people were leading the Congress in demanding a fight to the finish—freemen or slaves.

Paine, an immigrant of a few months, worked on his document within sight of the State House. Although 110,000 copies of his treatise sold within the first ninety days of 1776, he was not invited to address the Second Continental Congress, nor was he invited to the square room where it deliberated.

By April the people would be further along the road to liberty than their Congress. The British Army, in victory, would pillage and burn and confiscate. Paine's document convinced multitudes that efforts to reach "an accommodation with England" would not correct the wrongs of the past or those which would surely be inflicted on the defeated.

Washington spent the winter trying to organize an army which seemed to balance itself at sixteen thousand men. As new regiments came into Cambridge, soldiers who had enlisted for three months or six months were leaving to return to their farms. The general thought it impossible to have a military force under those circumstances. He asked Congress to alter the enlistment period to three years. The gentlemen were reluctant to do this; it would indicate that Americans thought the war would last that long. Congress would think about the matter. To assuage George Washington's sensitivities they gave him permission to borrow the big cannon captured at Fort Ticonderoga.

He used them well. In the early spring he ordered a surprise attack on Dorchester Heights, overlooking Boston from the south. It worked. At the same time he ordered General Thomas's forces at Boston Neck to make strong feints at the city. Howe had a small area to defend, equally small in which to deploy a large body of troops. The militia set the big guns up on Dorchester Heights. The first salvo convinced General Howe that his position was untenable. He requested Admiral Graves to issue sailing orders for the fleet to go to Halifax.

Thomas Gage heard the plea of thousands of Tories to take them to Halifax. Within a few days eleven thousand

Redcoats and a large delegation of Loyalists had embarked and sailed out of Boston. The ships were barely over the horizon when the militia burst across the Neck and took the city. It was a day and a night of rejoicing, distasteful to George Washington because he knew that Howe would be back with strong reinforcements. If he was pleased, it was because Howe left behind him great stores of gunpowder and musket balls and flints. Bunker Hill and Boston were now in colonial hands, and the word went forth by courier and sloop to the Colonies that it was a memorable victory because the Continental Army had not lost a man.

A euphoria dizzied the senses of the Colonies. In each of three engagements with the British, the militia had achieved the impossible. At Concord, in spite of the fears of the farmers, they had killed more Redcoats than expected and had seen them in hasty retreat; at Bunker Hill, Putnam's boys had inflicted much more damage on Howe than the mighty British general had been able to inflict on them; when George Washington was appointed Commander in Chief, this humorless officer had squeezed General Gage until he had been forced to flee for his life.

The news was beyond credence. No one believed that it was the end of hostilities; to the contrary, the British would be back in greater force at some day in some place. But where? The Continental Congress summoned General Washington to Philadelphia to discuss the next military move. Washington sent word that he dared not leave Boston for Philadelphia at once because no one knew when the British would be back, or in what force. Privately the Congress feared that William Howe and his brother would sail up the Delaware River and attack Philadelphia. A few thought that the brothers Howe might attack New York. In either case, the fears of the Congress were offset by the thigh-slapping joy of the colonists.

In the middle of May, 1776, Washington started from

Boston for the journey to Philadelphia, accompanied by a military secretary and an aide. The Congress, he found, seemed fearful of success. The body had appointed a committee of fourteen to confer with Washington, Major General Gates, and Brigadier Mifflin regarding the next "attack." Field generals abhor small committees of citizens and abominate large ones. General Washington could, with persuasion, convince some of the gentlemen that his tactics were both wise and conservative, but he could not convince all. The general admitted that he wasn't privy to General Howe's plans; he "thought" the British had retreated to Halifax; he "thought" the Redcoats would attack New York with heavy reinforcements; he had "no reason" to believe that they would attack Philadelphia.

To pacify the fearful, General Washington had to devise a military plan which would protect both New York and Philadelphia. He was more concerned with thousands of militia enlistments which would expire in four months—September, 1776. The committee did not want to confront the issue of a vanishing army. Washington and Gates worked out a plan, on May 29, called a "Flying Camp." It would consist of more than ten thousand militia, to be stationed at Amboy, New Jersey. The troops would be highly mobile, in the manner of British grenadiers, and would be able to hurry across the waist of New Jersey to Philadelphia—if an attack should develop there—or to New York if needed. The general agreed to bring his main army from Boston to New York. The Flying Camp would be a good holding force in either direction; the main Continental Army would follow.

The agreement was reached in secret. The Commander in Chief was learning that there are inherent weaknesses in a citizen army, one of which is that citizen soldiers are prone to desert whenever they are idle; the other is that responsibility for the conduct of an army to fifty members of a congress is an impossible task. The delegates, immersed in fear, demanded

199

to know Washington's detailed plans when he had none to offer. They arrogated to themselves the right to veto such plans if he had any. When he confided the details of his proposed military operations, the general had no guarantee that the delegates would conceal such secrets in their bosoms. Some could not resist writing home and relating such tactics. Others were known to be Loyalists who might consider it a duty to pass such information to British spies.

And yet the Continental Congress had no power to rule, was unrecognized by any nation as a government, and was beholden to thirteen separate colonial councils for its every action. Each group of provincial delegates was subject to recall by its colony, and sometimes was recalled. Almost all members of the Congress agreed that the governing power was back home in the provinces; few could resist election to a colonial council. Some, such as Patrick Henry of Virginia, were elated at the chance of returning to a colony where firm constitutions and laws were being hammered out by the real rulers of America.

If the Continental Congress had any power, it was to devise measures which were "mutually acceptable to all." This too was difficult because the political hues of the members ranged all the way from the radical-revolutionary sentiments of John Adams of Massachusetts to the conservative-Loyalist views of Dickinson of Pennsylvania. In addition, there is no known occasion when all fifty-five of the delegates were present to vote on any measure. On one occasion, when the gentlemen tried to estimate the population of the thirteen Colonies, the best they could do was to "believe" that there were 1,967,000 Caucasians and 539,700 Blacks. No one knew, or attempted to ascertain, the political feelings of the half-million slaves. No one appeared to ponder whether, as the Americans rose in revolt against their British masters, the slaves might rise against their American masters. If the delegates had a concern about an enemy within the gates, it was the 20 percent of colonists who were still loyal to Crown and Parliament. This amounted to 393,400 persons young and old, a formidable body of public opinion.

All of the members of Congress were propertied persons; each was expected to pay his way to Philadelphia, there to serve a year or two at his personal expense. New Hampshire, a frugal settlement, originally sent one delegate, Josiah Bartlett. He was a physician and attorney and could swing New Hampshire in any direction he chose by casting one vote. The unit rule was in effect—one vote per colony—and Bartlett watched with amusement as other colonial delegations argued and harangued their members to vote this way or that. The Congress, however, voted that at least one member of each of the thirteen Colonies should be on each standing committee. The result was that Josiah Bartlett was a member of all of them. The exhaustion of one man caused New Hampshire to take pity. The colony sent one more man, an Irish physician named Matthew Thornton.

It is safe to say that the word "democracy" was never used in Congress. The members understood the word, but the majority still thought in terms of thirteen states allied in a mutual defense pact. Rich New York and affluent Pennsylvania were not ready to countenance an equal vote for struggling Georgia. It is a certainty that Virginia, old and wise and most populous (504,264 persons), could not imagine itself on equal terms with sparse and rocky New Hampshire. To think otherwise is to impute to the Congress a charity and generosity to which it did not pretend. Quite properly, each delegation regarded its individual interests first, the common good second.

Only the radical revolutionaries believed that, in time, the thirteen Colonies could form a unity of interests which would bind them together in a thicket of arrows with one bow. George Washington, in spite of his pretensions to modesty, was glad to leave the Congress and serve as a military officer.

The same is true of Brigadier John Sullivan of New Hampshire. Christopher Gadsden left Philadelphia to organize a militia in South Carolina. Patrick Henry whooped with delight when he was called to Williamsburg to serve his native Virginia. Others from time to time excused themselves from serving because of pressing business at home.

Conversely, this rickety body of men could, on occasion, rise to make great decisions. General Washington, on the third day of spring, had asked the Congress for instructions on how to deal with British peace commissioners, if such should address themselves to him. Congress debated and tabled and debated the matter for six weeks. On May 6, 1776, the delegates surprised themselves by voting to send a firm response to the general:

> RESOLVED, That General Washington be informed, that the Congress suppose, if commissioners are intended to be sent from Great Britain to treat of peace, that the practice usual in such cases will be observed, by making previous application for the necessary passports and safe conduct, and on such application being made, Congress will then direct the proper measures for the reception of such commissioners.

The document was designed to force the British to recognize Washington as a general and the Continental Congress as a legal body. Neither Great Britain nor the Colonies had declared war. As June, 1776, dawned, the Congress saw that no avenue had been left to it except the path to independence. It was conscious and somewhat fearful of an Act of Parliament of December 22, 1775, which removed the American Colonies from the protection of Great Britain. The act forbade all trade with America and authorized General Howe to subdue the rebellious colonists; it also authorized the seizure of all "American" ships.

One by one, Great Britain had closed the doors to reconciliation. Confused, hurt, fearful, the conservative colonies of North Carolina, South Carolina, Pennsylvania, New York, and New Jersey were forced to alter their political stratagems toward independence and liberty. In the second week of June, 1776, the delegates nerved themselves to take the final step. Five members were appointed as a committee to draft a declaration of independence. They elected Thomas Jefferson to write the document.

☆ July 3, 1776 ☆

T HIS WAS A CLEAR, COOL MORNING. THE BREEZE was fresh out of the north, whispering that the heat spell had been broken. Elms and poplars spun green coins against an empty sky. At 6 A.M. most of the delegates to the Congress were up, opening shutters, drinking in a rare summer coolness, bathing, shaving, sitting to breakfast, and taking care of personal correspondence. John Adams, alone in a boardinghouse, dwelled upon the passing of the Lee resolution and was impelled to write his wife a short note.

Dear Abigail:
    Yesterday the greatest question was decided which ever was debated in America, and a greater perhaps never was nor will be decided among men.
    A resolution was passed without one dissenting Colony "that these United Colonies are, and of right ought to be, free and independent states, and as such they have, and of right ought to have, full power to make war, conclude peace, establish commerce, and to do all other acts and things which other States may rightfully do." You will see in a few days a Declaration setting forth the causes which have impelled us to this mighty revolution and the reasons which will justify it in the sight of God and man. A plan of confederation will be taken up in a few days.
    When I look back to the year 1761, and recollect

the argument concerning writs of assistance in the superior court, which I have hitherto considered as the commencement of this controversy between Great Britain and America, and run through the whole period from that time to this, and recollect the series of political events, the chain of causes and effects, I am surprised at the suddenness as well as the greatness of this revolution. Britain has been filled with folly, and America with wisdom. At least, this is my judgment. Time must determine.

It is the will of Heaven that the two countries should be sundered forever. It may be the will of Heaven that America shall suffer calamities still more wasting, and distress yet more dreadful. If this is to be the case, it will have this good effect at least. It will inspire us with many virtues which we have not, and correct many errors, follies and vices which threaten to disturb, dishonor and destroy us. The furnace of affliction produces refinement, in States as well as individuals. And the new governments we are assuming in every part will require a purification from our vices, and an augmentation of our virtues or they will be no blessings. The people will have unbounded power, and the people are extremely addicted to corruption and venality, as well as the great. But I must submit all my hopes and fears to an overruling Providence, in which, unfashionable as the faith may be, I firmly believe.

John Adams, the delegate with the high shiny forehead and the low-hanging, swinging stomach, was always a blunt and tactless man. In debate he was most articulate, alternating between strident shouts and a Jesuitical whisper. On this day, in his joy, he saw power reverting to the people, but his faith in the many as opposed to the few did not blind him to their "corruption and venality." He knew, for example, that his friend President John Hancock of the Congress owed $100,000 in fines as a smuggler. All men, he felt, had vices. The assumption held no risk; Adams feared that those with the most vices might achieve high station.

Adams, in the manner of Thomas Paine, viewed the thirteen Colonies as a latter-day undefiled virgin. It was an unrealistic conception. America had its share of thieves, armed robbers, murderers, confidence men, and adulterous relationships. The several colonies husbanded their prejudices. Maryland, the original home of Roman Catholics, excluded "Papists" from voting. Affluent New York, in which there were only 250 Jews, expressly excluded them from voting and holding public office.

In the Congress, Dr. Benjamin Franklin had said, "The franchise is the common right of free men." It wasn't true. Georgia ruled that a voter must own a minimum of fifty acres of land. Although it was stated that the forefathers of the Declaration of Independence fled Europe to find freedom of religion in the New World, they sometimes did not accord freedom in the individual colonies. The Puritans of Massachusetts Bay felt no kinship with the Quakers of Pennsylvania, who, in turn, were not on cordial terms with the Episcopal ministers and their flocks in Virginia. The colony of Maryland, founded by the Catholic Carrolls, was 92 percent Protestant in 1776. The 8 percent of "Papists" were disenfranchised.

Nor was patriotism to be confused with business. The Congress had asked the commercial houses of America to sell muskets and gunpowder. In Philadelphia and New York the plea had been heard in silence, and guns and powder were hidden. Few colonists would accept paper money from the Congress. General Washington would beg for clothing, for stockings, shoes, stores, coats for his army. When the call went out, these items disappeared from the shops and shelves to be hidden. A few patriotic businessmen were candid. "If the Congress could see its way to paying in pounds and shillings . . ." A Jew, Haym Salomon, gave generously of his personal fortune to help Congress and to fed and clothe units of the Continental Army.

At 8:45 A.M. Clerk Thomson could look up and down

Walnut Street and count the heads of approaching Congress-men. Because he was a Philadelphian, it is doubtful that Thomson remarked the incongruity of having a State House and stables surrounded by a seven-foot brick wall, knowing that the Walnut Street gate was always open. The citizens who arrived in Philadelphia this morning turned their carriages and rigs through the big wooden gates and ordered the stable-men to water and feed the animals, but no one turned to stare at the brick building and state, "History will be made here today." No one, except the Congressmen and their clerk, was aware that a portentous document would be read today, and that men, some in repressed ecstasy and others troubled and fearful for the future, would hammer out such a document of freedom as would stir the hearts of students hundreds of years from now.

If the farm shoppers thought of anything as they gave their animals and rigs to the stable, it was to remark why there were so many rusty cannon and a rotting platform within the yard. The guns were obsolescent. They had seen service in the French and Indian Wars and had been left in the State Yard. No one knew what to do with them; no one wanted to assume responsibility for them. In untidy rows, they gaped openmouthed at the pale-blue sky with yesterday's rain deep in their throats. The platform had been built by the American Philosophical Society so that Benjamin Franklin and his gentlemen of science could, on June 3, 1769, observe the transit of the planet Venus across the face of the sun. No one had been paid to take it down, so it had remained up. Now and then it creaked to the boots of a furious speaker who called the attention of all who would listen to a new and ob-noxious law or a restrictive tax.

The Congressmen walked through the gate, some up-right and smiling, some with hands twined behind backs, studying the hard clay underfoot as though to find there a clue to the future. Some nodded; some shook hands; many bowed formally. They had been here too long to remark on the brilliant sophistication of this city. Long ago they had exhausted the compliments. Philadelphia published books; it was host to learned societies in science and medicine; it paid contractors to collect and dispose of household refuse; the streets were watered by hand trucks and swept clean; constables patrolled its streets at night and sang out the hours. The gentlemen were not in a mood to dwell on the advantages of living in Philadelphia.

About fifty members were in the big room when the doorman closed and locked the double doors noisily. John Hancock, sometimes called "King John," sat behind his desk. He ordered the several committee meetings to be engaged and dispensed with quickly. Once more, Thomas Jefferson sat at the back of the room, the portable desk open on his knees. Today, for certain, his Declaration of Independence would be read. He would say later that he felt oppressed and gloomy at the prospect of all these men voting yea and nay on every phrase in the document. Collectively, they could reduce its sense to nonsense. Their corrections, their alterations could hardly make it a firmer declaration, but they could weaken or destroy it. Again Benjamin Franklin detected the depressed mood of the architect of freedom and sat beside him to smile, to chat, to lend support.

Caesar Rodney was not dwelling on the business at hand. His fingers kept stealing to his face, to press the big kerchief against the cancerous sore. He had slept poorly, fitfully, turning unconsciously to the wrong side of his face only to jump with pain. He was here to see this business through and, having been a part of it, go home to die. Death, like birth, is not always easy to court. He would spend years in the Delaware militia, fighting the battles of America by day and his personal one at night. This he did not know.

Elbridge Gerry, a small and slender merchant of Massachusetts, sat staring at the broad back of Benjamin Harrison of Virginia. Gerry was too solemn a man to appreciate the sallies of the fat Falstaff of the Congress. Elbridge Gerry had asked, if the Declaration was agreed to, whether all members of the Congress would sign or only Hancock as president, with Thomson as clerk attesting the signature. Falstaff had burst into laughter. All, all, he had said, would sign, every man Jack in the Congress. Of course, Harrison added, if the British defeated America, all, all, would be hanged. He had little to fear, said Harrison, because when he dropped at the end of a rope, he was so heavy that his weight would crack his neck at once. But Gerry, so light, so small, no doubt would dangle at the end of the rope, squirming for a half hour.

A committee on population and census studied a religious report filed in 1775. Why it was required reading on this day remained a secret. All it stated was: "No. of Churches —Congregational 668, Presbyterian 588, Anglican 495, Baptist 494, Quaker 310, German Reformed 159, Lutheran 150, Dutch Reformed 120, Methodist 65, Catholic 56, Moravian 31, Congregational-Separatist 27, Dunker 24, Mennonite 6, French Protestant 7, Sandemanian 6, Jewish 5, Rogerene 3." All committees hurried through their meetings this morning. Hancock was not going to delay the reading except for congressional letters and communications.

The president pounded his desk with his palm. He looked at his timepiece. There was a great noise of chairs being pulled back. The delegates sat. Clerk Thomson began to read. There was a communication from the Commissioners of Indian Affairs at Augusta, Georgia, asking for payment of expenses incurred. The letter had been posted seven weeks ago and had made the trip to Savannah by courier pony, then aboard a packet to Philadelphia. On a motion, Hancock ordered that the expense accounts be referred to the Board of Treasury, and paid. A second letter came from the New Jersey Convention. It was dated July 2—abnormally fast even though it had traveled only from Prince Town. The provincial convention wanted to know more about George Washington's Flying Camp, to be situated at Amboy.

This letter started a lively debate. The majority felt that such a camp, engrossing more than ten thousand soldiers, should be stationed at or near New Brunswick rather than Amboy. It was so moved and voted. This, presumably, would enable Washington to move these mobile units to Philadelphia or New York for the protection of either. A delegate pointed out that advices from General Washington indicated that General William Howe and his brother, Admiral Lord Howe, were in Lower New York Bay at anchor. If this were so, all the King's forces were at New York, and there would be no need for a flying camp. Someone else stated that the brothers Howe could feint at New York, land their troops on the New Jersey shore, and march overland to attack and pillage Philadelphia. The dialogue had become acrimonious when John Hancock asked the gentlemen their pleasure. It was voted to place the Flying Camp at New Brunswick, New Jersey, and to ask why no letter had been received from General Washington this morning.

Clerk Thomson searched through the papers on his desk. There was no message from Washington. The fretful ones concluded that he was under attack in New York and didn't have time to write. Others, somewhat more sophisticated, said he was probably busy shoring up his defenses around New York and had nothing further to say. All of them, the fearful as well as the practical, began to feel the viscous dread that comes with knowledge that war is at hand. Outside the closed windows, industrious Philadelphia went about its business of marketing and trading. Inside, fewer than three-score men knew that fiery cannon mouths and gleaming bayonets lay only eighty miles away.

The general was indeed busy. He was disconcerted to learn that his paper strength was greater than his actual strength. The roster showed 28,500 men under arms. Officers reported the actual "body count" to be nineteen thousand men. Most of these were young militia and recruits—men untested under fire. He could not find unanimity among his generals. Greene said that New York City was defenseless; it should be burned to the ground in a massive retreat toward White Plains. It would be difficult to defend a city, Washington conceded, that could be flanked by British men-of-war sailing up the Hudson or the East River. However, he had political as well as military reasons for fighting on this ground. One was that he thought the Continental Army, entrenched on Brooklyn Heights as well as Manhattan, could win a bloody fight. The other was that colonial emissaries were in France and Spain trying to float loans and buy gunpowder and stores; if it was learned that the army had burned its richest city and retreated to the forests, the loss of prestige abroad would be tremendous.

On Staten Island, General Howe was marshaling a force of 32,000 British soldiers. These were professionals. In the harbor, reaching down to Sandy Hook, three hundred warships and armed sloops rode at anchor. It was the most powerful military force ever poised at one place in history. The men were rested, well armed, and well trained. In London, the North government had invested $4,200,000 in this venture. Thirty-nine more ships of war, bearing 2,500 men, were beating the wind northward from Charleston, South Carolina. There, General Henry Clinton and Lord Cornwallis had been defeated attempting an amphibious landing. Within a week or two their forces would also be at the disposal of General Howe.

On July 3, General Washington committed himself to a plan of battle. It constituted a disastrous mistake; a mistake he would not repeat. Having the smaller force, and being on the defensive, he might have borrowed Prescott's plan at Charles Towne—keep his units close and taut in a small area, and wait for Howe to commit himself before adjusting to the assault. Washington decided to keep some regiments in Manhattan, send three divisions to Brooklyn, put a regiment on Governor's Island, put a brigade of 2,400 men on the northern tip of Manhattan, put another brigade at Kingsbridge, opposite Fort Lee, and keep the remainder in reserve on the Long Island side of the East River. It was as though this fine officer feared to be outwitted by his adversary and decided to be everywhere at once with forces too small to repel a strong attack. Tactically, New York City was almost indefensible; it was a tidy metropolis surrounded by a triple moat consisting of the Hudson River, the East River, and the Harlem River. The water would appear to assist in the defense of the city.

To the contrary, General Howe had several options for a successful attack. He could make a night landing at Gravesend Bay and chase three divisions of Americans across Long Island toward Manhattan, with an excellent opportunity to destroy the bulk of Washington's army when it tried to cross the East River to join Washington in New York. He could move westerly across Staten Island and land at Elizabeth Towne in New Jersey, and Bayonne, threatening the Flying Camp at New Brunswick and making an attack on Philadelphia while moving up the Hudson to cross above Riverdale and entrap the whole American Army in a cul-de-sac at Bowling Green. Or Howe could sail his army around Long Island, landing at Pelham for a quick march into New York. The opportunities for successful attack were several; for defense, one. General Washington's solitary fear would not be realized in the forthcoming battle—he felt that Howe might sail his ten ships of the line and his twenty armed frigates to an anchorage in the East River where they would cut off the retreat of his Brooklyn army and, at the same time, shell his artillery in position at Bowling Green.

Washington had little affection for New York. The friends of liberty were fearful of the British Army; the Loyalists in New York rejoiced that Howe was about to liberate the city. Neither was of any use to Washington. To him, New York was a poisoned well. He could not trust the civilians or the authorities. He saw treason and treasonable acts everywhere. Worse, the rank and file of his army regarded the British with awe. This induced pessimism in the ranks, an insuperable enemy in any army.

Howe, to the contrary, was in confident control of an optimistic army. He sat in his quarters at Staten Island, working out the details of a landing in force at Gravesend Bay, a full-scale attack on the left wing of the Continental Army aimed, not at winning territory, but in destroying that wing. He would rest his men for a few days, then cross the East River into Manhattan and chase George Washington north to The Bronx. At this point, he planned to send Cornwallis across the Hudson to attack Fort Lee and secure a landing point in New Jersey for the remainder of Howe's army.

And yet Howe had one additional duty before preparing for battle. Where Thomas Gage had failed as a diplomat, General Howe hoped to succeed. He would send a letter to George Washington under a flag of truce, offering amnesty for all who would lay down their arms. If, in return, Howe offered the benevolence of King George to the colonists, he might destroy their effectiveness as an army. He should have known that the course of history is hinged onto minuscule matters. He lost his opportunity by addressing his peace plea to "George Washington, Esq." instead of to "General George Washington."

In Philadelphia the public printers ran off the last of an assortment of German handbills. Congress, powerless to assist General Washington, had done its utmost to propagandize the British as the source of all evil, the Colonies as a font of pietistic goodness. When word reached Philadelphia that King George had contracted with German princes for the services of seventeen thousand soldiers, the press and pulpits of America roared "Shame!" Britain's cause was so weak that she could not recruit men from England, Scotland, or Ireland; she had to hire the hated Hessians, mercenaries of a foreign tongue who would cheerfully kill Englishmen or Americans, depending on which offered the most in return. Having scourged the English King with words, the Congress decided to utilize the opposite tack—print handbills and leaflets in German, promising the Hessians land grants, farms, and freedom, plus jobs with good salaries if they would desert the British for the American cause. The ploy did not work because neither Congress nor General Washington knew of a way to distribute the leaflets to the Hessians on Staten Island.

The sun was high in Philadelphia when Clerk Thomson reached for another paper. Jefferson could see that it was not his Declaration of Independence. The Marine Committee had reached a decision and required a favorable vote to execute it. The plan was to build a fleet of American ships on the southern edge of Lake Champlain, these armed vessels designed to keep British forces inside Canada. The measure was an afterthought when Congressmen saw that Howe could strike north out of New York City while British forces in Canada could head south and join him. If the English achieved this, New England would be effectively cut off from the middle and southern colonies.

The Marine Committee acted as though the British would be sufficiently cordial to wait until the American lake fleet was ready. Clerk Thomson read the terms for shipwrights to help build the fleet: salary thirty-four and two-thirds dollars per month, one month's pay to be given on signing the agreement; all personal tools and muskets to be assessed and paid for; one half-pint of rum per man per day; one extra day's pay to be given each man for every twenty miles between his home and the town or village of discharge. The Congress did not plan to reveal to the shipbuilders that George Washington's northern army had suffered dreadful attrition in the winter of 1775–1776 from Canadian attacks, Indian attacks, and subzero weather. In addition, the northern army had no timber. The ships of war would be cut from green forests at the edge of Lake Champlain.

The terms were generous. Another committee had set the emoluments of the American soldier at six and two-thirds dollars a month, of which one and two-thirds dollars would be deducted to pay for clothing. Uniforms would be, "as much as possible," brown with lapel facings of different colors to distinguish the various regiments. The Congress would issue "good firelocks with bayonets," each musket to have a barrel 3 feet, 8 inches in length, and attached thereto "a bayonet eighteen inches long." The rations, which would be seldom achieved, were more than generous. Each private soldier was to receive daily one pound of beef, or twelve ounces of pork, or one pound of salt fish. He would also be given one pound of bread or flour every day. For liquids the Continental Army would grant one pint of milk and one quart of spruce beer per day. Vegetables would be given at weekly intervals. Medical care and free quarters were guaranteed. Seldom did the Congress put Washington in a position to keep its agreement with the soldiers.

The clerk and the president conferred in whispers. John Hancock said that there were no more communications on the agenda. He would step down as Congress sat as a Committee of the Whole to hear the reading of the Declaration; Benjamin Harrison stepped up as presiding officer pro tem. Men in the room turned to get a better look at Thomas Jefferson. Benjamin Franklin moved his chair closer. "I'll tell you a story," he said softly. One or two Congressmen stood to ask for a postponement of the reading. It would be a long, irrevocable step from the stature of colonies to nationhood and independence, certainly too much of a step to take at once. Others observed that reading and voting at this time would be unfair to the colony of New York because the besieged province would have a state convention within a few days and would probably send new delegates with fresh instructions. Harrison observed that it had been the will and the sense of Congress to put this matter on its agenda for several weeks; further postponement would hurt the cause of the Colonies.

Benjamin Franklin whispered that there was a hatter named John Thompson. When he was prepared to open his shop he fashioned a big hand-lettered sign which stated: "John Thompson, Hatter, Makes and Sells Hats for Ready Money." Jefferson bowed his head to listen. Franklin said that, to emphasize the business, there was a drawing of a hat on the sign. A friend of Thompson studied the sign and said the word "hatter" was superfluous. It should be dropped. Thompson cut the word out. Another friend thought that the word "makes" was superfluous because the men who buy hats do not care who makes them. Besides, it was a shop for selling hats, not a factory for making them, that Thompson was advertising. The word "makes" was dropped. A third friend wondered why the reference to ready money; no one expected credit from Thompson. "Ready Money" disappeared. This left only "John Thompson Sells Hats." A regular customer gaped at it and said, "Ridiculous. John Thompson wouldn't give them away, would he?" What was left was "John Thompson" and a picture of a hat. Strangely, the business did well with the abbreviated sign.

Thomas Jefferson looked up at his old friend. He did not laugh. He was touched by Franklin's interest in his sensitivity. For a little while, the redhead stopped squirming in his chair. Instead he decided to listen to his critics and to take notes. In this manner he kept busy. And silent.

Harrison said that the draft of the Declaration would be read fully, without interruption, as a first reading. Immediately afterward, if the members had revisions in mind, it would be read again, slowly, paragraph by paragraph. When the document had been edited down to its final words, the Committee of the Whole would vote whether to adopt or negate the

Declaration of Independence. If the vote in favor carried, it would be properly enscrolled by a public printer, presented to the Congress sitting as a congress, and signed by the president and clerk of the Congress. If the measure lost, it would lie on the clerk's desk until such time as the Congress desired to resurrect it, if indeed such a time should arise.

Clerk Thomson cleared his throat. A distant peal of thunder was heard rolling off the heavens. The delegates glanced at each other. They were tired of a week of thundershowers. Some leaned forward tensely. A few cupped ears to hear every word.

When in the course of human events it becomes necessary for a people to advance from that subordination in which they have hitherto remained, & to assume among the powers of the earth the equal & independent station to which the laws of nature & of nature's god entitle them, a decent respect to the opinions of mankind requires that they should declare the causes which impel them to the change.

We hold these truths to be sacred & undeniable; that all men are created equal and independent, that from that equal creation they derive rights inherent & inalienable, among which are the preservation of life, & liberty, & the pursuit of happiness; that to secure these ends governments are instituted among men, deriving their just powers from the consent of the governed; that whenever any form of government shall become destructive of these ends, it is the right of the people to alter and abolish it, & to institute new government, laying it's foundations on such principles & organizing it's powers in such form, as to them shall seem most likely to effect their safety & happiness. prudence indeed will dictate that governments long established should not be changed for light & transient causes: and accordingly all experience hath shewn that mankind are more disposed to suffer while evils are sufferable, than to

217

right themselves by abolishing the forms to which they are accustomed. but when a long train of abuses & usurpations, begun at a distinguished period & pursuing invariably the same object, evinces a design to subject them to arbitrary power, it is their right, it is their duty, to throw off such governments & to provide new guards for their future security. such has been the patient sufferance of these colonies; & such is now the necessity which constrains them to expunge their former systems of government. The history of his present majesty is a history of unremitting injuries & usurpations among which no one fact stands single or solitary to contradict the uniform tenor of the rest, all of which have in direct object the establishment of an absolute tyranny over these states. to prove this, let facts be submitted to a candid world, for the truth of which we pledge a faith yet unsullied by falsehood.

he has refused his assent to laws the most wholesome and necessary for the public good:

he has forbidden his governors to pass laws of immediate & pressing importance, unless suspended in their operation till his assent should be obtained; and when so suspended, he has neglected utterly to attend to them.

he has refused to pass other laws for the accommodation of large districts of people unless those people would relinquish the right of representation, a right inestimable to them, & formidable to tyrants alone:

he has dissolved representative houses repeatedly & continually, for opposing with manly firmness his invasions on the rights of the people:

he has refused for a long space of time to cause others to be elected, whereby the legislative powers, incapable of annihilation, have returned to the people at large for their exercise, the state remaining in the mean time exposed to all the dangers of invasions from without, & convulsions within:

he has endeavored to prevent the population of

these states; for that purpose obstructing the laws for naturalization of foreigners; refusing to pass others to encourage their migration hither; & raising the conditions of new appropriations of lands:

he has suffered the administration of justice totally to cease in some of these colonies, refusing his assent to laws for establishing judiciary powers:

he has made our judges dependent on his will alone for the tenure of their offices and amount of their salaries:

he has erected a multitude of new offices by a self-assumed power, & sent hither swarms of officers to harass our people & eat out their substance:

he has kept among us in times of peace standing armies & ships of war:

he has affected to render the military independent of & superior to the civil power:

he has combined with others to subject us to a jurisdiction foreign to our constitutions and unacknowledged by our laws; giving his assent to their pretended acts of legislation for quartering large bodies of armed troops among us:

> for protecting them by mock-trial from punishment for any murders they should commit on the inhabitants of these states;
>
> for cutting off our trade with all parts of the world;
>
> for imposing taxes on us without our consent;
>
> for depriving us of the benefits of trial by jury;
>
> for transporting us beyond seas to be tried for pretended offences;
>
> for taking away our charters & altering fundamentally the forms of our governments;
>
> for suspending our own legislatures & declaring themselves invested with power to legislate for us in all cases whatsover;

he has abdicated government here, withdrawing his governors & declaring us out of his allegiance and protection:

he has plundered our seas, ravaged our coasts, burnt our towns & destroyed the lives of our people:

he is at this time transporting large armies of foreign mercenaries to compleat the works of death, desolation & tyranny, already begun with circumstances of cruelty & perfidy unworthy the head of a civilized nation:

he has endeavored to bring on the inhabitants of our frontiers the merciless Indian savages, whose known rule of warfare is an undistinguished destruction of all ages, sexes & conditions of existence:

he has incited treasonable insurrections in our fellow-subjects, with the allurements of forfeiture & confiscation of our property:

he has waged cruel war against nature itself, violating it's most sacred rights of life & liberty in the persons of a distant people who never offended him, captivating & carrying them into slavery in another hemisphere, or to incur miserable death in their transportation thither. this piratical warfare, the opprobrium of *infidel* powers, is the warfare of the CHRISTIAN king of Great Britain. determined to keep open a market where MEN should be bought & sold, he has prostituted his negative for suppressing every legislative attempt to prohibit or to restrain this execrable commerce: and that this assemblage of horrors might want no fact of distinguished die, he is now exciting these very people to rise in arms among us, and to purchase that liberty of which *he* has deprived them, by murdering the people upon whom he also obtruded them: thus paying off former crimes committed against the *liberties* of one people, with crimes which he urges them to commit against the *lives* of another.

in every stage of these oppressions we have petitioned for redress in the most humble terms; our repeated petitions have been answered by repeated injury, a prince whose character is thus marked by every act which may define a tyrant is unfit to be the ruler of a people who mean to be free. . . .

Nor have we been wanting in attention to our British brethren. we have warned them from time to time of attempts by their legislature to extend a jurisdiction over these our states. we have reminded them of the circumstances of our emigration & settlement here, no one of which could warrant so strange a pretension: that these were effected at the expence of our own blood & treasure, unassisted by the wealth or the strength of Great Britain: that in constituting indeed our several forms of government, we had adopted one common king, thereby laying a foundation for perpetual league & amity with them: but that submission to their parliament was no part of our constitution, nor ever in idea, if history may be credited: and we appealed to their native justice & magnanimity, as well as to the ties of our kindred to disavow these usurpations which were likely to interrupt our correspondence & connection. they too have been deaf to the voice of justice & consanguinity, & when occasions have been given them, by the regular course of their laws of removing from their councils the disturbers of our harmony, they have by their free election re-established them in power. at this very time too they are permitting their chief magistrate to send over not only soldiers of our common blood, but Scotch & foreign mercenaries to invade & deluge us in blood. these facts have given the last stab to agonizing affection, and manly spirit bids us to forget our former love for them, and to hold them as we hold the rest of mankind, enemies in war, in peace friends. we might have been a free & a great people together; but a communication of grandeur & of freedom it seems is below their dignity. be it so, since they will have it: the road to glory & happiness is open to us too; we will climb it in a separate state, and acquiesce in the necessity which pronounces our everlasting Adieu!

We therefore the representatives of the United States of America in General Congress assembled do, in the name & by the authority of the good people of these states, reject & renounce all allegiance & subjection to the kings of Great Britain & all others who may hereafter claim by, through & under them; we utterly dissolve & break off all political connection which may have heretofore subsisted between us & the people or parliament of Great Britain: and finally we do assert & declare these colonies to be free & independent states, and as free & independent states they shall hereafter have power to levy war, conclude peace, contract alliances, establish commerce & to do all other acts & things which independent states may of right do. And for the support of this declaration we mutually pledge to each other our lives, our fortunes, & our sacred honour.

It had been written. It had been read and said. It was, according to the historical perspective of individual Congressmen, either a long step forward into the bright sunlight of liberty or an interminable step backward into the darkness of the damned. James Wilson of Pennsylvania, who had spoken against it two days ago, stood to argue against consideration of it "now." It was too late a day for procrastination. Those who were still opposed to the Declaration no longer opposed; they fought for time. A month, a week would do. Congress would not hear of it. The members had listened to the vivid phrases of divorcement from Great Britain, and the ringing final sentences of independence. The gentlemen, still sitting as a Committee of the Whole, could no longer ignore this singular document. They asked to have it read again—slowly, a paragraph at a time. Most of the delegates, though in accord with a declaration of independence, had literary pretensions and these were about to be exercised in mutilating, amending, and excising Thomas Jefferson's work.

Mr. Jefferson was a most private person. He seldom criticized his confreres, and he had no appreciation of being criticized. He was squirming under his portable desk. His head inclined toward his quill. He was too proud to stand to defend a word or a phrase of his writing, but he would make notes and alter his copy of the Declaration of Independence as fast as the individual members insisted on changes. He would not comment publicly on what Congress did, but he referred to the changes as "mutilations" all of his life. He was so sure that his noble words would be mangled that after he had concluded the work on June 30 he wrote to Edmund Pendleton in Virginia, asking that a substitute Congressman be found to take his place so that he could go home to Monticello.

Jefferson would not give a reason, although he might have hinted that he was needed at home because Mrs. Jefferson was pregnant. He would not cite a reason because his public life was compartmentalized from his private life. Nor could he be persuaded to remain in Philadelphia longer than he chose. "I am willing to remain in Philadelphia," he wrote, "till the expiration of our year." On July 1, he wrote to his friend William Fleming and, for the first time, mentioned authorship of the great document. "If any doubt has arisen as to me," he wrote, "my country will have my political creed in the form of a 'Declaration &c' which I was lately directed to draw. This will give decisive proof that my own sentiment concurred with the vote they [the Virginia House of Burgesses] instructed us to give. Let this be proof that I am with you."

Old Joseph Hewes of North Carolina may have lifted Jefferson's spirits. He had been vigorously opposed to a declaration. When Clerk Thomson concluded the first reading, the seventy-six-year-old merchant sat bolt upright, got to his feet, and lifted his eyes and his hands to heaven. "It is done!" he shouted. "And I will abide by it." There was an unusual patter of applause; someone said "Hear! Hear!" and Hancock nodded from a table for Thomson to begin the second and much slower reading. The hour was late. If there were to be many changes, Congress would not complete its work today.

Remarkably, there were no more motions to table the document; there was no motion to name a new committee to devise a new declaration of independence; it was the sense of the members to work with this one. The clerk had barely read the preamble—"When in the course of human events it becomes necessary for a people to advance from that subordination in which they have hitherto remained"—when there was an assortment of hands in air trying to get the attention of Benjamin Harrison. The voices were disparate; the ideas variant; the choice of words like a cascade of coins; but the members finally hammered out the following:

"When in the course of human events it becomes necessary for one people to dissolve the political bands which have connected them with another, and to assume among the powers of the earth, the separate and equal station to which the laws of nature and of nature's god entitle them, a decent respect to the opinions of mankind requires that they should declare the causes which impel them to the separation."

"To advance from that subordination" had been changed to "to dissolve the political bands which have connected them with another." "Equal and independent" had been altered to "separate and equal." Jefferson's protest that he had tried to interpret the corporate mind of the people rather than use his own thoughts was about to become even more true. In the next paragraph, Thomson got no further than "We hold these truths to be sacred and undeniable," when there was a clamor to change it to "We hold these truths to be self-evident." Thomson, at times, could not complete the reading of a paragraph; he hesitated at the end of a phrase or clause and waited for objections. They were swift and loud. Jefferson the author cowered in the midst of fifty editors. He had written of "inalienable rights"; someone changed it to "unalienable." The members hacked at the Rights of Man section to such a degree that no one was certain what it said. Thomas Jefferson had written: "that from that equal creation they derive rights inherent & inalienable, among which are the preservation of life, & liberty, & the pursuit of happiness." When all the changes had been made, this section read: ". . . that they are endowed by their creator with certain unalienable rights, that among these are life, liberty and the pursuit of happiness."

John Hancock studied his timepiece. The clamor for alterations had not abated, and the supper hour, 4 P.M., was at hand. Benjamin Harrison caught the signal and adjourned the meeting of the Committee of the Whole so that Hancock could preside to adjourn Congress until tomorrow. Dr. Witherspoon of Prince Town College responded to the worriment of some members, declaring that the thirteen Colonies were "not only ripe for the measure but in danger of rotting for the want of it."

The president adjourned the Congress quickly, noting that he expected the members to agree on a final version of the Declaration of Independence and to vote on it tomorrow. It is doubtful that any of the alterations proposed on July 3 were intended to be mean or punitive; no record was kept of who proposed revisions; it is probable that many of the members, conscious of the long light of history, desired to make changes for the sake of having a personal hand in the writing of the Declaration. No one doubts that Jefferson felt crushed to silence by the dismembering of his lofty phrases, but at least one member looked upon Jefferson's work as redundant; the real measure of independence, John Adams thought, was the passage of the Lee resolutions of July 2. In addition to the hurried note to wife Abigail in the morning, he found time to pen an additional ecstasy in the afternoon:

> Yesterday the greatest question was decided, which ever was debated in America, and a greater perhaps, never was nor will be decided among men. . . .

His revolutionary zeal, aflame for so many years in a small company of men, burst its bounds and lighted his spirit with such a blinding glow that he burbled and babbled almost incoherently in sharing his happiness with his wife. He looked upon Jefferson's work as a formal document which, in hand-polished words, would endorse the Lee resolutions. He did not dwell upon the formal Declaration of Independence, even though he was one of the committee of five elected to draw the document and present it to Congress. The great deed of independence, severance forever from Great Britain, had been executed, in Adams's eyes, on July 2. He would remember that day always. Although Adams ranked second only to Dr. Franklin as a man who urged Jefferson to "think out and write" the Declaration, his comment on the work in late summer was that he was sorry that Jefferson had referred to King George as a "tyrant." Adams thought it was too harsh.

It was not that he did not appreciate and endorse the document. Rather it was that Adams seemed to feel that his young friend Thomas Jefferson had slain the King over and over. A terse, precise indictment would have been sufficient. Adams had a lifelong appreciation of simplicity and bluntness. If, as some theologians said, the sentence "Jesus wept" encompassed the entire spirit of the New Testament, then it is likely that John Adams understood and quoted Colonel Innis of the Virginia militia, who raised his goblet of rum in a Williamsburg tavern and thundered, "May God damn the King of England!" Surely that would be closer to the thinking of John Adams than anything Jefferson might write.

☆ July 4, 1776 ☆

At 6 A.M. THOMAS JEFFERSON NOTED IN HIS diary that the temperature stood at 68 degrees Fahrenheit. It would rise to 72 degrees at 9 A.M. and, at the same hour, tempers within the State House would begin to boil. For the first time, Clerk Thomson would have copies engrossed by Printer Dunlap. He would pass them out to each provincial delegation, and the gentlemen would hurry to hunt passages which were disagreeable. The big room would be locked again, as Hancock seldom tired of explaining, to keep the horseflies out and the disagreements within.

Before the president rapped for order, the delegations were busy trying to reconstruct words and phrases that had vanished or been altered so that they could proceed with the work at hand. For once, no one was late. Jefferson, dejected and silent, sat over his copy drawing lines through passages, seldom looking up to listen to a speaker. John Adams bustled happily from table to table, trying to hold acrimony to a minimum, acrimony he hoped would vanish in the afternoon. No one took a poll to find out which members were present in this historic day, or even to list the absentees. There were about fifty men in the room—give or take a few—including John Dickinson of Pennsylvania, who was present to add his vote to Benjamin Franklin's for independence and liberty. The members sensed that the passage of the Lee resolutions had made the thirteen Colonies an independent nation or conglomerate of nations. They looked upon the Declaration of Independence as their explanation to the world why they chose liberty.

It should be noted that in 1776 there was a literary trend away from the extravagant phrase, the capitalized word. Men of letters were given to starting sentences without a capital letter and favored such contractions as & and *don't,* *doesn't* and *isn't,* but not *it's,* which was Jefferson's weakness when he intended to write *its.* Man, having exercised his discretion to use the flamboyant phrase and to capitalize any and all nouns or verbs, had recently flown in the opposite direction, looking for simplicity and felicity of expression.

Thus, when John Hancock asked if the Congress wanted to consider letters and entreaties first, the members shouted no. They had worked on the Declaration of Independence yesterday, and they wanted to finish it this morning. There was a letter from George Washington, but it could wait. Hancock again resolved the body into the Committee of the Whole and stepped down to sit with Massachusetts Bay as Benjamin Harrison left the Virginia delegation to preside. Clerk Thomson stood to read the part of the Declaration which had been approved, and addressed himself to the remainder of the document.

"His majesty" was changed, in all references, to "the King of England." "Deluge us in blood" became "destroy us," and "everlasting Adieu!" had its exclamation point dropped to become "eternal separation." The word "subjects" became "citizens." The Congress was improving the Declaration, although Thomas Jefferson was so offended that in the years ahead he would send copies of *his* Declaration and *theirs* to friends, requesting that they tell him which one they liked better. Although he kept no record of the vote, it is doubtful that any of Jefferson's friends would wish to hurt one of the great statesmen of the century by conceding that *theirs* was the better of the two. Surely Jefferson must have known that his slavery paragraph would be anathema to at least three of the provinces—Georgia, South Carolina, and Massachusetts. As a slaveholder in Virginia, he understood the necessity of plantation owners to have the cheapest labor at hand, and he realized that the shipowners of Massachusetts bought the slaves in the African trade and sold them in the southern colonies. And yet in his charges against King George he wrote:

> he has waged cruel war against nature itself, violating it's most sacred rights of life & liberty in the persons of a distant people who never offended him, captivating & carrying them into slavery in another hemisphere, or to incur miserable death in their transportation thither. this piratical warfare, the opprobrium of infidel powers, is the warfare of the CHRISTIAN king of Great Britain. determined to keep open a market where MEN should be bought & sold, he has prostituted his negative. . . .

Contrary to Jefferson's views, Great Britain was much more enlightened in the matter of slavery than the Colonies. The King had countenanced the slave trade; he had not endorsed it. The big farm owners of America had embraced slavery because it was profitable. The cruelty of man toward his less enlightened brother was never a moral ethic. Nor did slaves come cheap. Planters at slave auctions often paid between five hundred and fifteen hundred dollars per slave, depending upon age, sex, and health. The cheapest way to proliferate the trade was to buy a few childbearing females, but even this required an investment spanning a decade before the plantation owners could expect Black children to work.

The only time, in the interminable reading and rereading of the Declaration of Independence, that anyone recalled who objected to what was during discussion of the slavery paragraph. South Carolinians and Georgians admitted that they were outraged, and proposed excising the entire passage. Massachusetts supported this on the floor and Jefferson, disconsolate, drew lines of ink through it.

If he had been wrong in dreaming that America would renounce slavery, he was equally remiss in believing that the Congress would not bristle over his disparaging reference to the Scots. In the paragraph beginning, "Nor have we been wanting in attentions to our British brethren," Jefferson wrote: "they are permitting their chief magistrate to send over not only soldiers of our common blood, but Scotch & foreign mercenaries to invade & deluge us in blood." Surely Jefferson knew that James Wilson of Pennsylvania and John Witherspoon of New Jersey had been born in Scotland. It is doubtful that either of them protested; others of their delegations probably got to their feet to state the obvious: that Scotsmen could not be fairly lumped with "foreign mercenaries." This too was stricken from the record.

Thomas Jefferson was a hot, busy redhead most of the day. When Congress shouted, "We will expunge," he wrote "alter." He was busy underlining, writing alterations in the margins, and bracketing words and phrases as the day dragged itself on leaden feet to a conclusion. His copy of the Declaration was so ink-marked and tracked that in sections it became illegible. When the Congress reached the twenty-seven indictments of King George III, it felt, in its collective wisdom, that Jefferson had gone too far. One of the amended items that the members found objectionable was: "future ages will scarcely believe that the hardiness of one man adventured, within the short compass of 12 years only, to lay a foundation so broad and so undisguised for tyranny over a people fostered and fixed in principles of freedom." It was stricken in its entirety.

Some of the members took the floor to offer capital letters in exchange for lowercase. They were especially irritated by the words "god" and "nature" in uncapitalized letters.

No one asked Jefferson about his foibles in grammar. The words, one by one, were killed and reborn. It was surgery without an anesthetic.

One man who cared deeply about every word in the Declaration and knew he would not sign it was John Dickinson. He would remain seated; he would listen attentively to the ebb and flow of dialogue; but the man from Pennsylvania could not, in good conscience, lend himself to an indictment of King, Parliament, and people. His colonial world was now opposed to his views, but he could not divorce himself from the Congress.

Near the end of debate, someone discovered a personal sentiment written by Jefferson. It amounted to a sorrowful reproach of Great Britain for what might have been. Jefferson and other members of Congress had kin and dear friends living in England; this document would alienate both sides forever. He had written: "these facts have given the last stab to agonizing affection, and manly spirit bids us to forget our former love for them, and to hold them as we hold the rest of mankind, enemies in war, in peace friends. we might have been a free & a great people together; but a communication of grandeur & of freedom it seems is below their dignity. be it so, since they will have it: the road to glory & happiness is open to us too; we will climb it in a separate state, and acquiesce in the necessity which pronounces our everlasting Adieu!"

It was in the penultimate paragraph, and some said there was room for a little display of sentiment because the next and final paragraph divorced America from Great Britain forever. Others took the floor to denounce sentiment and affection. The document and its message were too profound for personal longing and sorrow. The result was compromise. The paragraph could remain intact up to and including the words "enemies in war, in peace friends." The rest of it—"we might have been a free & a great people," et cetera—was stricken.

There was no reason to believe that having devised so many "mutilations," as Jefferson called them, the Congress would not change the final paragraph. This was the operative passage to freedom. One by one, members suggested alterations, until so many were on the floor that the section had to be read and reread. At times the sense of the Declaration was lost. This, beyond doubt, was the most painful time for Jefferson, because it was in the last and first paragraph that he allowed his words to take wing. Those who objected to parts of it seemed bent on shortening the last paragraph and, if possible, to place God on the side of the revolutionaries.

Where Jefferson had penned: "We therefore the representatives of the United States of America in General Congress assembled do, in the name & by the authority of the good people of these states, reject & renounce all allegiance & subjection to the kings of Great Britain . . ." was in time changed to: "We, THEREFORE, the Representatives of the UNITED STATES OF AMERICA, in General Congress, Assembled, appealing to the Supreme Judge of the world for the rectitude of our intentions, do, in the Name, and by Authority of the good People of these Colonies, solemnly publish and declare, That these United Colonies are, and of Right ought to be FREE AND INDEPENDENT STATES; that they are Absolved from all Allegiance to the British Crown. . . ."

God was now in the forefront of the paragraph; the word "united" in United States was reduced to lowercase, indicating that the proper name for the new country would be States of America, which were at the time united. The Declaration of Independence provides a portrait of thirteen independent nations with a common purpose. Each was to be as equal as the document stated all men to be.

And yet, as Jefferson squirmed over his portable desk, perspiring in the heat of a closed room, it is not too much to say that the deepest wound to his pride probably was the in-

232

clusion of Richard Henry Lee's graceful phrase "That these United Colonies are, and of right ought to be FREE AND INDEPENDENT STATES. . . ." It may have been a grievous hurt because some members of the Virginia delegation said that the phrase originated with Jefferson when he wrote a rough draft of Virginia's new state constitution. Jefferson's work was not acceptable to the Virginia House of Burgesses, but statements and sentiments were lifted from it and encompassed in the final constitution. If this is true, the Congress was stealing from Lee, who stole from Jefferson, who would not be credited in the final draft of the Declaration.

Hancock knew that adjournment would be late today. Congress was approaching the supper hour when the final changes were made. The Declaration of Independence was ready to be voted back from the Committee of the Whole to the Congress for a vote. A motion was made, seconded, and carried as Harrison left the presiding officer's chair and gave it to John Hancock. The president was not going to make a speech; he said that he was prepared to accept the will of the Congress and Clerk Thomson would call the roll from north to south. This was the moment for the enormous silence; the time when men brave and timid, excited and fearful, prepared themselves to take a long and irrevocable step in the name of the people of thirteen Colonies.

"New Hampshire!" bawled Thomson. Josiah Bartlett, physician and lawyer, a plain man in brown breeches and waistcoat, stood to say, "New Hampshire votes aye for the resolution."

"Massachusetts!" John Adams, swinging circuitously like a pealing chime, said, "Massachusetts votes aye for the Declaration."

And so it went. Rhode Island voted "Aye." So did Connecticut. New York, waiting for orders to vote for the measure, answered: "New York, at this time, abstains from voting." New Jersey, which had recently unhorsed its Royalist governor, Benjamin Franklin's estranged son, voted "Aye." So did Pennsylvania, Delaware, and Maryland.

When Delaware voted "Aye!" with Caesar Rodney bouncing and beaming, the Declaration of Independence became a fact. It was the seventh vote of thirteen. There was no pause; no cheer. The poll continued. Virginia voted "Aye." So did North Carolina and South Carolina. The last "Aye!" came from Button Gwinnett, representing the youngest colony, Georgia. New York asked for the right to vote when fresh instructions arrived. The chair granted the request.

The deed at last was done. Mr. Hancock instructed the clerk to record the vote as unanimous. No excitement, no huzzahs came from the tables around the room. The reaction was more a sigh of contentment, as though the men had climbed a formidable precipice and were ready to rest awhile. Thomas Jefferson slipped his heavily inked copy into the portable desk and closed it on his lap. Benjamin Franklin sat with his spectacles on his forehead, probably waiting for Hancock to adjourn the session. The president had other notions. He announced that a firm and true copy of the Declaration would be engrossed at the printer. It would be signed by John Hancock, and, attesting his signature, Clerk Thomson. There was no need for the members of Congress to sign the Declaration of Independence to make it valid, but there would be a hue and cry for all signatories within a few days.

Hancock announced that Dunlap the printer would print a great number of copies, these to be sent to the thirteen Colonies, additional copies to be sent to Selectmen, Councilmen, and members of Committees of Safety, also to military generals down to the rank of brigadier. Hancock would later state that he signed his name with a large and flourishing hand so that, if misfortune was to be the lot of the States of America, the King would not be forced to squint to find out whom he would hang first.

There was no objection to Hancock's directive. The final version of Jefferson's monumental work was, at best, a series of compromises wrung out of the minds and hearts of the Congressmen through two days of labor. It is possible that no one was completely satisfied with it, and yet, in its accepted form, it seems to have captured more nobility of purpose than Jefferson's version. Everybody wanted to have it read once more, even though the time for amendments had passed. It was done.

IN CONGRESS, JULY 4, 1776

THE UNANIMOUS DECLARATION of the thirteen united STATES OF AMERICA,

WHEN in the Course of human events, it becomes necessary for one people to dissolve the political bands which have connected them with another, and to assume among the powers of the earth, the separate and equal station to which the Laws of Nature and of Nature's God entitle them, a decent respect to the opinions of mankind requires that they should declare the causes which impel them to the separation.

We hold these truths to be self-evident, that all men are created equal, that they are endowed by their Creator with certain unalienable Rights, that among these are Life, Liberty and the pursuit of Happiness.—That to secure these rights, Governments are instituted among Men, deriving their just powers from the consent of the governed,—That whenever any Form of Government becomes destructive of these ends, it is the Right of the People to alter or to abolish it, and to institute new Government, laying its foundation on such principles and organizing its powers in such form, as to them shall seem most likely to effect their Safety and Happiness. Prudence, indeed, will dictate that Governments long established should not be changed for light and transient causes; and accordingly all experience hath shewn, that mankind are more disposed to suffer, while evils are sufferable, than to right themselves by abolishing the forms to which they are accustomed. But when a long train of abuses and usurpations, pursuing invariably the same Object evinces a design to reduce them under absolute Despotism, it is their right, it is their duty, to throw off such Government, and to provide new Guards for their future security.—Such has been the patient sufferance of these Colonies; and such is now the necessity which constrains them to alter their former Systems of Government. The history of the present King of Great Britain is a history of repeated injuries and usurpations, all having in direct object the establishment of an absolute Tyranny over these States. To prove this, let Facts be submitted to a candid world.

He has refused his Assent to Laws, the most wholesome and necessary for the public good.

He has forbidden his Governors to pass Laws of immediate and pressing importance, unless suspended in their operation till his Assent should be obtained; and when so suspended, he has utterly neglected to attend to them.

He has refused to pass other Laws for the accommodation of large districts of people, unless those people would relinquish the right of Representation in the Legislature, a right inestimable to them and formidable to tyrants only.

He has called together legislative bodies at places unusual, uncomfortable, and distant from the depository of their public Records, for the sole purpose of fatiguing them into compliance with his measures.

He has dissolved Representative Houses repeatedly, for opposing with manly firmness his invasions on the rights of the people.

He has refused for a long time, after such dissolutions, to cause others to be elected; whereby the Legislative Powers, incapable of Annihilation, have returned to the People at large for their exercise; the State remaining in the meantime exposed to all the dangers of invasion from without, and convulsions within.

He has endeavoured to prevent the population of these States; for that purpose obstructing the Laws of Naturalization of Foreigners; refusing to pass others to encourage their migration hither, and raising the conditions of new Appropriations of Lands.

He has obstructed the Administration of Justice, by refusing his Assent to Laws for establishing Judiciary powers.

He has made Judges dependent on his Will alone, for the tenure of their offices, and the amount and payment of their salaries.

He has erected a multitude of New Offices, and sent hither swarms of Officers to harass our people, and eat out their substance.

He has kept among us, in times of peace, Standing Armies without the Consent of our legislatures.

He has affected to render the Military independent of and superior to the Civil power.

He has combined with others to subject us to a jurisdiction foreign to our constitution, and unacknowledged by our laws; giving his Assent to their Acts of pretended Legislation:

For quartering large bodies of armed troops among us:

For protecting them, by a mock Trial, from punishment for any Murders which they should commit on the Inhabitants of these States:

For cutting off our Trade with all parts of the world:

For imposing Taxes on us without our Consent:

For depriving us in many cases, of the benefits of Trial by Jury:

For transporting us beyond Seas to be tried for pretended offences:

For abolishing the free System of English Laws in

a neighbouring Province, establishing therein an Arbitrary government, and enlarging its Boundaries so as to render it at once an example and fit instrument for introducing the same absolute rule into these Colonies:

For taking away our Charters, abolishing our most valuable Laws, and altering fundamentally the Forms of our Governments:

For suspending our own Legislatures, and declaring themselves invested with power to legislate for us in all cases whatsoever.

He has abdicated Government here, by declaring us out of his Protection and waging War against us.

He has plundered our seas, ravaged our Coasts, burnt our towns, and destroyed the lives of our people.

He is at this time transporting large Armies of foreign Mercenaries to compleat the works of death, desolation and tyranny, already begun with circumstances of Cruelty & perfidy scarcely paralleled in the most barbarous ages, and totally unworthy the Head of a civilized nation.

He has constrained our fellow Citizens taken Captive on the high Seas to bear Arms against their Country, to become the executioners of their friends and Brethren, or to fall themselves by their Hands.

He has excited domestic insurrections amongst us, and has endeavoured to bring on the inhabitants of our frontiers, the merciless Indian Savages, whose known rule of warfare, is an undistinguished destruction of all ages, sexes and conditions.

In every stage of these Oppressions We have Petitioned for Redress in the most humble terms: Our repeated Petitions have been answered only by repeated injury. A Prince, whose character is thus marked by every act which may define a Tyrant, is unfit to be the ruler of a free people.

Nor have We been wanting in attention to our British brethren. We have warned them from time to time of attempts by their legislature to extend an unwarrantable jurisdiction over us. We have reminded them of the circumstances of our emigration and settlement here. We have appealed to their native justice and magnanimity, and we have conjured them by the ties of our common kindred to disavow these usurpations, which would inevitably interrupt our connections and correspondence. They too have been deaf to the voice of justice and of consanguinity. We must, therefore, acquiesce in the necessity, which denounces our Separation, and hold them, as we hold the rest of mankind, Enemies in War, in Peace Friends.

WE, THEREFORE, the Representatives of the UNITED STATES OF AMERICA, in General Congress, Assembled, appealing to the Supreme Judge of the world for the rectitude of our intentions, do, in the Name, and by Authority of the good People of these Colonies, solemnly publish and declare, That these United Colonies are, and of Right ought to be FREE AND INDEPENDENT STATES; that they are Absolved from all Allegiance to the British Crown, and that all political connection between them and the State of Great Britain, is and ought to be totally dissolved; and that as Free and Independent States, they have full Power to levy War, conclude Peace, contract Alliances, establish Commerce, and to do all other Acts and Things which Independent States may of right do.—And for the support of this Declaration, with a firm reliance on the protection of Divine Providence, we mutually pledge to each other our Lives, our Fortunes and our sacred Honour.

John Hancock
President

Charles Thomson
Secretary

It was a good instrument; perhaps a noble one. The members of Congress realized it was not a perfect instrument. Within six months their fire had been directed away from Parliament to the King. He was to be the archvillain. Calling George III a tyrant did not make him one. The bumbling, fumbling, fuming sovereign was still a constitutional king who looked upon himself as a stern father prepared to reward his subjects or to punish—as the need arose. All of the sound advice he had received from his ministers and the military urged him to send troops, to defeat the colonists in a few skirmishes, to burn a few towns. He was assured that this would cause the radical revolutionaries to run. If the King made a mistake, it was in assuming that the rebellion was confined to the few; that the many in the thirteen Colonies were fundamentally loyal. It can hardly be said that the belligerent acts of the Congress won the Colonies to revolution; the people listened to the logic of Thomas Paine and his *Common Sense*. It was this tract, passed from hand to hand, which won the minds of men to a point where they were willing to follow the radical dictates of a Congress which moved slowly to a declaration of independence.

The compelling paragraphs—"When in the Course of human events"; "We hold these truths to be self-evident"; and "We, therefore, the Representatives of the united States of America"—would capture the admiration of historians and statesmen, but the people of the Colonies needed a long list of offenses and usurpations against the King to persuade them that they were forced to face a long conflict to achieve peace and independence. The Messrs. Jefferson, Adams, Franklin, Harrison, Hancock, and others who literally lifted or dragooned the timid to vote for this document were determined that the stout and humorless King made an ideal scapegoat.

To achieve this it was necessary not only to exaggerate the charges against the King but to divorce the British people from him. Thus the paragraph: "Nor have We been wanting in attention to our British brethren. . . . We have appealed to their native justice and magnanimity, and we have conjured them by the ties of our common kindred to disavow these usurpations . . ."

In like manner, it became important to tie the presence of British forces in America to the heinous actions of the

King. To achieve this, the Congress proposed no less than five paragraphs to hammer the link into place. "He has kept among us, in times of peace, Standing Armies . . ."; "For quartering large bodies of armed troops among us"; "For protecting them, by a mock Trial, from punishment for any Murders which they should commit on the Inhabitants of these States"; "He has abdicated government here, by declaring us out of his Protection and waging War against us"; "He is at this time transporting large Armies of foreign Mercenaries to compleat the works of death, desolation and tyranny. . . ." There was craftiness as well as philosophy in the words of the Declaration; logic and hyperbole ran in contrasting threads.

There was no time for Congress to assess what it had done. The president called the body to order. He reminded the members that the hour was late and there was important work which could not be postponed. He asked that a great seal of the united States of America be designed, and directed —if there were no objection—the appointment of Dr. Franklin, John Adams, and Thomas Jefferson as a committee to ask for designs and submit the most appropriate to the Congress. There being no objection, it was so ordered.

Hancock submitted an emergency request from the Continental Army in New York. There was a shortage of troops and flints for muskets. There ensued considerable debate, though to no known purpose. It was settled with this resolution:

"RESOLVED: That an application be made to the committee of safety of Pennsylvania for a supply of flints for the troops at New York: and that the Colony of Pennsylvania and Delaware be requested to embody their militia for the flying camp, and to march them, without delay, to the City of Philadelphia."

The business at hand proceeded. The feverish revolutionary Caesar Rodney penned a letter to his brother Thomas, while half listening to the voices of contention:

Philadelphia July the 4th, 1776

Sir:

I arrived in Congress (tho detained by thunder and rain) in time enough to give my voice in the matter of Independence. It is determined by the Thirteen United Colonies, without even one decenting Colony. We have now got through with the whole of the Declaration, and ordered it to be printed, so that you will soon have the pleasure of seeing it. Hand-bills of it will be printed, and sent to the armies, county towns, etc. To be published or rather proclaimed in form. Don't neglect to attend closely and carefully to my harvest and you'll oblige
Yours, etc.

Caesar Rodney

Hancock pushed the measures with as little debate as possible. He ordered that Robert Morris of Pennsylvania and Joseph Hewes of North Carolina be appointed a committee of two to lease a vessel owned by a "Mr. Walker." No one recollected later the purpose of the boat. It seems to have been connected with building fortifications for Philadelphia at the mouth of the Delaware River. Morris had been opposed to the Declaration of Independence, as strongly in opposition as John Dickinson. Dickinson would not sign. Morris would. His reasoning is known: "I think that the individual who declines the service of his country because its councils are not comfortable to his ideas, makes but a bad subject; a good one will follow if he cannot lead."

In good time Hancock ordered Thomson to read the note from General George Washington. The sense of it was depressing: "Since I had the honor of addressing you and on the same day several Ships arrived within the Hook; making the number that came in then, 110, and there remains no doubt of the whole of the Fleet from Hallifax being now here. Yesterday evening 50 of them came into the Bay and anchored on the Staten Island side. Their views I cannot precisely determine, but am extremely apprehensive, as a part of them only came, that they mean to surround the island and secure the whole stock upon it. Our reinforcements of Militia are but small yet. . . ."

The letter was punctuated by shocked silence. The Congressmen looked at each other and at Hancock. Having agreed to send flints and additional militia to his Flying Camp at New Brunswick, New Jersey, the members could think of nothing more within their power to help. It did not lift their flagging spirits to know that the commanding general was "extremely apprehensive." Washington did not sound like a heroic victor. Hancock roused himself from lethargy to suggest that Congress might do something about the defense of Philadelphia. Delegations from New Jersey, New York, and Pennsylvania were ordered to confer with the Philadelphia Committee of Safety to discuss measures to minimize an attack by the brothers Howe. Congress cheerfully guaranteed the expenses of such conferences.

Another committee was instructed to ascertain that thousands of musket flints stored in Rhode Island be delivered to the Continental Army forthwith. Considerable time was lost in repetition of the rhetorical question "If our gallant men cannot fire their muskets, what good are they in battle?" Someone suggested that Henry Wisner send a man to Orange County to get a sample of flint; if the quality was good and the supply great enough, the man would be empowered to order forty or fifty thousand.

The Declaration of Independence seemed to recede within the memories of the members as the specter of defeat in battle emerged in their consciousness. The Congress was bent on crossing *t*'s and dotting *i*'s in an effort not to dwell upon the imminence of invasion. They made much of two vacancies in the "middle department" for Commissioners of Indian Affairs. After discussion and spirited voting, Jasper Yeates and John Montgomery were elected. James Wilson of

Pennsylvania and Benjamin Franklin of the same province were asked to notify the men of their election. Hancock had requested a private secretary to handle his work. The Congress addressed itself to this matter. After the pros and cons were enunciated, Hancock was instructed to find himself another private secretary, the salary to be guaranteed by the Congress.

A courier who had brought dispatches from Trenton to Philadelphia was ordered—by vote—to be paid. The summer sun was blazing bronze in the west when the Secret Committee was authorized to sell twenty-five pounds of gunpowder to John Garrison of North Carolina. The members were in a state of lassitude, creatures spent by decisions great and small. John Hancock brought the palm of his hand down sharply. It hit the table and he announced that this session of the Continental Congress, July 4, 1776, was adjourned. For a time, no one rose to leave. Thomson knocked on the inside of the door for the doorman to open it; two members lifted windows. A breath of air moved shyly indoors and lifted cross-hatched papers from desks, only to drop them back where they had been.

A few members stood to chat. A few pored over the Declaration to find, as perfectionists, what the Congress had done to Jefferson's monumental work. Sixty-eight changes had been made. Eighteen hundred seventeen words had been cut to 1,337. Four hundred eighty words had been killed. Someone patted Josiah Bartlett on the back and made a jest. He smiled wanly. Dr. Bartlett had been the first man to vote aye for the Declaration of Independence but he was not a jovial person. He was laconic and uttered words as though coins were spilling from his purse. At home in Kingston, New Hampshire, Bartlett was a physician, a member of the colonial legislature, a justice of the peace, a colonel of militia. He was also a man careless of appearance, wont to appear with a vest half buttoned, breeches partly laced below the knee. If he despised anything, it was probably a speech.

The members of Congress left in groups. The hour was close to sunset and those who ate in boardinghouses as well as those who supped in taverns would be asked, "What kept ye?"

The faces would not light with joy; the tongues would not ladle the brave words of liberty; the gentlemen would remain secretive about the business of Congress. "We were busy," some would say. "The British are outside New York, you know." Others would shrug. "A long day of work," they would say.

The public printer Dunlap would ask his assistants to work tonight. They had a document to engross in the finest script; they would have to run off a thousand copies before dawn; copies without a blot or smudge. It could be done. It would be done as long as the Congress guaranteed prompt payment.

☆ Postscript to Freedom ☆

A MEMBER OF CONGRESS SHOULD HAVE SUPER-vised the all-night work of John Dunlap. Surely the designer of the Declaration of Independence would be present to proofread the corrections. Thomas Jefferson, silent and de-pressed, bowed an adieu to his confreres and walked back to his boardinghouse. Benjamin Franklin, the best-known printer in the Colonies, might have assisted Dunlap. But the wise old doctor was suffering from a recurrence of gout. At the age of seventy, he was beyond the median life-span. His physician had warned him that good company and a mastery of the social graces would not kill him, but that his love of rich food and rare wines would.

Dunlap was pleased that no member of Congress was present to oversee his work. He was an independent man much given to correcting copy sent to his shop. His common mood was irritability. A messenger handed him an interlined copy of the Declaration of Independence with quill-and-ink corrections cross-hatching the work. The printer did well with what he had, with the exception of the word "unalien-able." In the morning his broadsides were ready. He did not return the original copy to Congress. Either it was lost or

Mr. Dunlap felt that it was not presentable and left it with discarded proofs.

July 5, a Friday, was a day of mailing. Copies of the Declaration were rolled, placed in cardboard cylinders, and sent by courier, by coach, by packet ship and sloop to the northernmost reaches of New Hampshire, the southernmost settlements of Georgia, and all the towns and hamlets between. There would be formal readings everywhere. Philadelphia had its reading Tuesday, July 8. On the same evening, the Declaration was read publicly in Trenton, New Jersey, and Easton, Pennsylvania.

Colonel John Nixon chose to stand on the rickety platform in the State House yard to wait for a gathering of public-spirited citizens. He was commander of the Philadelphia Associators, a military regiment organized and outfitted by Benjamin Franklin thirty years before. When the colonel concluded bellowing and trumpeting the exciting words, he waited for applause. There was little. It was as though the people had expected this moment for a long time. A boy ran from the State House to tell the warders of the churches to ring the bells, that freedom had been proclaimed. A half hour later the din of bronze tongues was so great that citizens ran from their homes asking what had happened.

Some thought it unseemly to use church bells to propagate a resolution. The Reverend Henry Muhlenburg made a fresh entry in his diary: "This—the Declaration—has caused some thoughtful and far-seeing *melancholici* to be down in the mouth; on the other hand it has caused some sanguine *miopes* to exult and shout with joy. *In fine videbitur cuius toni*. The end will show who played the right tune." Charles Biddle wrote: "I was in the State House Yard when the Declaration of Independence was read. There were very few respectable persons present."

In New York, General Washington read the Declaration and sent an order of the day to his troops:

The Hon. Continental Congress, impelled by the dictates of duty, policy and necessity, having been pleased to dissolve the Connection which subsisted between this Country and Great Britain, and to declare the United Colonies of North America free and independent STATES: The several brigades are to be drawn up this evening on their respective Parades, at six OClock, when the declaration of Congress, shewing the grounds & reasons of this measure, is to be read with an audible voice.

The General hopes this important Event will serve as a fresh incentive to every officer, and soldier, to act with Fidelity and Courage, as knowing that now the peace and safety of his Country depends (under God) solely on the success of our arms: And that he is now in the service of a State, possessed of sufficient power to reward his merit, and advance him to the highest honors of a free Country.

The Brigade majors are to receive, at the Adjutant General's Office, several of the Declarations to be delivered to the Brigadiers General and the Colonels of Regiments. . . .

The main body of the militia was drawn up as a hollow square at the foot of Broad Way at 6 P.M. Outside the square, bands of young hoodlums listened. The Commander in Chief looked upon the day as a solemn one accompanied by a dignified reading. Instead, as a young officer bellowed the document from side to side, the soldiers began to cheer. The hoodlums huzzahed as they listened to each of the many charges against King George III. When the reading was over, some of the militia broke ranks and joined the ruffians. Within an hour they had a dozen ropes around the gilded lead statue of the King. They yanked and cheered and toppled it into the street. They stomped on it and built bonfires. Soldiers fired guns into the night sky, forgetting General Washington's order to conserve gunpowder.

That night the New York State Convention, which controlled the politics of the big middle province, met at White Plains Courthouse to change its vote. It was voted that the Second Continental Congress had "cogent and conclusive" reasons for writing a declaration of independence. Therefore New York, besieged by British forces, ordered its Congressmen to vote for independence at once, thus achieving unanimity. General Washington remained up late to vent his personal feelings on his troops. The order was published in the morning:

Headquarters, New York, July 10, 1776

'Tho the General doubts not the persons who pulled down and mutilated the Statue in the Broad Way last night, were actuated by Zeal in the public cause; yet it has so much the appearance of riot and want of order, in the Army, that he disapproves the manner, and directs that in future these things shall be avoided by the Soldiery, and left to be executed by proper authority.

The Declaration was two weeks old when it was read to a wildly cheering crowd in Boston. The day was Thursday, July 18. Abigail Adams had attended church services and was on her way home when she noticed a large crowd walking toward the State House. She followed and heard the immortal words come down from a man standing in an upper window. Again, the people seemed impervious to the high philosophy of the first, second, and last paragraphs. They begged to hear more about the horrible deeds of the King upon the innocent Colonies. And again it was the young—the people with the least to lose—who moved off from State House to tear down tavern signs that expressed allegiance to King and Crown; to start street-corner fires; to shout defiance to Great Britain. In Dover, Delaware, militiamen burned a portrait of the King and formed a cheering circle around the flames.

The unspoken fear of Congress, that "the Unanimous Declaration of the thirteen united States of America" wasn't quite unanimous, had receded into history by July 19. New York had made it unanimous. John Hancock was so pleased that he asked permission of Congress to have the document "engrossed on parchment," which would make it look more stately and dignified, but more difficult to read. Permission was granted. It was the consensus of the members that the work would be given to Timothy Matlock, a big-nosed, dour-mouthed perfectionist of Philadelphia. Hancock assured the Congress that the parchment would be ready toward the end of July. As usual, no records were kept of the meetings, but it was probably at this meeting of July 19 that someone proposed that all members of Congress sign the parchment copy. Some said that the proposal was made so that the guilt could be spread among the fifty-six members. Others maintained that it was pride which motivated the suggestion. In any case, John Hancock suggested that Friday, August 2, be set aside as signing day.

Congress, it is certain, had the best of motives, but the signing would lead to a miasma of names. Assuming that the original document was legal—which it was—a second and more proliferating signing could not make the Declaration of Independence more legal. Further, no one took a poll of names on July 4 to ascertain which members voted for the Declaration or even how many were present. Among those who would sign the parchment were members elected after July 4, men who had not voted for the instrument.

On the morning of August 2, the popinjay of the revolution, John Hancock, sat at his table and read the new copy. He used a silver inkstand and a tall quill. Once again he signed with large strokes in dead center, pressing heavily on the downstrokes. It is probable that Button Gwinnett of Georgia stood beside him because he signed at the extreme left. Under Gwinnett's signature, the remaining two delegates of Georgia signed—Lyman Hall and George Walton. This established a pattern; delegates would sign in groups, each group to constitute a state. When completed, there would be six columns of names.

North Carolina did not want to sign under Georgia, so William Hooper started a second column and signed sufficiently high so that no state could get between North Carolina and the last paragraph of the Declaration of Independence. He was followed by confreres Joseph Hewes and John Penn. South Carolina signed next. Edward Rutledge left a broad space under the North Carolina delegation, then squiggled his signature. He was followed by Thomas Heyward, who seemed to feel that the Rutledge signature should stand alone. He left a goodly space under Rutledge, and signed. Close behind were Thomas Lynch, Junr., and a firm and legible signature from Arthur Middleton.

The top of the third column was captured by Maryland. The penmanship was small, growing slightly darker in its descent. Samuel Chase signed, followed by Wm Paca, Thos. Stone, and Charles Carroll of Carrollton. The strong Virginia delegation signed under Maryland. Here, if anyone hoped that the author and designer of the Declaration might be permitted to sign first, he would be disappointed. Virginia signed in order of seniority: George Wythe, Richard Henry Lee, Th Jefferson, Benj Harrison, Ths Nelson jr., Francis Lightfoot Lee, and Carter Braxton.

Pennsylvania started a fourth column, flirting its quills adjacent to the *k* in John Hancock: Robt Morris, Benjamin Rush, Benj. [a] Franklin, John Morton, Geo. Clymer, Ja^s Smith, Geo. Taylor, James Wilson, and Geo. Ross, the last of whom drew a heavy line under his name to set Pennsylvania apart from others. At the bottom of the fourth column, Delaware's heroic Caesar Rodney signed, followed by Geo. Read and Tho. M'Kean.

New York's newly designated Congressmen started a fifth column, signing with sweeping flourishes: Wm Floyd, Phil. Livingston, $Fran^s$ Lewis, and Lewis Morris. New Jersey, which left a large space under New York's signers, decided that all names should have a graceful line of penmanship under the signatures: Richd Stockton, Jno. Witherspoon, Fra^s Hopkinson, John Hart, Abra Clark.

There was plenty of room in the first column under the three signatures of Georgia, but New Hampshire decided to begin a sixth column on the right side: Josiah Bartlett, the workhorse of the revolution, who had been on every standing committee of Congress, signed first. Wm Whipple signed underneath. Samuel Adams of Massachusetts Bay signed Saml Adams close to Whipple. John Adams left enough room so that Samuel Adams appeared to be a part of the New Hampshire grouping. He was followed by the heavy lines of Robt Treat Paine, and then the small signature of Elbridge Gerry.

Rhode Island followed with a shaky signature by Step. Hopkins, who was sixty-eight years old. The remaining delegate, William Ellery, graced the page with a Spencerian hand as excellent as that of John Hancock. There was room for Connecticut's four Congressmen, but not much more. They squeezed their names under each other: Roger Sherman, Saml Huntington, Wm Williams, and Oliver Wolcott.

Whatever order in which they were signed, or over what span of time, or even why they crowded the right side of the page leaving empty spaces on the left, is not known. It is certain that the third delegate from New Hampshire, Matthew Thornton, was not present at the original signing. He found no room to sign with his state, so he wrote small and placed his signature at the bottom of the sixth column, making himself the thirteenth man in that line. There was a rush of signatories on August 2. For several weeks afterward, tardy Congressmen arrived to flesh out the document.

On August 10, the news of independence reached Georgia. A packet from Philadelphia, idled by the vagaries of summer breezes, hove to off the Battery at Savannah. The port was wild with celebrants. Officials read the Declaration at the

Savannah Liberty Pole and again at the Battery. A holiday was declared. Guns boomed. Plantation owners set up tables under moss-dripping magnolias to eat well and drink a toast to a nation already five weeks old. The news was everywhere in the Colonies; the Declaration of Independence had been published in newspapers, read aloud in homes and on commons, been nailed to trees before courthouses, copies given to the old and young for silent study, sung solemnly from pulpits. Captain Alexander Graydon of the Third Pennsylvania enunciated the politically conservative view: "The Declaration of Independency is variously relished here, some approving, some condemning—for my own part, I have not the least objection did I know my rulers and the form of government . . . popular government I could never approve of . . . delaying the [Declaration] a while longer would have kept the door open for a reconciliation, convinced the world of our reluctance to embrace it and increased our friends on t'other side of the water. . . . However the matter is settled now and our salvation depends upon supporting the measure."

To the citizens, Whig and Tory, the Declaration was a final step. To Congress it was a first step. Patriots celebrated the end of something; Congress worried about its ability to midwife the beginning. The men in Philadelphia did not delude themselves to believe that independence was something granted by a piece of paper. Independence, to them, was a far-off goal, a state of eventual serenity to be earned in bloody battle, through winters of starvation and summers of despair. The brave men of Congress—the braver because many were afraid—realized that hundreds, perhaps thousands of decisions would be thrust upon them. They must make the right ones. Liberty could be shouted anywhere; it existed nowhere.

Military men feared that thirteen agricultural colonies could not amass and marshal an assortment of men and weapons strong enough to match and defeat the world's most powerful nation. The pious hope in the ranks of the Continental

Army was that on some distant day the British would tire of whipping the Colonies. It could be too expensive and too exhausting. Neither George Washington nor Lord Cornwallis could see that day in the haze of the future. But it would come. The frail buds of spring would shiver on branches and twigs five more times before Cornwallis, more surprised than George Washington, would stand on a field at Yorktown to surrender and withdraw.

The parchment document of the Declaration of Independence would survive the bloody battles, the valor on both sides, the feeble calls of the dying. It was guarded in the State House at Philadelphia until the end of 1776. Then the British threatened Philadelphia, and Congress took itself and its valiant words to Baltimore. There the members voted for a second public printing of the Declaration, this time with all the names appended. Within a few months it was back in Philadelphia.

July 4, 1777, came and went. No one marked the date; no one celebrated. In the autumn, Congress fled to Lancaster, then to York, Pennsylvania. Congress became a running, hiding body of men. At York, the Declaration was placed in the courthouse under perpetual guard. The Congress and its paper were back in Philadelphia in June, 1778. Both were home and five years went by. In July, 1783, the men and the parchment moved to Prince Town, New Jersey. Next they went to Trenton. Then to Annapolis, Maryland. In June, 1785, they moved to New York. The Declaration of Independence, well traveled and brittle, was given to the first President, George Washington, in 1789.

He felt that the original copy was too precious to repose in the hands of a chief executive. It was given in perpetuity to the Secretary of State. John Jay put it under guard. A new Secretary of State was returning from Paris to assume the office. Once more it curled in a tight circle under the strong hands of Thomas Jefferson. In 1790, the Virginian took it to his offices in Philadelphia. He was prone to admonish friends not to touch it; the document was beginning to show its age. Successive Secretaries of State had it until 1800, when it was moved to Washington, D.C. In all those years, little was said publicly about the authorship of the document. It was as though America wanted to perpetuate the fiction that all the members of the Second Continental Congress had contributed bits and pieces to the great banner of liberty.

On March 4, 1801, Thomas Jefferson was the recipient of the ultimate accolade. He followed John Adams as President of the United States. He had been thirty-three years of age when he wrote the Declaration of Independence. He was now fifty-eight, the red hair turning rusty, the gait firm, the integrity immovable. He walked to his inauguration listening to the ear-shattering explosion of American cannon.

It was another day, another time. If he dwelled at all on his fellow Congressmen of 1776, Jefferson must have evicted the thought as dolorous. John Adams had palsy. Josiah Bartlett was dead. So were Carter Braxton, George Clymer, Benjamin Franklin, Button Gwinnett, Lyman Hall, John Hancock, Benjamin Harrison, John Hart, Joseph Hewes, William Hooper, Stephen Hopkins, Francis Hopkinson, Samuel Huntington, Richard Henry Lee, Francis Lightfoot Lee, Philip Livingston, Thomas Lynch, Jr., Arthur Middleton, Lewis Morris, John Morton, Thomas Nelson, Jr., William Paca, John Penn, George Read, Caesar Rodney, George Ross, Edward Rutledge, Roger Sherman, Richard Stockton, Thomas Stone, George Taylor, William Whipple, James Wilson, John Witherspoon, and Oliver Wolcott. Many of the others were too infirm to attend the inauguration.

There were fresh, bright, and strange faces in the north wing of the Capitol when Thomas Jefferson took the oath of office. His blue eyes darted across the scene. He must have wondered if, among the young and intrepid, there might be another George Washington, another John Adams, a Peyton

255

Randolph, a Franklin. Sometime after he became President, Thomas Jefferson was asked by a friend to list his most notable accomplishments. He took pen in hand, half amused, half serious, and began to write a few achievements that would not be abrasive to a mind disciplined to modesty. After several notations, he hesitated. Then, with a firm hand, he wrote it at last: "The Declaration of Independence."

☆ Bibliography ☆

American Heritage History of the American Revolution, The.
McGraw-Hill, 1958.

Andrist, Ralph K., ed., *George Washington, A Biography.*
The Founding Fathers series. Harper & Row, 1972.

Ayling, Stanley, *George the Third.* Alfred A. Knopf, 1972.

Beard, Charles A., and Beard, Mary R., *The Rise of American
Civilization.* Macmillan, 1927.

Berky, Andrew S., and Shenton, James P., eds., *The Historians' History of the United States.* G. P. Putnam's
Sons, 1966.

Brodie, Fawn M., *Thomas Jefferson, An Intimate History.* W.
W. Norton & Company, Inc., 1974.

Brooke, John, *King George III, A Biography of America's
Last Monarch.* McGraw-Hill, 1971.

Butterfield, Herbert, *George III and the Historians.* Macmillan, 1957.

Chidsey, Donald Barr, *July 4, 1776.* Crown Publishers, 1958.

Collins, Alan C., *The Story of America in Pictures.* Doubleday
& Company, 1935.

Commager, Henry Steele, and Morris, Richard B., eds., *The
Spirit of 'Seventy-Six.* Harper & Row, 1958.

Fast, Howard, *Citizen Tom Paine.* Random House, 1943.

Fleming, Thomas J., *Now We Are Enemies*. St. Martin's Press, 1960.

Jackson, John W., *The Pennsylvania Navy, 1775–1781*. Rutgers University Press, 1974.

Kinnaird, Clark, *George Washington, the Pictorial Biography*. Hastings House, 1967.

Lloyd, Alan, *The King Who Lost America*. Doubleday & Company, 1971.

Lorant, Stefan, ed., *The New World*. Euell, Sloan & Pearce, 1946.

Malone, Dumas, *The Story of the Declaration of Independence*. Oxford University Press, 1975.

Miller, John C., *Origins of the American Revolution*. Little, Brown & Company, 1943.

Morris, Richard B., *The American Revolution Reconsidered*. Harper & Row, 1967.

Neumann, George C., *The History of Weapons of the American Revolution*. Harper & Row, 1967.

Paine, Tom, *Selected Work,* edited by Howard Fast. Modern Library, 1946.

Preston, John Hyde, *Revolution 1776*. Washington Square Press, 1933.

Sarles, Frank B., Jr., and Shedd, Charles E., *Colonials & Patriots*. U. S. Government Printing Office, 1964.

1776 Guide for Massachusetts, The. Harper Colophon Books, 1975.

Smith, Frank, *Thomas Paine Liberator*. Frederick A. Stokes Company, 1938.

Snell, Tee Loftin, *The Wild Shores, America's Beginnings*. National Geographic Society, 1974.

Street, James, *The Revolutionary War*. The Dial Press, 1954.

Ward, Christopher, *The War of the Revolution*. Macmillan, 1952.

Woodward, W. E., *Tom Paine, America's Godfather*. E. P. Dutton & Company, 1966.

☆ Index ☆

259

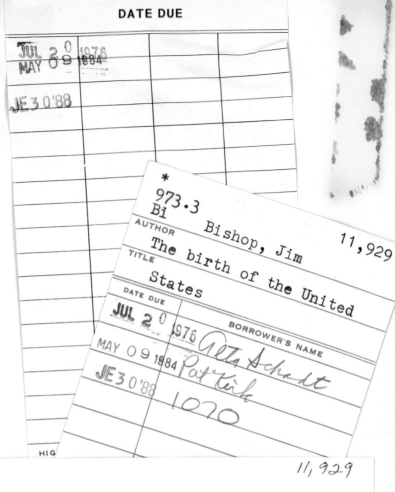